World Class Production and Inventory Management

World Class Production and Inventory Management

Darryl V. Landvater

John Wiley & Sons, Inc.
New York · Chichester · Brisbane · Toronto · Singapore

ISBN 0-471-13218-7

Printed in the United States of America

10 9 8 7 6 5 4 3 2

To Oliver W. Wight

Acknowledgments

I was more fortunate than most in that I had the opportunity to work closely with Oliver Wight from 1975 until his death in 1983. During that time he shared his insight, his wisdom, and his humor. He was a delight to work with, and asked only that I make my clients successful. In a number of instances within this book, I hope you'll see some of that remarkable person.

The depth of experience in the Oliver Wight group is so great that I've taken the unusual step of acknowledging several of the leading thinkers at the end of many chapters. You'll see them mentioned, with a short explanation of their contributions to this rapidly expanding body of knowledge. I have only the greatest respect for each of these exceptional people.

Jim Childs, our publisher at Oliver Wight, is a true professional in every sense. His vision for our publishing efforts is superb, and his insights on this book in particular have been invaluable. Without Jim, this would have been a different book.

Steve Bennett, the writer I worked with, is another member of the team that made this book possible. Steve worked with me as we electronically fired sections of the book back and forth in a somewhat unique and thoroughly enjoyable literary version of the blacksmith hammering out a forging.

Walt Goddard and Tom Wallace were the two "great critiquers." Walt used to be Ollie's critiquer, and has lost none of his skill over the years. Tom's critiques were so brutally honest, and so clearly on target, that I could do little but laugh out loud, and then proceed to fix the problem.

I'd like to mention Jim McLaughlin, who like Ollie, died long before his time. It was Jim who first motivated me to become involved in MRP II.

Finally, my hope is that this book makes a contribution which is in addition to the profits that companies achieve through the use of more competitive tools. I hope it does something to elevate the quality of life for those thousands of people who today struggle to manage manufacturing companies without the proper tools to do their jobs.

Darryl Landvater
October 1992
Williston, Vermont

Contents

World Class Production
and Inventory Management

Chapter One

The Emergence
of a Profession

Try getting a degree in manufacturing management—you can't.

But you can get one in veterinary medicine, embalming, Etruscan history, or French literature. This symbolizes a serious misunderstanding on a national level. Few fields make as great a contribution to our economic well-being as manufacturing. Manufacturing accounts for 22 percent of our gross national product, and provides more than 20 million jobs.

Why don't business schools offer courses on managing a manufacturing company? Ask them and you'll get answers like "Well, we do have a few courses on operations management. But if you can operate a business in general, you can run a manufacturing company."

This is a misunderstanding of enormous significance. A lot has happened in manufacturing over the last several years, and more is happening all the time. There is a body of knowledge that is specific to running a manufacturing company—knowledge about the new competitive tools and how to use them.

Nevertheless, on a very basic level, the institutions you speak with would be right—all businesses, regardless of what they make, must maintain payables, receivables, payroll, and other standard accounting functions.

But the similarities to manufacturing companies stop there. Manufacturing companies have particular needs that require specialized technologies such as manufacturing resource planning (MRP II), Just-in-Time,

3

total quality management, CAD/CAM/CIM, distribution resource planning (DRP), design for competitive advantage, and employee empowerment, to name a few. Each of these involves a specific body of knowledge in its own right.

What has left the colleges and universities behind, as well as many manufacturing companies, is the rate of change in managing manufacturing companies.

MANUFACTURING: FROM A QUIET POND TO A HURRICANE AT SEA

Many of today's managers cut their teeth in manufacturing during a period of relative tranquillity. They formed their sense of what's important—their set of beliefs on how to manage—during this calm. Today, *calm* is not a word many people use to describe what's happening in manufacturing management. These same managers now live in what can only be described as a "hurricane" of change.

From the 1940s through the late 1960s, most of the competitive advances in a manufacturing company revolved around improvements in equipment. Significant advances in the science of how to manage a manufacturing company were relatively scarce when compared with the rate of changes today. Changes in thinking like scientific inventory management and MacGregor's Theory X and Theory Y seem meager in view of what has happened recently.

In the late sixties, the science of managing a manufacturing company began to accelerate with the development of material requirements planning (MRP). This acceleration continued through the seventies, as MRP evolved into manufacturing resource planning (MRP II) and the track record for success became compelling. By the midseventies, quality became a major issue, as statistical process control evolved into total quality control, and total quality control evolved into total quality management. Other incentives for change came in the early eighties, as Just-in-Time, employee empowerment, design for competitive advantage, and other technologies came into their own. Today, companies on the cutting edge use multiple technologies to achieve outstanding cost savings and improvements in productivity and quality.

In many cases, the subsets of these different technologies are substantial bodies of knowledge in themselves. For example, within the area of total quality management you'll find fields such as statistical process control and problem solving skills and tools, as well as design tools such as quality function deployment (QFD). Just-in-Time includes setup reduction, kanban, cellular manufacturing, and competitive benchmarking, and so on. Some of the subsets within manufacturing resource planning include sales and operations planning, master production scheduling, material requirements planning, and supplier scheduling.

These are all tested and proven approaches for improving the competitiveness of manufacturing companies, not just theoretical musings of academicians. Each technology has a demonstrated record of success in a wide range of manufacturing companies, with returns on investment in the range of several hundred percent.

This rate of change, as shown in Figure 1.1, is not linear, or even exponential; it represents a quantum leap in knowledge in a span of only a few years. The science of managing a manufacturing company went from having little that is new to suddenly having a great deal on the cutting edge.

Prior to this leap, managing a manufacturing company was, as the business schools stated, "pretty much the same as managing any other business." Most manufacturing people learned early in their careers that better machinery could improve productivity and increase profits. This

Figure 1.1   Time Line for New Technologies

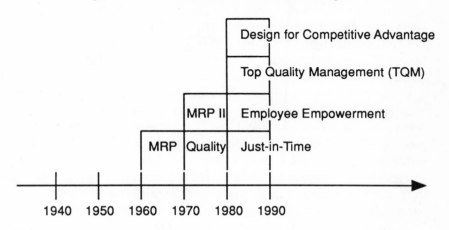

became a set of shared beliefs for most manufacturing people. Everyone "knew" that having better equipment was good, and it was only a question of whether a company could justify such equipment.

The flip side was that people didn't "know" that adopting new management approaches would result in significant financial and competitive improvements. Changing the way you managed a manufacturing company as a way of improving the bottom line seemed strange. Even when these technologies demonstrated ROIs of 200 percent and more, everyone still "knew" that the way to improve productivity and profits was to buy better equipment.

Consequently, this stable period in American manufacturing management taught managers not to seriously question the way a manufacturing company is managed, and not to expect change in this area. And it set the stage for conflict, characterized by two opposing deep-seated convictions:

- "Changing the way we manage is the most significant action we can take to improve the bottom line."

- "Changing the way we manage isn't the way it's 'done,' and everybody knows that. Let's get back to fundamentals—faster feeds and speeds, attacking labor costs, automation, things like that. . . ."

People holding these opposite views cannot act as a team. One group won't see what all the fuss is about, and the other group sees the need for major change. One group may concede the need for a small team focused on a narrow task, and the other will want broad involvement throughout the organization. Communication will be difficult and frustrating because the basis for communication is so different.

It's like what would happen if an ancient alchemist were somehow transported into the Brookhaven National Laboratories. The alchemist believes he can turn lead into gold—it's just a matter of finding the right process. To him, the particle accelerators, supercomputers, and other resources are new and wonderful ways to meet his goal. "Let's start trying different chemicals," he says. The scientists throw their hands up in frustration. The underlying beliefs are so different that there is no basis for communication.

To create a basis for companywide communication, executives and managers today need to be well versed in diverse technologies and must understand how they interact with one another. And while this book is primarily about planning and control systems, it is important to have a basic sense of the other technologies and techniques currently in use. Nothing operates in a vacuum, and these other technologies affect how people use their planning and control systems. In this chapter, we'll take a brief look at what companies are doing with these different technologies, and how they work together. In later chapters, we'll identify the specific points at which the various technologies can be integrated with the planning and control systems.

Two Steps Forward, One Step Back

A good question to ask at this point is: Who invented the specialized bodies of knowledge needed to run a manufacturing company? The answer: no one. That is, no single person. No single person could have developed what we know today; there aren't enough man-years in a person's life, not enough opportunities to learn in a single career. Rather, it evolved from the collective experimentation of dedicated people who were motivated by the need to find a better way to run a business.

Planning and scheduling a typical manufacturing company was often a frustrating and overwhelming experience—frustrating because you never had the tools to do the job, and overwhelming because the rate of change could drown you in a sea of data. Changing the manufacturing process was an uphill battle. Who would have believed that changeovers on large pieces of manufacturing equipment could be reduced from several hours to a few minutes?

The struggle to develop the different bodies of knowledge took decades. For those involved, it felt like an eternity. Taking two steps forward often meant taking one step backward. A problem solved usually meant that another would emerge from nowhere. In some ways, it was like peeling the onion. For each layer removed, what appeared was not the solution but another layer of problems to be addressed.

For example, in the development of planning and scheduling systems, the advent of high-speed digital computers meant that companies could suddenly afford to purchase computer power that could carry out key scheduling calculations in a reasonable period of time—hours, not weeks.

Just when everyone thought that the scheduling problem was solved, the other half of the problem emerged from the sidelines. Up to this point, the question was "When do we need to order?" Suddenly, it became more important to answer the question "When do we really need it?" The reality of manufacturing is that the world is constantly changing, and a valid plan today might be worthless tomorrow.

The need date is a moving target because of customer changes, engineering changes, inventory adjustments, scrap, overruns, capacity problems, vendor problems, and so on. These changes all have the same effect—some items are needed earlier than before, while others are needed later. Therefore, the scheduling problem must be continually solved; today's answer is not tomorrow's answer—you can't just launch an order and work to an unchanging schedule.

And so it went. With each new advance, there was a new set of challenges to conquer. But people persisted, and each contributed a piece to a growing foundation. Finally, after several decades, with thousands of companies and many thousands of people participating in the work, a very substantial structure emerged. That structure is not static, but is constantly changing, continuing to evolve, becoming somewhat different, with every day as people show up for work.

Today you have a choice: You can use this accumulated body of knowledge and build upon it, or you can rediscover it. Clearly, no company can afford the time or resources required to re-create the basic body of knowledge that has accumulated over the past several decades. Besides, what company has the resources and can afford to make all the mistakes that other people in other companies have already made? Throughout two decades of evolution in manufacturing planning systems, the mistakes were spread out over thousands of companies, one or two per firm. But if many of these were combined into a single "megaton" mistake within a single organization, the fallout would likely be lethal.

Yet there are people and companies that continue attacking the problems of competitiveness in the nineties armed only with their own experiences and their own native intelligence. While it might be admirable that these gladiators will step into the ring armed only with limited tools, the outcome is unfortunately predetermined. In the battle for competitive supremacy, they are using clubs against tanks, swords against missiles.

Unlike in warfare, in competition the real reasons for victories are not always obvious. In the late seventies, Xerox realized that its joint venture Fuji Xerox was able to produce a copier at a cost that was 50 percent less than the cost in the United States. Xerox undertook an aggressive benchmarking program to understand the reasons for the difference, and ultimately reduced its costs by this amount.

Some years later, Hewlett-Packard encountered a similar situation in which competitors were selling a printer product for what it cost HP to actually make the piece of equipment. HP's first reaction was denial— the competing product couldn't work as well . . . it couldn't be the same quality. Hewlett-Packard bought several to find out for sure. In fact, they worked well and had excellent quality. This led to Hewlett-Packard's implementation of Just-in-Time.

Unfortunately, Xerox and HP are exceptions. Countless other companies experience competitive losses and have no inkling what's behind their competitors' improvements in cost, quality, and delivery.

The game has changed, and what used to work no longer does. More insidious is the fact that many proud and successful companies continue to operate as they have in the past. Their history works against them. Changes in the "soft stuff" of managing did not account for their success in the past, much of which happened during the period of relative calm mentioned earlier. Yet today, the technologies we've been discussing have become an essential element for survival. It's hard to win sales when customers can choose products that perform as well or better, reach the market first, cost about half as much, and are delivered in less time.

So given the availability of technologies and techniques for remaining competitive, why don't more companies adopt them? The answer: Their pain threshold is too high.

THE FEAR AND PAIN FACTOR

Experience shows that companies don't adopt certain new ideas because they're good or because they improve financial performance—they do it because of *pain*.

Business schools teach what might be called the "opportunity model," in which the chance to save a million dollars will send people scurrying to do whatever has to be done. Various alternatives are studied, and the ones with the best financial returns are accepted and implemented.

This model presupposes a set of beliefs. For example, if the set of beliefs in a company is that the most effective way to compete is through better equipment, different equipment will be evaluated, and the most effective alternatives will be selected.

Yet what if the most attractive alternatives are in conflict with that set of beliefs? What if there is a 200 percent return on investment from implementing a new management technology, and a 50 percent return on investment from acquiring new equipment? Which way will the decision go now? Typically it will fall in the direction of the set of beliefs (the new equipment), not in the direction of the greatest competitive impact (new management technologies).

Generally, it takes some level of fear and pain to cause an organization to change its beliefs or management paradigm. It happened at Xerox, and it happened at Hewlett-Packard. They realized that when a competitor is building a product for 50 percent less cost, it can't be cheap labor. Direct labor costs only account for about 5 to 10 percent of the sales dollar in most manufacturing companies.

Today, companies have a choice: They can actively choose to change their set of beliefs about what makes a company competitive in manufacturing, or they can wait for the competition to get tough and give them a few really difficult years, during which time they have to survive, make shipments, and at the same time carry out significant changes or risk sinking into very deep water. While the proactive stance is the more sensible approach, it is by no means more popular.

Reinforcing the fear and pain model is the fact that most companies do what they can to avoid having to deal with major change. For example, the first thing many companies will do is hope the problem goes away on its own. Some problems do indeed go away, but the majority of major problems come back to haunt their owners.

Another step is to repeat an old solution. For example, someone might say, "The last time we had this problem, we had the general manager sign all purchase orders over $500—that's how we kept the inventory down. So let's get the general manager to sign all the purchase orders again." Is the general manager going to sign the purchase orders forever? Why do we have purchasing people if we need the general manager to, in effect, be the purchasing agent? Such an approach, of course, merely attacks the symptoms, not the problem itself.

A frequent response to problems is to change people. When something goes wrong in an organization, the tendency is to ask *who's* the problem, not what's the problem. In many cases, though, the problem isn't a "who," it's something else. For example, let's say the product mix changes and the company goes out of control. Typically, the materials manager or VP of manufacturing gets fired. In this case, the real problem turns out to be the company's limited systems, which weren't designed to cope with unexpected changes. Firing the materials manager is just another way of attacking the symptoms instead of fixing the real problem. Worse, next time the problem crops up, the company will just fire the next crew.

At some point, a number of companies begin to look a little deeper. Maybe it's time to go beyond the patchwork fixes of the past and the revolving door for key managers. Maybe it's time to do some things differently on a more broad-based level. In the example above, the company needs to implement a better control system. Then it will be able to handle a change in product mix without going out of control.

This type of self-examination is harder to do than it sounds. It takes a degree of courage and self-confidence that isn't present in all management teams. Yet in nearly all cases it ends up being an extremely positive experience. Once people understand the real causes of the problems they've been experiencing and see that there are effective, proven solutions, they feel positive and motivated.

That's where this book can help. Each chapter points out the current body of knowledge in the field of production and inventory management (P&IM), with solutions that can help people do their jobs better and with less frustration. In the following pages, you'll learn about key techniques, such as sales and operations planning, demand management, master production scheduling, material requirements planning, capacity planning, and material planning. You'll learn how to implement MRP II and how to operate your company more effectively through an MRP II closed-loop system. And along the way, you'll learn how MRP II integrates with the other techniques and technologies that are so important today. Before moving on to descriptions of individual techniques, let's take a few moments to consider why the integration of multiple technologies is so important.

MULTIPLE TECHNOLOGIES FOR A CHANGING WORLD

The most striking reality of American manufacturing today is the massive competitive advantage available to companies willing to break with tradition. Not only do the different technologies offer enormous competitive benefits in their own right, but they work together in a remarkable synthesis.

John Mammoser, MRP II project leader at Schrock Cabinets, managed a multiple technology implementation and offers the following insights into the process: "The main idea is to spread the load out as much as possible. We had our quality control manager running the TQC part, our P&IM manager running the Just-in-Time part, and a newly named master scheduler taking care of the MRP II pilot. I worked pretty closely with the team [employee empowerment] concept. We tried to spread it out as much as we could.

"We had a JIT task force, which acted as a project team for the JIT effort, with a variety of different spin-off task forces. At one point we had around a hundred people, each of whom was involved on a JIT task force or spin-off team—we were trying to get everybody involved. And most of those teams were made up of people from the floor, the hourly people.

"On the MRP side, we pretty much followed the classical advice—we had spin-off task forces for inventory record accuracy, bills of material, master scheduling, and all that. It was pretty much a standard proven path implementation.

"In TQC, our QC manager had an overseeing task force of his own. He tried to get the high-performance teams involved up front in TQC. The high-performance work teams were structured pretty much by department. Rather than really trying to get a whole series of spin-off task forces for TQC, he went to those teams that were already functioning and got them to use the TQC tools to attack problems. I will say this, though: One or two small TQC task forces were working on several different problems outside the boundaries of the high-performance work teams."

Unlike Schrock, most companies used to implement one technology at a time. They might start with MRP II; when that was completed, they might begin working on Just-in-Time. Today, competitive pressures are such that companies no longer have the luxury of a sequential implementation approach to multiple technologies.

Valleylab felt that pressure, as general manager Ed Fitzgerald explains: "We were working toward Class A MRP II when we were directed to jump right into JIT. Some of us thought that wasn't a prudent decision—to get into JIT before we felt comfortable with the MRP II process. We were dragged into it kicking and screaming. In retrospect, it worked out well. We did have the ability to do both, and we did both well. It didn't slow up the MRP II implementation significantly, if at all. At the end, we felt we had made the right decision—to do both at the same time."

As Schrock and Valleylab discovered, the various technologies complement rather than fight each other. If, however, multiple initiatives appear to be the "flavor of the month," people lose confidence and the company appears to have no direction other than bouncing from one buzzword to another. One foreman for an automotive supplier summarized it well when he said, "I've learned three things about these new programs over the years. First, never oppose them. If you do, you'll get fired. Next, never do any work on them. That's because of the third thing, which is, in three months you'll never hear about them again. I've been here twenty-three years, and I've seen twenty-three of these things come and twenty-three of them go." While this foreman's skepticism may be extreme, many people share his concerns, although they may be reluctant to express them quite as directly.

To provide direction and stability, many companies have established an overriding theme that integrates the different initiatives. Valleylab is typical with its total quality initiative. Under its symbolic total quality "umbrella" you'll find Just-in-Time, MRP II, and a reward and incentive program. This communicates the message "We're going from here to there, and these are some of the steps along the way." In this case, people perceive multiple initiatives to be interrelated, complementary, and mutually reinforcing.

Because the different technologies complement one another, some connections need to be made between them.

"In our environment, some JIT activities needed to be done before major steps in our MRP implementation could be done," explains Al Gronlund, plant manager at Diamond Cabinets. "I think you need to do process changes—JIT activities and kanban activities in your factories—prior to developing shop-floor controls and determining how you are going to cost them because there are so many things hung on that process.

"We started MRP II first," Gronlund continues. "After our pilot teams got rolling, we slapped ourselves on the sides of our heads and said, 'Now, wait a minute, we need to define how we're going to run our business first before we can proceed much further with any of this.' We took a step back and emphasized the need to get point-of-use inventories *where they need to be*, to go through a major inventory reduction so we didn't have to spend a tremendous amount of time and effort learning how to deal with inventory that wasn't going to be there."

Gronlund's experience is typical. Implementing multiple technologies is somewhat chaotic, and movement isn't always in a straight line. There is enormous change happening, and the interrelationships between the different technologies mean that the sequencing and direction of the work can be confusing.

"We also had a problem with kanban and bills of material," explains John Mammoser at Schrock. "We were cutting bottoms for our drawers out of sheets of plywood. We were cutting them by work order, and we had big piles of inventory. One of our JIT spin-off groups came in and changed the whole situation. Since most of our drawers are the same depth, the people from the spin-off group would cut strips of plywood to that depth, and then just slice off the width needed for each drawer bottom. That was all well and good, except that changed the structure of how the product was built, added some parts, and took away the stock so we didn't inventory actual cut-to-size drawer bottoms. The people from the JIT spin-off group ran afoul of the bill of material people, who said, 'Hey, you can't do that.' So for a couple of weeks the JIT leader and the bill of material leader were at odds with each other. 'They can't do that,' the bill of material people were saying. And the JIT people were saying, 'Now, wait a minute, we're not going to stop progress just to please the bill of material people.' I got the sides together and said, 'We have to keep the bill of material right, and we can't just stop progress.' "

John Lewis, plant manager at Continental Can Co., explains how his company integrated its MRP II and quality initiatives. "When we first started with MRP, we had already started the quality process. The quality process brings organization to our company by making us identify our requirements. When we started MRP, we used the same process and asked, 'What are the requirements of this process?' So we integrated the two of them, and they played off each other very well."

INTEGRATION

Clearly, each new initiative affects everything else. When John Lewis talked about how his company integrated MRP II and its quality program, he was identifying one of these interrelationships. At Schrock, the effect of the JIT team's initiative on the company's bill of material group, as described by John Mammoser, is another of these connections. And Al Gronlund at Diamond Cabinets identified another connection when Diamond decided that it made more sense to do some Just-in-Time activities before proceeding with MRP II implementation.

A good way to illustrate the manufacturing integration concept is to use the analogy of the human body (Figure 1.2):

Figure 1.2   Human Body Analogy

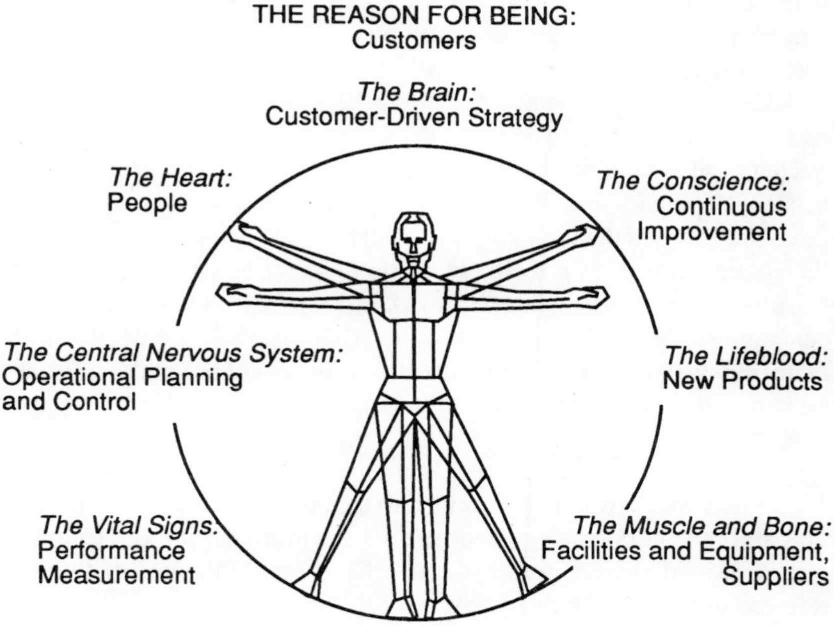

THE REASON FOR BEING:
Customers

The Brain:
Customer-Driven Strategy

The Heart:
People

The Conscience:
Continuous
Improvement

The Central Nervous System:
Operational Planning
and Control

The Lifeblood:
New Products

The Vital Signs:
Performance
Measurement

The Muscle and Bone:
Facilities and Equipment,
Suppliers

The **people** of an organization are the *heart*. They're what keeps it alive.

The **facilities and equipment** and **suppliers** are the *muscle and bone*.

New products are the *lifeblood* of any organization.

Continuous improvement is the *conscience* of the organization, always prompting it to get better.

Performance measurements is the *annual checkup*, the EKG to check the *vital signs* of the organization.

Operational planning and control is the *central nervous system* that coordinates all the various aspects of the business.

Customer-driven strategy is the *brain* that makes decisions on where to invest, where to use resources, and so on.

Finally, in addition to blood and sinew, we have the **customer**, the *reason for being*. Everybody needs a reason for his or her existence. This can be family, work, church, and so on. For a company, the customer serves this purpose.

The usefulness of this mental image is that the human body can't live without all the parts, and all the parts must function in harmony with one another. Similarly, within a company all the parts are needed, and each must work effectively with the others.

Another way to represent the interrelationships that exist in a company is shown in Figure 1.3.

Here, the symbol in the center shows the integration of the different parts of the business. As companies attempt to improve their effectiveness, they have to deal not only with independent elements, but also with the connections among them. In each of the following chapters, you'll learn how key technologies can work in harmony and how integration can augment their effectiveness. When this happens, the whole manufacturing operation becomes greater than the sum of the parts—just as a human body is more than the sum of its various organs and systems.

With this as background, let's return to the subject of this book, production and inventory management and its integration with key technologies. The next chapter presents a set of key P&IM themes that will be referred to throughout this book.

Figure 1.3   An Integrated Structure for Operational Excellence

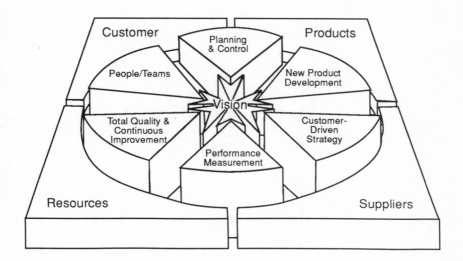

Chapter Two

Major Themes in PIM

THE PRODUCTION CONTROL EXPERTS

(with apologies to "the Blind Men and the Elephant" by John Godfrey Saxe)

It was six men of management,
To learning much inclined,
Who discoursed on production control
And the answers they did find
—From experience, and the lessons
That reward an inquiring mind.

"Order to mins and maximums,"
The first was heard to say.
"You'll have neither too much nor too little
When production's controlled this way."

"But the answer lies in a forecast,"
Said the second man in line.
"Just anticipate your sales
And everything will be fine."

"I doubt it," said the third one.
"You've forgotten the EOQ.
With balanced setups and inventories,
What problems can ensue?"

The fourth one said, "Use order points
To get the desired control.

When you order materials soon enough,
You'll never be 'in the hole.' "

"But you really need a computer,"
Said the fifth—"PC's a dream,
With loads run from last week's payroll cards
And exception reports by the ream."

Said the sixth, "Materials management
Is a concept to which I'm devoted—
Instead of learning production control,
I've escaped by getting promoted!"

So study each book and seminar,
Attend every one you can, sir!
You'll find a thousand experts
—each with *part* of the answer.

O. W. WIGHT

EVERY ONE FOR HIMSELF

If you asked the blind men in the traditional ode to build an elephant, each would create a very different beast. The same thing has happened in manufacturing: Each company used to create planning systems based on its own individual view of the world and driven by its own unique logic. One company would be running a system it called "STARS," another would be running "MARS," while still others would be running "ZIP," "ZAP," and so on. The problem was that everyone reinvented the wheel rather than generalizing from everyone else's successes and failures.

Today, you have a choice of starting from scratch or drawing on the body of knowledge that has been distilled from the experience thousands of manufacturing companies have accumulated over the past two decades. While the decision may seem obvious, there are two reasons why many companies prefer to start from square one.

First, many manufacturing companies are loath to generalize from the experience of other firms, even those in the same sector. "We're unique," they claim. "We have a one-of-a-kind ordering system—no one else's problems and solutions could possibly apply to us!"

True, every company *is* unique if you look at its combination of products, manufacturing processes, marketplace, culture, and financial ratios. And it's natural for people to ask, "How can we use the same kind of planning system as the company next door? Its products are different, it doesn't use the technology, it has fewer employees, its debt-to-equity ratio is twice ours, and so on."

But imagine what it would be like if you attended an accounting convention and someone stood up and said, "Our company can't use double-entry bookkeeping because we're different from other businesses." You and your colleagues would certainly wonder how a person could be so misguided. In the manufacturing world, though, managers use the same argument every day to reject standardized manufacturing planning systems. And the amazing thing is that so many people agree!

At PYOSA, a major manufacturer of pigments and industrial compounds, it would have been easy to say, "We're unique . . . MRP II won't work for us." Pigments are difficult products to schedule because they're processed in batches, yet there is very high volume, that literally flows through the factory. Instead, the people at PYOSA said, "We can make it work." And they did. As the director of the pigments unit, Rubén Sáez, puts it, "MRP helps us put the spotlight on the problems that we can solve. A year ago, our customer service was, at best, 50 percent— we usually couldn't deliver a customer order within five days, as we were supposed to. Now our fill rate is 95 percent. Customers who said horrible things about us before now think we're terrific, and it's showing up in our increased market share!"

At Heekin Can in Cincinnati, which manufactures almost a million cans per shift, people could have said, "MRP II will never work in our environment." At the time, no other company had ever applied MRP II to a repetitive, high-volume manufacturing operation like can making. But Heekin's president, Harry Uehlein, began to explore the concept, and later acted as "executive torchbearer" for his company's implementation. Heekin's customer-service rates were good before the implementation, but with MRP they can only be characterized as excellent—orders arrive on schedule 97 to 98 percent of the time.

Another reason companies tend to build planning systems from scratch is that they have a natural inclination to develop their own solutions to problems. After all, there's a certain pride in saying, "We fixed it ourselves." Also, people tend to operate in a "seek-and-destroy mode"—find a problem and solve it—rather than stepping back and looking at what others have done in a particular area. The most intelligent form of pioneering entails building on what's already been discovered—it makes no sense to rediscover what's already known and proven.

Finally, there's the issue of morale. People can only do so much when you drag them through endless nights and weekends to make small increments of progress—which is exactly what happens when you try to build a manufacturing planning and control system from the ground up.

The alternative is to recognize that there are more similarities than differences among manufacturing companies, whether they make potato chips or microchips. The knowledge and experience of others can therefore give you a "jump start" in your own efforts. During the past twenty years, a number of fundamental principles that transcend all business types have been discovered and articulated. Some of these principles appear to be just statements of the obvious, such as the difference between planning and execution. But others represent hard-won lessons that could only be learned through difficult experimentation.

For example, it took ten years of trial and error to fully understand the limits of computers and the proper role of people, and to establish a balance for each. Issues such as planning versus execution and humans versus computers set the backdrop for this book. Let's start by looking at the differences between formal and informal systems.

THE FORMAL VERSUS THE INFORMAL SYSTEM

Most executives would be surprised to learn that in the planning and scheduling areas, their procedure books are really more collections of theoretical ideas than actual operating principles. This would come as a shock, because even though they realize that the procedure books may be somewhat out of date, top managers assume that, by and large, the procedures are followed. Sure, they accept the fact that there will be some variations, since people must be given flexibility to deal with unusual situations. But overall, they believe that their companies are being run "by the book." The truth is, there's often a wide gap between the formal system—the company as outlined in the procedure books—and the informal system—the idiosyncratic methods and techniques that individuals develop to do their jobs.

John Lewis, plant manager at Continental Can Co., explains what it was like before his company implemented a formal planning and scheduling system: "We would schedule a can size. At three o'clock in the morning the lift-truck driver is half awake and half asleep. He goes out to the warehouse, can't find the material, then goes to the supervisor. The supervisor looks at his schedule and there's nothing else on it to run. So he calls a scheduler, waking him from a sound sleep. The scheduler says, 'I don't remember.' They shut down the line. You come in the next day, they've gone to another item. Then you find there are ten bundles of material out there and we've missed a customer delivery. It's been over four years now since that type of thing has happened."

In the old days, Radio Cap Company, an advertising specialty firm that manufactures products like Koozie™ beverage-can holders, hats, and mugs, was typical of many companies with informal systems. Job folders littered the factory floor from one corner to another; piles of half-finished orders and raw material sprang from the floor like giant stalagmites; people roamed the floor looking for any material they could find to get their jobs done. Recalls facilitator Glenda Saucedo with a smile, "We were so disorganized that chaos would have been paradise. It's a wonder we got *anything* out the door!" "Things were so bad," adds cell facilitator Mary Thomas, "that you'd get an order due to ship the next day, and you'd go to get inventory and there wouldn't be any. Instead of doing anything about it, you'd put the order down and go on to the next order. Jobs were all over the place with 'committed' ['hot'] stickers on them and the priorities were based on how many stickers were on a folder. The only way you knew that an order would actually ship was to escort it through the factory and make sure it got put on the truck." Two years later, Radio Cap's sales per employee had risen 62 percent, inventory turnover was up by 22 percent, overtime had been reduced tremendously, and cycle time for products through the plant had been reduced from 15 days to 5 days.

But the most poignant example of the informal system comes from MRP II pioneer Oliver Wight following his experience with Stanley. If nothing else, Stanley was the embodiment of a formal system gone awry and an informal system that arose out of pure need.

When Ollie first graduated from college, he joined Raybestos Corporation as a trainee in production control. The boss asked Ollie to help Stanley, a 32-year veteran, to become more systematic. At first Wight questioned this task: Stanley had a spotless record, never missing a schedule for lack of raw material. The boss told Ollie that Stanley did indeed do a fabulous job, but since Stanley kept all on-hand balances on little scraps of paper inside his jacket pocket, the company would literally stand still if Stanley ever got into an accident. To avoid this unpleasant possibility, the boss wanted Ollie to get Stanley to play by the rules in the procedures book, which required updating all the Kardex inventory files on a daily basis.

Now, Ollie was a confident young man with a college education. Stanley was also confident, and at that point he had survived at least 32 college-trained assistants. The first day, Ollie immediately suggested that the two of them update the Kardex file. Stanley, in turn, suggested that Ollie just "follow him around for a week or so" to see how the place worked. Ollie agreed, and watched in amazement as Stanley recorded a torrent of information on little slips of paper and cards stored in various pockets. "You can't use the systems around here," he'd say. "They're too out of date. This load of tire waste is needed in department five this afternoon. It'll be sometime next week before it shows up in the receiving system."

And so it went, with Stanley making notes on what was happening in the factory and Ollie trying to understand why his boss wanted him to update the Kardex records; the records clearly had nothing to do with Stanley's keeping the company going, and didn't seem to offer any hope of being able to do the job nearly as well as Stanley was doing it by manually recording the quantities of raw materials in the plant.

At one point, Ollie thought he had him. Stanley unscrewed the top from a resin tank, put a stick down the hole, and announced, "Five hundred gallons."

"Now, if we'd used the consumption reports, you wouldn't have to put the stick in the tank to see how much is there," Ollie eagerly pointed out.

"Ollie," Stanley said, "ten years ago we changed the formula for the Chevrolet brake shoes, and the bill of material hasn't been changed yet. If you use the consumption report, you'll have no idea what's in that tank. Around here, you can't trust anything that's on a sheet of paper. Look—there's a lot of things I don't know, but I do know this: If it's on the stick, it's in the tank." Ollie didn't say much for the rest of the day.

At the end of three weeks, Ollie announced that Stanley was indeed doing a terrific job, and no book of procedures could replace him. John, Ollie's boss, got angry. "Well, what happens if he gets hit by a truck?"

John asked. "What are we going to do then? Have you thought about that?"

"Yes, I've thought a great deal about that over the last few weeks. If Stanley gets hit by a truck, I wouldn't even know which pocket to look in. John, I go to church every Sunday and pray for Stanley. I suggest that you do the same."

Why didn't Stanley update the Kardex record as required by the procedure book? Because it didn't give him the information he needed to run the business. This is the common thread that runs through all informal systems: If the formal system doesn't provide people with the necessary information to do their jobs, an informal one will appear.

In general, there are three reasons why a formal system doesn't work:

1. *It's based on an invalid model.* The underlying logic of the system may be incorrect; that is, it's based on an invalid model of the way the world works. Take an order point system based on the notion that you should have a little of everything around all the time. Of course, in a world of limited resources—cash, material, inventory, and so on— that's not realistic. The inventory needed to support such a system would drive you into a noncompetitive position.

A valid model would tell what you need and when you need it. The order point system fails on both counts. First, the fact that you just used up material has nothing to do with when you'll need it again. You might need it tomorrow or you might need it next month. Second, the system tells you to order a specific quantity, which may in reality turn out to be too little or too much. One thing is certain: The order quantity isn't based on anticipated future needs, but rather on past average usage. For example, the average usage for an item might be 100 per month. That doesn't help you if you need 150 next month to fill a customer order. This is called "steering the ship by the wake."

The result of this mode of piloting the manufacturing ship is that you may not be able to meet customer demand, or you may needlessly tie up valuable dollars in raw material inventory. Since people are given the objective of meeting customer delivery dates and keeping inventory down, and since the formal system doesn't tell them how to do that, they invent an informal system—just as Stanley did.

2. *The formal system is based on sound logic, but the data feeding into the system are inaccurate.* MRP II is certainly a valid model, but there

are many companies that have both MRP II *and* an informal system. How can that be? Answer: The formal system doesn't give them the information necessary to run the business, because the data aren't accurate. The best MRP II system in the world won't tell you what you need and when you need it if your inventory records are only 30 percent accurate. If the system says, "Get this material right away," and someone thinks, "The last time I listened to the computer we had five years' worth of material on hand and I got chewed out by the boss," the formal system will give way to the informal system—that person, like Stanley, will find some other way to order what's really needed.

Similarly, if no one updates bills of material, formulas, or recipes, there is no way for MRP II to know that, say, one integrated-circuit chip has been replaced with another one. As a result, the proper chips won't be available as they are needed. This will induce people to invent their own system for determining what's really on hand and what's really needed. And when push comes to shove, people will start expediting, developing bigger shortage lists, carrying out spot checks on the inventory of specific items, ordering more than what's really needed, and requesting delivery of raw material and components before they're needed—just to make sure they're covered. As people slip into crisis mode, they expend a lot of nervous energy without being productive, which in the long run leads to poor customer service, reduced profits, and burnout.

The plight of a large maker of pharmaceuticals demonstrates what can happen when the data are not accurate. This company had good data accuracy on its raw materials, but poor accuracy on its bottles, labels, caps, and other packaging materials. When it was time to manufacture a product, the materials weighing room sent the materials to the blending and mixing operations. This was the trigger that set off a flurry of activity to make sure all the items needed to package the product were on hand. The clock was ticking because once the blending had begun, it was only a matter of hours before the product would be ready for packaging.

Typically, because the data were inaccurate, the company would find it was short on some packaging items, and then go into panic mode in an attempt to have labels printed on short notice or have another delivery of bottles scheduled. The informal system was alive and well for the packaging supplies because the formal system was unable to tell people what was needed and when. For this company, having an in-house printing shop for labels was both a blessing and a curse. The blessing was that it could perform miracles by producing labels on short notice (the informal system had a short horizon). The curse was the amount of money lost and a sky-high frustration level in the packaging area.

3. *The formal system is valid, the data are accurate, but the management is poor.* A good model and sound data will still not yield a workable situation if managers abuse the system. Consider the classic overloaded master schedule. Many people believe it is necessary to put more on the schedule than can actually be produced. The logic goes as follows: "Today we miss the schedule and only produce 85 percent of plan, right? We also have to make the billing numbers or we run out of money, right? Then we have to put more on the schedule so when we miss it we still get enough to meet the billing numbers, right?" Wrong! By putting more on the master schedule than is doable, the only thing you ensure is that the formal system will break down and the informal system will rear its head.

Let's assume that there is more on the master schedule than can be realistically built. The material planning system asks for all the material required to support the bloated schedule, and the computer generates a list of all materials needed for the following weeks. People in purchasing take one look at the list and realize that they don't have a prayer of getting all the materials on time. So what do they do? They go out to the assembly supervisor and say, "Hey, Jack, what do you need from us to make this week's schedule?" The assembly supervisor responds by making a list of all the items he's short, and says, "If you can just get me these materials, I can make it through the week."

What's just happened here? The purchasing people and the assembly supervisor have created an informal system *so they get their jobs done.* The formal system is the giant list of materials spewed out by the scheduling system, but everyone knows that it's unrealistic, so everyone disregards it in favor of a system that solves the immediate problem.

THE PROBLEM WITH INFORMAL SYSTEMS

At this point, you might wonder, "If an informal system has been around for years and keeps the company going, why change?" Here are three good reasons. First, success in this context is an illusion. While an informal system might enable this week's shipments to get out the door, it does so at a price. *Informal systems are inefficient and costly.* They also detract from the quality of work life; living with an informal system is like being locked in a dark room with a madman armed with a baseball bat—the blows come out of nowhere.

Second, *the informal system will eventually break down.* The person who runs the system in his or her head will eventually get sick, quit, change jobs, or retire. When that happens, all the information locked in his or her head will vanish. That means the informal system is highly susceptible to personnel changes.

Even if you wanted to propagate the informal system, it has a long learning curve, possibly ten years or more, because it is based on personal knowledge and experience.

The final major drawback of the informal system is that *it paralyzes your ability to manage effectively* by compromising one or more of the four basic and well-accepted principles of management:

1. Set objectives.

2. Assign accountability.

3. Provide tools (as simple as a screwdriver or as complex as a planning and scheduling system for a plant or factory).

4. Measure performance.

When a company operates by an informal system—i.e., without the tools people need to get their jobs done—it can't set objectives and hold people accountable, other than at the very top level. There is no mechanism for translating high-level plans into day-to-day tasks. The company can ask, "Did things work? Did we ship product on time?" But it can't ask, "Who was supposed to do what?" Further, unless each person in the company knows what he or she is supposed to do to meet the top-level goals, the ability to hold people accountable is dramatically reduced. And accountability is fundamental to management.

The informal system also destroys a company's ability to measure performance objectively. How can performance be measured when the company's basic operational plans exist only in the minds of one or two people?

In contrast, if a company provides a formal system that generates valid numbers, management can say with certainty what has to be done by specific dates and who is responsible for making the plan happen. Then everyone will be working in concert toward a mutually understood goal.

PLANNING AND EXECUTION

During the early days of MRP, many practitioners fell into the trap of thinking that just because they had a good plan, the plan would actually happen. What they quickly learned was that good planning often reveals problems, which must be resolved through a separate process.

The most successful companies do a good job of *both* planning and execution. An excellent example is Steelcase, one of the pioneers in both MRP II and Just-in-Time. When talking about their planning system, the people at Steelcase are careful to explain, "The planning system doesn't make parts. It gives you information. When you realize the items you need are in another city, then the people have to find a way to get them here on time."

In contrast, companies that focus only on execution without having a valid plan tend to operate with a brute-force, "we'll make it happen" mentality. This approach is self-defeating because it leads to more overtime and burned-out employees. One company, for instance, got a new general manager with a "hands and hours" approach to planning. Rather than invest in new tools and technology, his approach was to put in more hours, make bigger and bigger shortage lists, and work more and more overtime. After more than a year of this approach, people were burned out, and shipments to customers, while better than before, were well below the results a sister division was achieving through the use of better planning tools. This company learned that while putting more into the business is beneficial, it cannot take the place of necessary and fundamental controls.

Of course, the opposite situation—a good plan without the means to execute it—is no better. Perhaps the plan requires getting 15,000 units of product per week for the next four weeks from a particular line. Historically, though, that line has never produced more than 10,000 units per week. So the choices are:

1. Find a way to get the line to produce more.

2. Find another line to get the job done.

3. Find an outside subcontractor.

4. Change the product so it can be manufactured differently.

5. Change the schedule so the products will ship later than when they were originally called for.

Ultimately, what distinguishes the real competitors from the rest of the pack is their ability to make a plan happen by identifying and resolving problems and working out the fine details that spell the difference between success and failure. People ask, "How quickly can I get to top levels of performance?" The answer is within each company's control. How fast can you resolve problems? How fast can you get to the root causes and make them go away? The planning and scheduling system makes these issues visible. The top organizations are the ones that tackle these issues, as well as identify opportunities and resolve pressing problems.

HUMAN VERSUS COMPUTER

Some people understand MRP II to be largely a hardware/software issue. Over the past two decades computers have been excellent at manipulating massive amounts of data, for example, retrieving and updating the on-hand balance of item 2254938-40. This is far superior to having someone thumb through stacks of index cards. In fact, with most manufacturing companies having between 2,000 and 30,000 items to control, the computer can do things that are almost impossible for a human brain. But in the areas of evaluation, judgment, and creativity, people are better. People have the ability to innovate, evaluate various options, and make decisions—computers have not demonstrated an ability to do these things.

There have been attempts over the last twenty years to program decision logic into computers for things like master scheduling and capacity planning. These efforts have been mostly unsuccessful for three reasons. First, *not every decision can be reduced to numbers.* More important, *programs have no ability to be creative*—they can't look at a problem with unconventional approaches. And sometimes it's the unconventional approaches that work in a given situation. The moral? Marry the brute processing power of the computer with the capacity of people to make informed decisions. This fulfills what management expert Peter Drucker calls the primary purpose of an organization: to maximize strength and minimize weakness. That is, maximize the strength of the computer—its ability to retrieve and manipulate data. Allow people to use their strengths—their ability to innovate, analyze, and make judgments. Third, *computers cannot be held accountable.* If, when something goes wrong, people can shrug their shoulders and say, "I was only doing what the computer told me to do," then accountability goes out the window.

The bottom line is that computers are useful tools for helping people make the best possible decisions, but when they are left to run the business, expensive mistakes are likely to be made. At one instrument manufacturer, for example, a buyer developed the habit of doing whatever the computer recommended. He was certainly surprised when 6,000 pounds of molybdenum steel—a 20-year supply—showed up on the loading dock. "That's what the computer called for," the buyer muttered as he cleaned out his desk.

HONESTY: A SINGLE SET OF NUMBERS THAT SIMULATES REALITY

If you were going to start a manufacturing company from scratch, how would you organize it? You would most likely want to have a single set of numbers communicated throughout the entire organization. Unfortunately, that's not how most companies work. Anyone who's been to a two-hour meeting in which the first hour was spent arguing about which numbers are valid will appreciate the importance of the single-set-of-numbers approach.

To be effective, the single set of numbers has to be an accurate representation of reality. Is the master production schedule accurate? Are the bills of material, formulas, or recipes accurate? Do the numbers accurately reflect the introduction of the new product? People ask, "Can you do this in MRP II? Can you do that?" The answer is, What can you do in the real world? Can you produce 10,000 units this week? How are you going to manufacture the product? What's the realistic timing for the new product? In other words, you must represent in your system what is happening in the real world. If you can make these things happen, then show them in the formal planning and scheduling system. If not, then work together to develop your best estimate of what will happen, and represent that in the system.

Honesty is a word that did not appear in the early writing and discussion of planning and control systems. Today, honesty is a subject of almost continual discussion as companies manage the numbers in their planning and control systems. One company, a food manufacturer, will tell you it "winks" at the plans. What does it mean to "wink" at a plan? It means nobody really believes the plans, but it's considered poor manners to go up to the top executives and tell them their plans are unrealistic.

If people don't really believe the plans, are they expected to go out and execute the plans? Should they buy the material, get the necessary capacity? If not, how are they supposed to know how much to wink? Should they buy 80 percent of the material and capacity? And if so, which 80 percent? What if one person gets 80 percent of what's called for in the plans, another gets 70 percent, and a third gets 100 percent? Or what if they all get 80 percent, but for different products? Now the company has the worst of all worlds because it has material and capacity it can't use.

In addition, the company creates a high level of frustration, as the person who had to put in hours of work on Saturday and Sunday finds that it was all for nothing. The other materials and the capacity needed to manufacture the materials he or she provided are not available. From now on, whoever asks this person to put in the extra effort to get "needed" material or capacity will probably be told to drop dead, or, even worse, will be politely ignored.

Marshall Byrd, from Martin Marietta Astronautics Group's Defense & Space Communications, knew what it was like to work with inaccurate data. "As a supervisor, I had no priorities. I could work on anything I wanted because everything was past due. There was no sense or rhyme or reason in what we did from day to day. It was stressful on everyone, from the worker all the way through the program manager who was trying to deliver to his customer's end date." One of the keys to reaching top levels of operating performance is what Byrd calls "an honest system." By *honest* he means a system with accurate data that enables people to make proper decisions and operate in the most efficient, cost-effective manner. "We never had that flexibility before," says Byrd, but with accurate data "we're in a better cost-competitive position. We give customers the most efficient processes as well as deliver high-quality products."

Summary/Checkup

1. The days of inventing approaches and techniques in the field of planning and control are over. Most companies recognize this, and few, if any, pursue this path any longer. Have there been instances when someone in your company has felt the need to rediscover what was already available from other sources?

2. The informal system is alive and well in many companies today. To what extent, if any, does the informal system exist at your company?

3. Most organizations focus on execution, with less attention and emphasis on planning. These companies will benefit greatly from improved tools in the planning area. Other companies like to plan, but just don't seem to be able to "make it happen." This is a more difficult challenge. What does your company reward with regard to planning and execution?

4. The role of the computer has not been well defined. Does the computer have a mystique at your company, or is there a levelheaded understanding of what it does well and what people do better?

5. Today, a company can run its business using a single set of numbers that people believe and that are agreed upon by all departments. Does such a situation exist in your company?

With these major themes as background, let's turn now to two companies and the way they do business.

...ter Three

...siness
Usual

All comp ....ng for sales and production. They might do it with a state-of-the-art computer system, or they might scratch out the numbers on the back of a napkin over coffee and doughnuts.

All companies run into capacity problems at one time or another; they need another filling line, another plastic injection molding machine, or another chemical reactor. The question is, when do they discover the need for more capacity—before it becomes a problem, or when orders are overdue and work is stacking up on the factory floor?

And at one time or another, all companies have a problem with inventory—too much or too little. It could be that they made valid and realistic plans and the marketplace zigged when they predicted it would zag. Or they may not have a good planning and control system so they didn't know what they needed and when they needed it.

Those companies that do their planning on the back of a napkin are run by the informal systems described in Chapter 2. Those that use powerful planning and scheduling tools, like MRP II, are run by formal systems.

There are any number of misconceptions about formal systems. The most common is that formal systems are perfect, and that using them will make the day-to-day problems that plague most manufacturing companies vanish. This doesn't happen in the real world. What does happen with formal systems is that people are given better, more effective tools to

35

deal with the kinds of problems that happen every day. They have better visibility, better data, and a better understanding of the implications of various options in running the business.

In most companies, new tools carry with them some unrealistic expectations. In one equipment manufacturing company, the materials manager said, "Even though we were extremely careful to explain to people that the new systems wouldn't solve all our problems, that was still the impression many people developed. 'Don't worry about it, the new system will take care of that problem' was something you'd hear nearly every day. When we actually started implementing, we had to counter those expectations."

The reality of new tools is that they don't eliminate obstacles in the real world. There will still be problems in search of solutions, and much work to be done—identifying problems, developing creative solutions, and implementing plans.

In a company in which the planning and control systems are not working well, the challenge and achievement of work have been replaced by the frustration that comes from being overwhelmed by problems. The realistic objective, therefore, is not to eliminate the problems inherent in running a manufacturing company, but rather to turn them into challenges that result in success and accomplishment.

To be sure, virtually all companies fall somewhere in between total chaos and excellent planning. If they're closer to the total chaos end of the spectrum, they probably ought to be doing something to improve their management approach. If they're closer to the other end and have good planning and schedules, they should continue to invest the time, energy, and resources needed to maintain their status, and to look for ways to refine their efforts.

A Tale of Two Companies

To illustrate the difference in planning approaches, let's consider the differences in two companies. The first operates in an informal, reactive manner, focusing its attention on saving the day. Its employees are stressed and strained from expediting and making diving catches in the ninth inning. Yet the culture of this company rewards people for perpetuating what is ultimately a chaotic environment.

In contrast, the second company has developed and refined a formal planning system that provides a window on the future and prevents crises from happening in the first place. People in this company work just as hard as their counterparts in the first company, but they don't feel as if the world is about to end every ten minutes—they have the tools to help them see the developing problems, and they can approach the solutions in a more methodical, well-informed way. Their tool? A "closed-loop" planning system integrated with other leading-edge management technologies. Information is shared among departments, and plans are changed to reflect agreed-upon solutions and agreed-upon limitations. There are inevitable compromises, decisions some people don't like, and "least-worst" choices. But people work together to accommodate changes within the company, the marketplace, and the economy.

Again, there are no perfect companies, and businesses that are totally out of control and chaotic don't last very long—most companies lie somewhere in between. The following descriptions are food for thought about ways to improve your company's competitiveness, profitability, working environment, and quality of life.

Chaos, Inc.

People in Chaos, Inc. spend most of their time madly stomping out brushfires rather than working to prevent them in the first place, even though preventive actions are more efficient than "heroically" saving the day. For example, they frequently shut down production for lack of raw materials, purchased items, or manufactured components. They react to the crises by expediting the missing items. If the missing items are purchased, they call the vendors and insist on immediate delivery, which is not nearly quick enough for a company that "needs everything yesterday." If the missing items are manufactured, they do the same thing with the factory or plant.

The chaos at Chaos becomes self-catalyzing, feeding on itself and creating ever more confusion. It's further fueled by management's practice of rewarding—and thus perpetuating—"heroic acts." Here's how it works: Every day the weight of the world hangs on getting the shipments out, the clock is approaching midnight, and things aren't looking good. Out of nowhere a fleet-footed "hero" steals parts from a half-finished product, commandeers the toolroom, has the fabrication area stop everything to make one item that's desperately needed, threatens to tear the heart out of a poorly performing supplier, and pulls it all together with just a few minutes to go. With cheers from his co-workers in the background, he slumps into his chair exhausted. It's a hard act to follow.

The problem is, no one ever examines the legacy of such acts of corporate bravery. In reality, someone has to find another part to replace the one that was cannibalized. The toolroom was behind schedule already, as was the fabrication area; now they're in even worse shape. And the next person to deal with the supplier who's been put through the wringer will have an even more difficult time. Rather than fixing the problems, the company has just guaranteed that they will all happen again in another 30 days or so.

To continue this scenario, the people at Chaos, Inc. experience serious problems with capacity. They tend to find out that they need equipment or manpower when it's too late to do much about it. When jobs start backing up at a particular piece of equipment, the number of options is reduced to just a few, because there's so little time to do anything.

For example, the option to buy new equipment or subcontract is no longer available. There isn't enough time to buy new equipment, get it installed, and produce products. There isn't enough time to find a supplier, send the material out, and have it return in time to meet the schedules. The options that are available include overtime, extra shifts, and off-loading work to different equipment. But while these will solve some capacity problems, they can't be counted on to solve *all* the capacity problems.

Chaos, Inc., like all businesses, is attempting in one way or another to solve what Oliver Wight identified years ago as "the universal manufacturing equation":

1. What do we need to make?

2. What does it take to make it?

3. What do we have?

4. What do we have to get?

To understand this equation, consider the process of making Thanksgiving dinner. What do we need to make? Dinner on Thanksgiving. What does it take to make it? We need turkey, stuffing, cranberry sauce, and so on. What do we have? We have the cranberry sauce. What do we have to get? All the other ingredients.

Of course, there are several key differences between Thanksgiving dinner and the work of most manufacturing companies. One is that Thanksgiving doesn't change. In contrast, most manufacturing companies are constantly changing their schedules to meet the volatile demands of the marketplace. Another difference is that Thanksgiving happens once, while manufacturing companies are making different products every day.

In a manufacturing company, the questions would be answered in the following way:

1. *What do we need to make?* The master production schedule (anticipated manufacturing schedule).

2. *What does it take to make it?* The bills of material (BOMs), formulas or recipes, and the routings. The BOM says what's needed to make the product, and the routing indicates what kind of capacity—manpower or equipment—is needed.

3. *What do we have?* The inventory records for material and the planned capacities for equipment.

4. *What do we have to get?* The company's detailed schedule for both material and capacity. It tells us not only what we need, but also when we need it.

At Chaos, Inc., the difficulty is that people can never get beyond the next few days when answering these questions. They know what's preventing them from making today's shipments. However, they're never in a good position to know what they should be working on today to prevent these problems in the future so they can make next week's or next month's shipments.

The net effect is that shipments to customers suffer, inventory is too high, and productivity is low. The company's sales and marketing departments get angry and accuse manufacturing of not doing its job.

Manufacturing responds by blaming sales and marketing for wishful thinking, lousy forecasts, and unrealistic customer promises. Next, the spotlight shifts to quality. Quality assurance people, who have rejected products that have been rushed through plant, are under pressure to ship anyway, which in turn creates resentment. Finally, management begins to scream at everyone as margins slip because the costs of confusion find their way into the product; buyers have been forced to purchase materials at premium costs and pay premium shipping rates so that deliveries can be expedited, overtime is used extensively to deal with capacity problems, and productivity suffers as people attempt to build good products despite bad planning.

To stop the hemorrhaging, top management, under pressure from the company's directors and investors, issues monthly edicts, such as "Cut inventory 10 percent . . . or else." This type of "kick-butt" approach rewards hasty decisions and penalizes formal analysis. Instead of working with people to arrive at common solutions, management, without realizing it, forces adversarial relationships. And instead of serving as resources, managers become opponents. Heads begin to roll and certain key positions—materials manager, vice-president of manufacturing, and inventory manager—become like bucking broncos, throwing their riders onto the ground one after another.

Can life at Chaos, Inc. continue in this fashion indefinitely? Possibly, but the sad thing is that Chaos could offer its people a healthier, more productive working environment, and in doing so achieve a competitive and strategic advantage. Compare Chaos with the following company, which runs more like a team and less like a tug-of-war.

Clockwork Corporation

In contrast to Chaos, Inc., Clockwork Corporation has the ability to identify most problems weeks or even months into the future. Clockwork's COO characterizes his company this way: "We work to try and solve problems rationally, in most cases as part of a team. We can't solve every problem. For example, last month we had a piece of equipment that should be able to produce 180 standard hours per week, but we were getting 120. We're attempting to do some things with this equipment that really push the limits of its design. We're working with the manufacturer of the equipment, with our quality people, with our supervisors, and with our suppliers. Unfortunately, it's not going to reach that rate of output overnight. So we had to go back and change the plan, recognizing what we're able to do in the short run. Our people work with facts now, and with accurate data, and then they evaluate the options."

Clockwork still experiences emergencies, but these are the exceptions rather than the rule. Unlike Chaos' employees, who spend their time frantically fighting skirmishes at every turn of the day, Clockwork's people use planning tools to work smarter and therefore more efficiently. And whereas Chaos' employees leave work feeling frustrated and stressed, employees of Clockwork, in their COO's words, "leave tired, but much more satisfied than years ago, and certainly challenged."

Clockwork's ability to see problems stems from the fact that its high-level business plans are connected in "rack-and-pinion style" to its lower-level detail plans (see Figure 3.1); when the top-level plans have to be changed to accommodate the realities of the marketplace, the lower-level execution plans change in sync.

The flow of planning information at Clockwork is shown in Figure 3.1. It all starts with the business plan. The business plan is stated in dollars, while the plans that people will ultimately be accountable for meeting are stated in terms of units or hours. The first step in converting financial plans into operational plans happens in the sales and operations planning process. Sales and operations planning evaluates anticipated sales and planned production in terms of product families (5 to 10 families in most companies). One output from this process is the production plan, which is typically stated in terms of rates of output by product family—for example, 200,000 small electric motors per month, or 400,000 gallons of silicone fluid per week, or 3 steam turbines per quarter. Sales and operations planning is the responsibility of the general manager (or president) and staff.

To give the production plan developed in the sales and operations planning process a "reality check" and ensure that it can be achieved, people use an abbreviated form of capacity planning called rough-cut capacity planning. "Rough-cut" is a technique that looks at the demands on key resources. In most companies, 10 or 20 key resources are evaluated before the plan is taken to the next level of detail. If the plan is not achievable, then it is changed before people proceed.

The box labeled Demand Management refers to forecasting, customer order promising, distribution and interplant demands, and service

Figure 3.1   Manufacturing Resource Planning
(MRP II)

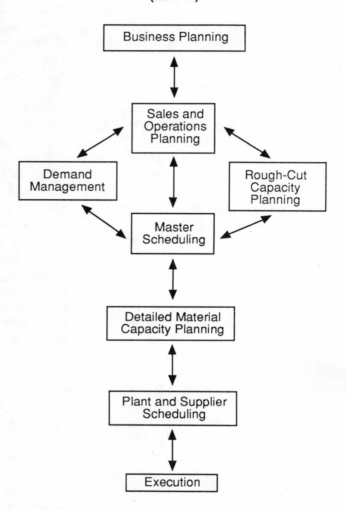

demands (where these exist). It is necessary to take all of these activities into account in order to represent the specific needs of the customers within the planning and scheduling system.

The next level of detail is the master production schedule (MPS). This is the statement of production by item, date, and quantity. Within the family of small electric motors, there may be two hundred different types of motors. The master production schedule shows how many of one type are scheduled to be built today, how many of the next type, and so on for all the types of small electric motors. It reveals the schedule for as far out as the planning system extends (at least a year for most companies). The MPS, when summed up by product family, must equal the production plan for that family.

The material plan is also based on the master production schedule. The material plan describes what material you need and when you need it. *Material* is a general term that can mean assemblies and subassemblies, fabricated items, purchased items, raw materials, intermediates (solutions, mixtures, formulations), bulk production, and so on. Material planning solves the fundamental manufacturing equation for material. A material plan exists for every item, and goes out as far as the planning horizon.

Once you know what material is needed and when it is required, the next (sometimes optional) step in the planning process is to determine what capacity is necessary and when it is needed in a more detailed fashion than is possible with rough-cut capacity planning. Capacity can be either equipment or manpower. Detailed capacity planning solves the universal manufacturing equation:

1. *What do we need to make?* The material plan.

2. *What does it take to make it?* The routings.

3. *What do we have?* The planned capacities.

4. *What do we have to get?* Any additional capacity.

When Clockwork or any company performs detailed capacity planning, it creates a plan for every work center or line and manpower level, one that extends across the full planning horizon. In some industries, such as chemical processing, the company may not need detailed capacity planning. It has a limited number of mixing vats and packaging lines, so rough-cut capacity planning may be sufficient for this company.

At this point in the planning process, the top-level plans have been broken down into specific tasks that need to be accomplished. People can evaluate the plans and ask, "Where are the problems? What would have to happen in order to make the plan succeed?" For example, it may be necessary to get 1,000 pounds per week of a particular raw material in order to meet the plan. Or the plan may require that a purchase order be pulled up for delivery four weeks earlier than its current due date. Capacity could also be a problem. The plan may call for 300 standard hours per week from a particular work center or line over the next six weeks.

Is there a way to make these things happen? If so, the plan is valid, and people's energy should be channeled into executing the plan. Note that it's important to differentiate between a plan that can be achieved and one that's easy. The best companies put an enormous effort into hitting the plan once they determine it's achievable and valid. If, however, the plan simply isn't realistic, it's important to tell the truth. There are a number of reasons why it just may not be possible to make a plan happen, most of which usually involve time or money. It may not be possible to increase capacity next week from 200 to 300 standard hours per week at a particular work center or line. And while it may be theoretically possible to charter a 747 to deliver material in order to meet a delivery, the cost would likely be impossibly high. In situations in which there is no other recourse, the plan is changed to accurately reflect what is actually going to happen.

After the plan has passed the validity test, it must be communicated to the people who will be accountable for making it happen. This is plant and supplier scheduling, as shown in Figure 3.1. The material plan is communicated to suppliers, and the material and capacity plans are communicated to the factory or plant. At this point, the top-level plans of the company have been broken down into the specific tasks that people can be held accountable for hitting.

With a closed-loop system in place, people are willing to be held accountable because they have been part of the planning process and part of the decision to make changes where necessary. In other words, they have *ownership* in the plan.

Accountability is fundamental to managing any business, and manufacturing is no exception. With a closed-loop plan in place, accountability can be maintained. People can be measured. Overall management effectiveness goes up dramatically when the informal system no longer runs the business. This is represented by the box labeled Execution in Figure 3.1.

Another advantage of the closed-loop approach is that it helps you manage change better. Even the best-laid plans may have to change when unexpected events happen within the company (a strike, equipment breakdown, etc.), within the marketplace (a competitor goes out of business, a new technology makes your product obsolete, etc.), or within the political/economic arena (currency rates change, new regulations affect your product, etc.). As thousands of companies have learned, with an effective closed-loop system, the business can quickly see the impact, adjust for unexpected changes, and position itself to meet increased or decreased customer demand. It can also count on information that will lead to informed decisions likely to benefit the company—which is another aspect of life at Clockwork Corporation.

The Decision-Making Process at Clockwork

Managers at Clockwork participate in making decisions about what the company will produce, based on anticipated market demand. As Clockwork's general manager puts it, "We look at different scenarios, like 'What happens if business goes up or down 10 percent—how will we respond to the changes in demand?' 'What if the dollar drops 5 percent—how will that affect our European business?' 'What if our main competitor experiences a rumored labor strike—how can we meet the "opportunity orders" we think we'll get?'

"For example," he continues, "two months ago we evaluated a proposed 10 percent increase in business. The analysis showed that two new pieces of equipment would be needed to handle the increased demand. But then we said, 'What if the business doesn't increase as expected?' Could we afford to have expensive new equipment sitting idle? Since the equipment wouldn't have to be delivered for another four months, we had time to do a pretty good market analysis, whereas in the past we've had to make these decisions quickly, based on gut response."

Since each department at Clockwork participates in the planning process, the department managers have a realistic view of how increases or decreases in the business could affect them. (Quite a difference from having someone at corporate decide what can or cannot be done and hand it down on a plate to the people at the production sites.) The result is a process that takes advantage of the knowledge and creativity of all the people in the organization.

Things are not perfect at Clockwork, but people are satisfied and the company achieves its delivery and quality objectives. Ideas are evaluated, although not every new idea gets adopted.

Clockwork is also improving its overall effectiveness by implementing technologies in addition to MRP II. Says Clockwork's general manager, "As part of Just-in-Time, we recently implemented kanban in a number of manufacturing areas, replacing some aspects of our shop-floor control system. In addition, we're working to implement a major total quality control initiative. We began the implementation of Just-in-Time and total quality management after MRP II was up and running. If we had it to do over again, we would have done a more simultaneous implementation—that is, we would have implemented aspects of Just-in-Time and TQM while we were working on MRP II."

Most outsiders will notice that Clockwork is not without problems—there are certainly many—but the way Clockwork's people *deal* with them is the important factor. There is still too much to do in a day, and the least-worst choice is sometimes the best option available. While not ideal, the environment at Clockwork is sane and reasonable, and it contributes to the sense of a job well done at the end of the day.

Finally, and most important, at Clockwork top management can work with middle management to set reasonable objectives, measure performance, and hold people accountable. And whereas managers at Chaos, Inc. are often rewarded for deflecting spears to others, people at Clockwork are rewarded for bona fide top performance. This merit system and the ability to create the future gives the company every possibility of becoming a world-class manufacturing firm.

Chaos, Inc. and Clockwork Corporation: The Real Identity

Chaos, Inc. and Clockwork Corporation are really the same company six years apart. As in most companies, six years have brought some change to the organization. There has been some turnover in people, although less than in most companies. There are new products and new manufacturing processes, as would be expected. People's memories are fuzzy when asked about things six or seven years ago. They'll say things like "Yeah, it was a lot worse then. It's hard to believe we actually made a profit in those days."

If anything, the people tend not to congratulate themselves about what they've accomplished—"Wow," they say, "when I sit down and go through an objective assessment of where we were and where we are today, we've made a lot more progress than I realized." They tend more to focus on the problems/opportunities that exist today, saying things like "We have a quality problem in the blending department, and we're too slow in fixing it. It shouldn't take this long."

Where a company falls on the spectrum—that is, whether it's more like Chaos, Inc. or Clockwork—is a choice. It's not part of the company's "organizational DNA—a company isn't stuck for eternity with whatever systems (or lack of them) it has in place today. One of the best ways to think about this change is to assess your organization, then compare it to where you want to go.

Rate Yourself

The generally accepted assessment tool for operational audits is *The Oliver Wight ABCD Checklist for Operational Excellence.* The checklist was originally developed by Oliver Wight in 1977. It's now in its fourth generation and has been expanded significantly from its earlier versions. Companies can use the checklist to assess how well they manage their business operations. The letter grades are like grades in school: Class A companies are at the top of the list, with the best scores, Class D companies are at the bottom, and Classes B and C are in the middle.

There is more to the checklist than what's shown in Figure 3.2. For each of the overview questions shown, there are a number of detail questions. These help to determine the rating on the overview question, and provide additional detail for improvement in the different subject areas. The questions below indicate the types of overview and detail questions in the checklist.

Figure 3.2   ABCD Checklist—Sample Series of Items

OVERVIEW ITEM:

14.0   Sales Planning
There is a formal sales-planning process in place with the sales force responsible and accountable for developing and executing the resulting sales plan. Differences between the sales plan and the forecast are reconciled.

DETAILED ITEMS:

14.1   The sales force understands the impact of sales planning on the company's ability to satisfy its customers.
14.2   Actual sales are measured against sales plans. Measurements are broken down into sales responsibility areas.
14.3   The sales-planning process is designed in such a way as to minimize the administrative impact for the sales force.
14.4   The incentives of the sales compensation system are effective and do not inject bias into the sales plan and forecast.
14.5   The sales force is actively pursuing customer linking. It is working with the

Figure 3.2 (Cont.)

customers' planning systems and communicating this information to the company.

14.6 Aggregate forecasts are reconciled with the sales plan.

14.7 Sales participates with marketing, forecasting, and manufacturing in a demand planning meeting to prepare for each sales and operations planning meeting. A system is in use to communicate customer intelligence information to forecasting.

14.8 Sales areas are provided with useful feedback regarding their performance to plan at least monthly. Sales plans are stated so that they are meaningful to the sales force, yet translate into the sales and operations process.

14.9 The assumptions underlying the sales plan are documented. They are reviewed on a regular basis and changed as necessary.

The Oliver Wight ABCD Checklist for Operational Excellence is a direct measure of business results. Figures 3.3, 3.4, and 3.5 are from The Oliver Wight Companies' surveys of manufacturing companies. Two surveys were done, spaced four years apart, and the results were surprisingly consistent: For most questions there was less than a 2 percent difference in the results, even though the companies responding were different and four years had elapsed. There were 1,100 and 1,600 companies, respectively, that responded to these surveys. The data show a direct correlation between letter grade on the ABCD Checklist and tangible business results. In addition, the data show that it costs no more to be Class A than Class D. Class A is not something a company can buy, but rather the result of management activities. Those that manage well get excellent results.

Take a few minutes before proceeding to the next chapter in this book and answer the overview and detail questions listed above as a quick evaluation for your company. In addition to filling out the checklist yourself, we recommend that several people in your company do the same exercise, then compare the results. This exercise is not a complete self-assessment, since only a single question is listed and the responses of one or several people do not constitute a comprehensive evaluation, but it can be an excellent eye-opener.

Figure 3.3   Survey Results: Individual Benefits by Class

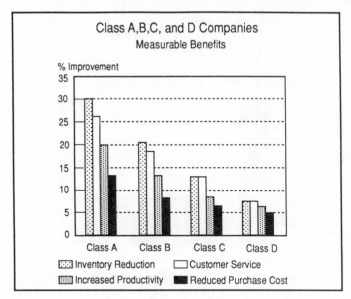

Figure 3.4   Survey Results: Cost/Benefit by Class

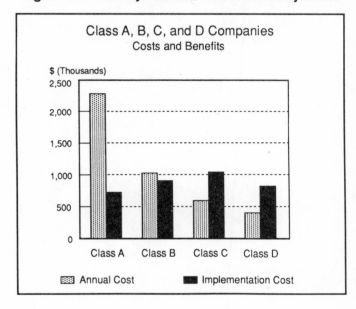

Figure 3.5   Survey Results: Return on Investment by Class

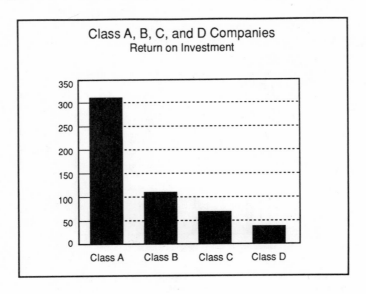

Chapter Four

Sales and Operations Planning

SALES AND OPERATIONS PLANNING (S&OP) BASICS

"When business would turn down, a tidal wave of materials would wash over us for the next thirty to sixty days," says Al Gronlund, plant manager of Diamond Cabinets. "Our business would be going down, but our inventories would be climbing. Then we'd see our business start to tick up, but since we'd reacted to an inventory excess, inventories would fall and we'd have stockouts. We don't have that kind of problem anymore.

"Sales and operations planning [S&OP] brings people together," he continues. "People in sales and marketing realize that their forecasts really commit the company to resources and materials. That kind of ownership wasn't there before. But as a result of the sales and operations planning process, all areas of the company now take ownership of that final unit number we're going to build, and the information gets disseminated formally."

Another company, Thunderbird Products, which manufactures high-performance boats, also found itself in a situation in which precise coordination among sales, marketing, and other divisions became critical to survival. The luxury tax enacted in 1991 caused sales to drop like an anchor in still water.

Thunderbird's CFO, Mike Landrigan, attributes the sales and operations planning process with helping the company through the difficult times. "When we started with S&OP it was really a new concept for us because we didn't have any real coordinated plan. Every year we'd go around the room and everybody would give us an estimate of sales for that year. Sales, being the eternal optimist, would come up with a high number. Production's number was roughly ninety percent of sales' estimate because the production people knew that sales couldn't achieve its goal. Finance, of course, had the lowest number. Generally, the finance people were the closest. The end result was that we'd be overstocked in inventory. With S&OP we've been able to focus not only on what's happening internally—how many orders we're getting—but also on what's actually happening in the marketplace with our boats.

"With our S&OP process we meet monthly during stable periods of time," Landrigan explains. "Now, we're actually meeting weekly, because there are enough things changing that we need to have a short-term focus as well as long-range vision. With S&OP, we're able to relate the changes throughout the company without one manager dictating a change that nobody else agrees on. We come out of the S&OP process with consensus on how we're going to proceed—it really benefits us because people aren't looking over their shoulders saying, 'Am I doing the right thing? Am I doing what I'm supposed to be doing?' Everybody heads in the same direction.

"Things aren't as good as we'd like them to be," Landrigan admits, "but they'd be a whole lot worse if we didn't have sales and operations planning. S&OP is in itself probably worth the cost of the whole MRP II implementation because it forced us to focus on the retail inventories. You see, we have two kinds of customers— the dealers themselves and the retail customers. For example, we introduced a brand-new boat and made 25 over a two-year period. The first time we did a field inventory, we found there were 23 out there, and most of those were over a year old. We recognized at that point that we had a problem and stopped making that model. In 1989, had we been using S&OP, we'd have seen that the dealers' inventories were overstocked by 100 boats, which was 10 percent of total production for the year! We could never envision that we'd have that many boats in inventory. Over the last few years we've been forced to work off that excess number of boats, and it's hurt each of the subsequent years."

Diamond Cabinet and Thunderbird, like many manufacturing companies, have found that effective sales and operations planning can pay big dividends. A common misunderstanding is that sales and operations planning is just manufacturing to the forecast—if the forecast says you'll sell 50, then make 50. End of story, right? Not quite. Intuitively, it *does* make sense to follow your forecast, yet there is more to sales and operations planning than meets the eye.

Just manufacturing to a forecast doesn't really focus on satisfying the customer. It doesn't take into account the possibility that it may be wise to actually build inventory in anticipation of a peak selling season, or deplete inventory if you're approaching the end of a peak season. Backlogs may be too short or too long and may need to be adjusted. Or, the marketplace may be highly volatile and your factory or plant can't respond without creating high levels of inefficiency, lost productivity, and added costs. Therefore, in order to satisfy customer demand and run an efficient manufacturing operation at the same time, you may need to stabilize production. In other words, to satisfy the customer, you may need to do some planning.

Think back for a moment to the universal manufacturing equation introduced in Chapter 3, which asks, "What do we need to make?" As you can see, the answer is not nearly as obvious as it appears at first blush. The forecast is certainly one of the factors in arriving at an answer, but other issues such as backlogs, inventory levels, and the need for stability also have a major impact on your production needs.

The best way to determine what to make and when to make it is by using a process in which all departments meet regularly to assess future market demand and determine whether the factory or plant can meet this demand and, if so, how. This process, as you might have inferred from the beginning of this chapter, is known as sales and operations planning. (For an in-depth review of sales and operations planning, see *Orchestrating Success* by Richard Ling and Walter Goddard, published by Oliver Wight Publications.)

Sales and operations planning generates a number of different high-level plans, including the sales plan, production plan, engineering or R&D plan, and financial plan. One of the most important aspects of the

S&OP process is that these plans are in sync with one another. The sales plan doesn't fight the production plan. The financial plan agrees with both the production plan and the sales plan. And the engineering or R&D plan identifies what has to be done and when in order to make the other plans happen.

S&OP is conducted in the aggregate, and deals with families and rates of production. The strength of this process is that it enables a company to translate overall plans, converted into dollar values, into production plans that can be used by the factory or plant. The flow of information used in sales and operations planning is shown in Figure 4.1.

- The sales and operations plan serves as a "budget" for the master production schedule, which translates the aggregate family data into specific items and specific quantities.

- The master production schedule feeds into material planning, which indicates how much material will be used.

- The material plans are used to calculate how much capacity is required and when it will be needed. Both the material plan and the capacity plan are thus directly linked to the higher-level plans; as the high-level plans are formulated and altered, they have a direct effect on the detail plans below.

- After the material and capacity plans have been formulated, the next step is to evaluate them. Are they realistic? If so, the plans are executed and then monitored, much as financial controls are used to measure variance from budget and determine why the deviations occurred.

But what if the plans aren't realistic? If left alone, unrealistic plans will cause the informal system to reappear, with all the loss of customer service, cost, and frustration that accompany it. If the plan is unrealistic, it will have to be changed—you can't hold people accountable for a plan that won't work. Unworkable plans become wish lists that simply drive people to the informal system.

WHY IS SALES AND OPERATIONS PLANNING IMPORTANT?

Every company does some kind of production planning, whether it's through a formal process like the one described in this chapter or an

Figure 4.1   Manufacturing Resource Planning
(MRP II)

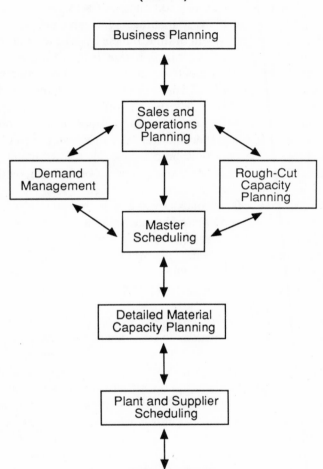

informal process of talking in the hall. There are a number of major benefits to the formal sales and operations planning process, including the following:

1. *It makes customer service objectives happen through better management of finished goods inventory and/or backlog.* In a customer-driven

organization, this is the most important reason for sales and operations planning. Rather than managing in terms of "motherhood" slogans like "We pride ourselves on having good customer service," the top management team defines its plans so that it gets the customer service levels it wants. For a small investment of time and energy, the top management team is rewarded with an organization that is far more effective in meeting customer service objectives. Saying "We pride ourselves on having good customer service" isn't effective because there is no *right* level of finished goods inventory; there is only a process of managing inventory in response to the constant fluctuations of the marketplace. For example, if sales are higher or lower than anticipated, inventory will fluctuate above or below the desired levels. Therefore, managing finished goods inventories is not so much a matter of deciding on the right number as it is of responding to the marketplace.

The same thing is true for backlogs in a make-to-order product. Sales and operations planning is the right place for making decisions about finished goods inventories or backlogs and the factors that affect them, namely, sales and production. This is because the right people are available to make the best decisions, the planning process is structured, and management's expectations are known.

2. *It connects strategy and operations.* S&OP ties the company's high-level business and strategic plans to the operations of each department, guaranteeing that they're in harmony. Many organizations have financial plans that, while not created in a vacuum, are at the same time not directly tied to the numbers in the operating system either. This creates the potential for loss of control and significant miscommunication within the organization. Loss of control arises because there's no "rack-and-pinion" relationship between the business plan and the tasks that people are held accountable for hitting on a day-to-day basis.

Miscommunication happens because one set of numbers is being used to answer questions in one part of the business while a different set of numbers is being used to answer questions in another part. A good example would be an overstated shipping budget that's used to order material so "we have coverage," while a different set of budget numbers is submitted to corporate as part of the business plan for the division. This duality makes it difficult to answer the key questions "What are we going to buy?" and "What are our cash requirements for material?" The answers become less meaningful if they vary depending on which set of numbers you use.

3. *It breaks down language barriers.* In its simplest form, MRP II can be thought of as a companywide communication mechanism that translates high-level plans into specific tasks. Sales and operations planning is an essential link in the communication process. Specifically, S&OP takes the business plan, which is stated in dollars, and translates it into standard hours, pounds, gallons, and so on—the language of production.

John Lewis, plant manager at Continental Can Co., explains how this has worked for his company. "What's been most effective for us has been the ability to speak the same language. Sales traditionally wants to talk dollars and cents, and manufacturing typically wants to talk units. When you talk in dollars and cents, you are never going to get to the level you need to. So we talk purely in scheduling quantities. Then we convert that to dollars and cents of sales afterward. This has made a big difference in how we work together, and it's also reduced our obsolete inventory. Also, our meetings are structured so that everyone is a participant, not a receiver. You have to come to the meeting to give something—everyone who comes to the meeting has to be a presenter of some information that is valuable to the process."

4. *It provides a common plan for the entire company.* When the company has a single game plan, each department functions in harmony with the other departments. What happens if the company doesn't have a common plan? One group of people works very hard at its plan while other groups work equally hard at their own plans, but because the plans are different, each group is effectively working on the "wrong" thing.

For example, purchasing buys the materials for a set of plans and wants to make sure that there are no shortages and plenty of material to choose from. At the same time, manufacturing is reluctant to add capacity based on past experience. In the past, manufacturing has added capacity only to find that there was a lack of material. People wound up standing around with no work, and the vice-presidents were upset with the supervisors because of the idle time. Meanwhile, the finance department is lining up the financing for yet another set of plans, the ones that the general manager gave to corporate, which were designed to meet corporate's profit and cost-cutting objectives. When things don't work out—when there's too much inventory, not enough capacity, and the cost targets are exceeded—each group is convinced that the others are the problem. Frustration skyrockets, and everyone leaves work at the end of the day convinced that the real competition is inside the company.

Ed Fitzgerald, general manager of Valleylab, explains how his company agrees on a common plan. "At least now we're all in agreement on how to respond to our customers. We receive good direction from marketing, and we talk with the customer service people almost on a daily basis to make sure we are filling their priorities. The communication is much better, especially considering that the marketing and customer service group is out in Boulder, Colorado. We're all singing from the same song sheet now."

"Generally," adds Phil Presti, purchasing manager at Valleylab, "we like to ship from stock, and we usually carry a small safety stock. Marketing is fully aware of our approach from the S&OP meeting. Lately, we've had some big increases in demand and our inventory has gotten too low. Our plan shows when it's going to be back and when we're going to build the systems. And the marketing people attend the S&OP meeting, so they know what's happening. They can relay that information back to the customer service people."

"In the past," says Fitzgerald, "there would have been a lot of finger pointing. Marketing would have just kept taking customer orders and asking manufacturing, 'When can you ship it? Why isn't it there?' Now, they've already agreed to build eight a week this month and nine a week the month after that. They know what to tell the customers up front in terms of realistic ship dates. They can say, 'OK, we got your order, but it's going to be six weeks before we're going to be able to deliver it.' They have some upfront knowledge, so they don't leave the customer hanging for a long period of time. This year we'll get 24 turns on our finished goods inventory, which would have been impossible three years ago without a lot of yelling, finger pointing, changing priorities, and so forth."

5. *It yields a workable plan.* Most plans are unworkable; in a world of competitive pressures, unreasonable customers, and increasing expectations from top management, there's a tendency to overstate what can realistically be done. This is not a matter of lack of business acumen or lack of experience—it's done with the best of intentions.

To make a plan workable, a series of "reality checks" is needed, starting with the sales and operations planning process. At the top level, a rough-cut capacity analysis must be done (see Chapter 8) to verify that the plan is attainable. If the plan passes the rough-cut test, the detail material and capacity plans need to be checked to verify that they're attainable as well. Without such reality checks, unrealistic plans are the norm, not the exception, leading to confusion, additional costs, and reduced customer service.

In addition, "random decisions" that affect the whole company are made on the plant floor, at a vendor's plant, or within a particular department. Any time more work is due today than can actually be done, someone has to decide what gets done and what doesn't. That decision should be made by someone who can see the "big picture" in terms of customers, products, due dates, and so on. Otherwise, the decisions may as well be made by flipping a coin.

The feedback loops in Figure 4.1 force people to verify that plans are attainable at different levels. And since each department participates in the process, all key functions of the plans are accounted for, eliminating surprises.

6. *It makes it possible to manage change.* Companies that carry out sales and operations planning are not driven by knee-jerk reactions or shoot-from-the-hip responses to unexpected situations. This means they can effectively respond to change, taking advantage of opportunities and steering clear of disasters.

Managing change has two aspects: One is making a change at the right level, the other is making sure that the change happens—period. Sales and operations planning is the appropriate place to make significant changes because it ensures that all departments are in agreement. Moreover, because sales and operations planning is the top-level driver and links the high- and low-level plans, changes made at the S&OP level are automatically passed down and translated into detailed plans.

7. *It provides a basis for measuring performance.* This is related to the development of a common, workable plan agreed to by all. Such a plan then becomes the basis for measurement. If there is more than one plan, the answer to the question "How well did we do?" depends on which plan we're talking about. The answer also depends on whether the plan

was achievable. There are no real consequences to failing to meet an unachievable plan. If the general manager asks, "Why didn't we meet the plan for the month?" the response could be "We never meet the plan, it's always overstated." If someone in sales asks, "Why didn't we ship this customer order?" the response could be "Look, we promise more customer orders in a week than we can ship so we have some flexibility in order to meet the monthly goal for billing dollars. If something goes wrong on one customer order, we have others to draw from." In each case, there is someone else who needs to accept some part of the blame, and there is little real accountability. Consequently, sales and operations planning is critical to maintaining accountability and effectively managing the company.

A typical question at this point is "If sales and operations planning is so important, why have companies been able to live without it?" The answer is that while it is possible to exist without a formal sales and operations planning process, companies that do so incur significant hidden costs in terms of increased inventory, decreased productivity, and decreased levels of customer service.

Anatomy of the S&OP Process

The focus of the sales and operations planning process is a meeting that is typically held monthly. For some volatile businesses, it may be necessary to hold sales and operations planning meetings more frequently, as is the case at Thunderbird Products. Or a special situation that can affect production, such as a product recall or a competitor on strike, will necessitate an unscheduled meeting. In any case, the experience of a broad range of companies shows that it is not effective to hold S&OP meetings less frequently than once a month.

The meeting is attended by the general manager (or president) and staff (or VPs). These people make decisions about adding a shift, major subcontracting, responding to customer service issues, and other issues. Given the significance of these problems, the decisions can't be delegated—they're the responsibility of top management. Other types of decisions that are made in the S&OP meeting include: increasing production on a particular product to assure high customer service levels in a new market; reducing production on one or more product families because sales are lower than expected, or because manufacturing cannot support the higher rate; setting new targets for finished goods inventories or backlogs by family; and so on.

The meeting focuses on an aggregate review of the company's products. This means working with product families rather than individual items. By focusing on a handful of families rather than getting bogged down in hundreds or even thousands of individual items, the general manager and staff can keep a clear focus on the "big picture" and make better decisions.

Figure 4.2 is an example of an S&OP spreadsheet for a family of products. This spreadsheet shows the sales, production, and inventory or backlog information—each in a separate section. For each of these, the plan, the actuals, and a cumulative difference are shown. The left side of the spreadsheet shows a number of months of history, in this case three. The right side of the spreadsheet shows the plan extending into the future. For the future months, the Actual and Cumulative Difference boxes would be empty. The history is used to evaluate how well the company is doing compared with the plan. The future plans, to the right of the history, are used in discussions of the current plan for the family of products.

This type of spreadsheet is typical of what's used in most manufacturing companies. In some organizations, additional lines of information are necessary. Consider Hillshire Farm & Kahn's, which produces meat products with a limited shelf life. Explains Ed Wohlwender, manager of inventory control/central planning at Hillshire, "We put an interactive graph on the S&OP spreadsheet so, as we change the proposed plans, we can see how many days of inventory result to better manage shelf life. We also show the target inventory levels and track actual deviations." The modifications that Hillshire Farm & Kahn's has made are innovative, but typical of the kind of creativity that companies can bring to bear to improve the effectiveness of the sales and operations planning process.

The family review process itself is a collaborative effort to develop the appropriate company response to an ever-changing world. "How will we handle a 10 percent increase in market demand for a particular line?" "If there is a change in mix because some product families are selling faster than expected and others are selling less, how will we deal with it?" There are no formulas for answering these kinds of questions. They can only be resolved by applying product knowledge, company knowledge, and proper preparation for the S&OP meeting.

Figure 4.2 Sales and Operations Planning Spreadsheet

Sales Plan	-1	-2	-3		1	2	3	4
Sales Plan								
Actual								
Difference								
Cumulative Difference								

Production Plan

Planned								
Actual								
Difference								
Cumulative Difference								

Inventory or Backlog

Planned								
Actual								
Difference								

Preparation means knowing the likely alternatives and the implications of each one. For instance, if production is increased by 12 percent on a particular product line, what are the likely problems and how will they be resolved? Having the data to answer questions like this is critical to the process. Sometimes the data may only require a cursory analysis—some quick penciling on a piece of paper. Other times they may require computer simulation using your MRP system.

By anticipating and preparing for the future with contingency plans, a company gains the greatest possible control over its environment. In this way, sales and operations planning truly *is* the general manager's process—it provides an opportunity to control the business and maximize the company's chances for achieving the objectives laid out in the business plan.

SALES AND OPERATIONS PLANNING ACTIVITIES

Richard Ling, an innovator in this field, has identified the following activities that are essential for the process to work.

1. *Everyone must understand the mechanics of the sales and operations planning process.* Since the top management group must do sales and operations planning, it needs to understand the mechanics. These mechanics are not complicated, but they are a necessary prerequisite to a productive meeting.

2. *The company must define product groupings or families.* It would take many hours, maybe even days, to review the plan for each salable item in a typical manufacturing company. It therefore makes more sense to review the plans for a handful of product families. To do so, however, you must first group items into product families. This is sometimes difficult, because sales and marketing might look at products one way, in terms of *customers,* while manufacturing looks at the products in terms of *manufacturing processes.*

It doesn't matter to them whether an electric motor goes to the commercial or industrial market. While sales and marketing are closest to the customer, and their viewpoint is extremely important, manufacturing will ultimately be responsible for putting product in the customer's hand. So it's typical in situations like this to shift back and forth between marketing and manufacturing families. In the situation just cited, the industrial and commercial markets would be differentiated for the purposes of sales and marketing, and combined for the purposes of production.

3. *Each department must do its premeeting "homework."* S&OP can only work if each department has assembled its own data and compared past performance to plan.

Sales and marketing must not only project future customer demand, but also document their assumptions about why things will change or stay the same. What's happening in the economy? What are our competitors doing? What promotions, advertising, and other sales activities are we pursuing? These are all important to document, and, once documented, they serve as a basis for analysis. Why are we selling more than planned? Which of our assumptions is incorrect?

Just as sales and marketing have the task of documenting the assumptions behind their forecasts and plans, manufacturing has the pre-S&OP-meeting task of assessing material and capacity needs for the current plan or any proposed changes in the plan. This is especially important if the plan calls for an increase in production.

Ed Wohlwender of Hillshire Farm & Kahn's describes the sequence of events at his company this way: "Sales and marketing sit down before the pre-S&OP meeting and go over the proposed plans. Then at the pre-S&OP meeting we talk about what the schedulers and inventory control people think about the plan, and what the reasoning is behind the sales plan. We also review the inventory picture. After the pre-S&OP meeting, we go to the executive committee and present the proposed plans, and answer any questions."

4. *The company must commit the necessary time and resources.* Responsibility for the sales and operations planning process cannot be delegated. While the detail work and research can be done by middle managers and their subordinates, the department heads must be accountable for the plans, and they must attend the formal meetings. The general manager must also be willing to set aside the time to participate in the monthly meetings—the presence of the general manager indicates the seriousness of the process, and serves as an incentive for others to make it a high priority. Figure 4.3 lists mandatory attendees who make up the core team at monthly S&OP meetings, as well as attendees who might be called in to provide information during special situations.

The schedule of the meetings for the entire year should be distributed well in advance, so that people can arrange their travel and other plans *around* the S&OP sessions. Meetings should start on time and should not be interrupted by telephone calls.

Figure 4.3   Attendance List for S&OP Meetings

Mandatory Participation	Potential Participants
General Manager	
Sales	
Department Manager	Customer Service Manager
	Distribution Manager
	Service Parts Manager
	Demand Manager
Marketing	
Department Manager	Chief Forecaster
	Product Manager(s)
Manufacturing	
Department Manager	Manufacturing Manager
Materials Manager	Master Scheduler
	Purchasing Manager
	Quality Assurance Manager
Engineering	
Department Manager	Drafting Manager
	Engineering Scheduler
	Manager, Design Engineering
Finance	
Department Manager	Budget Manager
	Cost Accounting Manager
Human Resources	
Department Manager	
Programs/Special Projects	
Appropriate managers	

5. *Prior to the formal meeting, distribute a sales and operations planning "kit."* In *Orchestrating Success,* Richard Ling and Walter Goddard suggest a kit containing the following:

- all of the premeeting plans created by the various departments
- analysis of the plan's assumptions and vulnerabilities
- an agenda, with the following topics:
  1. special issues
  2. company performance review
      a. review of customer service
      b. review of financial and business performance
      c. department-by-department (sales and marketing, engineering or R&D, and manufacturing) review in aggregate

3. review of assumptions and vulnerabilities
4. family-by-family review
5. new product discussion
6. review of special projects
7. review of meeting decisions
8. critique of process

COMMUNICATING THE RESULTS, IMPROVING THE PROCESS

It is vitally important to keep a set of minutes as the formal S&OP meeting unfolds—memory is fleeting, and as different alternatives are proposed people are likely to remember different versions of what was said. That's why step 7 of the preceding agenda is so important. Once a companywide plan is adopted, your sales and operations planning team should review the minutes so that everyone is in agreement as to what was actually decided. The final minutes should be posted so that everyone in the company will be aware of the current plan and how it was developed.

The last step before the formal meeting is adjourned, critiquing the meeting, is the key to ongoing improvement. Even companies that are proficient at sales and operations planning find that they can always improve the process. Like most functions within a manufacturing company, the more people work at sales and operations planning, the more they'll get out of the process. Improvements in sales and operations planning, because of the enormous leverage, always generate significant savings to the company.

INTEGRATION ISSUES

Engineering or R&D Plan

Most of the attention in the typical sales and operations planning process is on the sales and production plans. The engineering or R&D plan, however, can be a "sleeper" for many organizations.

There are two reasons for this: (1) The first to market with a product has a powerful advantage over all other competitors, and (2) product life cycles in many industries are shrinking at an accelerating rate. With the advent of technologies like concurrent engineering, design for manufacturability, and design for competitive advantage, companies are able to reduce the time to market dramatically and better position themselves for ongoing success.

Consequently, management teams are making decisions to ramp up production of new products, and phase out older products, before the new products are completely designed, and well before they are tested. Materials, tooling, and even capital equipment are being ordered earlier in the design process. Conversely, materials for the older products are not being ordered in anticipation of the new product release.

More than ever before, it's imperative to have high confidence levels in new product plans. If a plan is too conservative, and the new product is available before the old products have been ramped down, the company is left with the unpleasant choice of either delaying the introduction and potentially losing the first position, or taking a significant write-off on the unused material. If the plan is too aggressive, and the new products are not available on time, the company may not be able to manufacture anything, or it may have to incur a significant cost to make more of the old products.

The major issue here is the need to integrate the new product development plans into the sales and operations planning process as well as the material planning system. For example, when should material be ordered for the new product? Sales and operations planning tells everyone when the new product lines will be introduced. The new product development system informs the development people when their specific tasks and activities must be completed. And the material planning system lets the purchasing people and the plant know what to buy or make, and when.

Some companies use their MRP II systems to plan and schedule both manufacturing activities and the nonmanufacturing activities (design, drawings, methods, tooling, etc.). Material and capacity planning are done for all of these new product introduction activities, as well as for the materials and capacities needed to manufacture the new products. Other companies use scheduling systems developed for new product development, and integrate these with their MRP II systems. The systems "communicate" on dependent events. Either method is workable, and successful companies use both. In Chapter 7 both scheduling approaches will be explained in more detail.

Employee Empowerment

Ultimately, sales and operations planning is a group process. While the general manager is accountable, if the group cannot work effectively as a team the results are going to be disappointing. Therefore, another integration issue is how well the group works together. If your company has been subjected to twenty years of autocratic management, in which everyone waits to see what the highest-ranking person in the room says before speaking, then you'll probably need to do some work on employee empowerment and group process skills. In such a situation, the S&OP process is an excellent forum for developing these skills.

S&OP MEASUREMENTS

The single most important S&OP measurement is performance relative to the production plan, which should be at 98 percent or better. In other words, a company should be able to perform within 2 percent of its goal by product family. Some of the individual items may be off by more than 2 percent. One might be off by plus 5 percent and others by minus 5 percent. In total, though, a deviation from the goal of 2 percent or less by family should be achieved on a monthly basis.

Other plans should also be measured, including the sales and finance plans. It is not possible to provide hard-and-fast performance criteria for these, because the nature of different industries varies so much. In the high-fashion business, for example, 30 percent accuracy relative to forecast may be acceptable (see forecast measurements in Chapter 5, "Demand Management"). In a stable industrial market, such as replacement parts for grinding machines, you would, however, expect greater accuracy.

In addition, the engineering and R&D plans must be measured. As mentioned above, the integration and integrity of these plans is critical in today's increasingly competitive markets. Most companies measure these plans in the same way that they measure manufacturing and purchasing on-time performance (see Chapters 9 and 10 for details).

Finally, a nonquantitative measurement of the S&OP process is the ability to achieve consensus as a group—consensus on the company plan and on specific issues regarding the marketplace, the economy, the competitive arena, and how fast the company can adapt to a changing world. The ability to come to consensus and work as a team is a vital measurement of how well the process is working.

SUMMARY/CHECKUP

1. Sales and operations planning is the top-level handle on the sales and operations aspects of a manufacturing business. How firm a grip does

your top management have on that handle? Do the top-level managers accept responsibility for this process? Or do they manage in terms of pleasant platitudes—"Have good customer service," "Don't have too much inventory," and so on?

2. The sales and operations planning function resides between the business plan and the master production schedule. How well do your sales and operations plans give definition to the business plan? How well does the production plan serve as a "budget" for the master production schedule?

3. When done effectively, S&OP breaks down communication barriers and provides a common, workable plan for the entire company. How do you rate the communication in your company? Are the plans common and workable? Do people just wink at the plans, or do they pay them serious attention?

4. The arithmetic of S&OP is simple. The real work is in making decisions. What is the quality of discussion that takes place in your sales and operations planning meetings? Is it short and superficial, or do people struggle with difficult decisions?

5. There is a set of tested and proven activities that, if followed, will greatly improve the quality of the sales and operations planning process. Does your company carry out these activities, and if so, how well?

6. Are you measuring your performance relative to the production plan? If you do, is it within plus or minus 2 percent?

The forecast is one of the important items used to do effective sales and operations planning. In the next chapter we'll look at forecasting, as well as the other elements of demand management.

SPECIAL ACKNOWLEDGMENTS

Richard Ling and Walter Goddard, two innovators in the field of sales and operations planning.

Chapter Five

Demand Management

WHAT IS DEMAND MANAGEMENT?

For most people, demand management is a contradiction in terms. "Why, you can't manage demand," they say. "It's something that happens *to* you and there's little if anything that can be done about it." A war in the Middle East increases demand for oil. Closer to home, a strike, a competitor's new product, a sales promotion, or a pricing change influences customer demand. A cold winter in New England burns out automobile starters at a record pace. A recession drops the number of housing starts, reducing demand for building materials. An economic recovery kicks capital spending into high gear, and the machine tool industry enters another one of its ongoing boom-and-bust cycles.

Each of these occurrences is outside your company's control. So the natural question is "What can I do about this?" The answer: Most companies are able to influence demand, and when they are unable to influence it, they can at least plan for it in an effective manner. Of course, one company cannot control world events, economies, or overall market demands. Yet companies *do* control the release of new products, sales promotions, pricing, customer order promising, on-time deliveries, product quality, and a number of other factors that all influence customer demand patterns.

Sometimes it takes a bit of ingenuity to influence demand. Mike Landrigan, chief financial officer at Thunderbird Products, explains, "We've tried to design our selling programs so that each dealer will give us a quarterly commitment at the start of each model year. The dealers tell us the number of units they're going to take and give us a forecast of desired units by quarter. They don't have to take those commitments, but if they do, we give them a cash rebate. We've tried to develop a program that helps us identify the needs of our dealers, and consequently our future production needs."

Alternatively, when a company cannot influence customer demand, it can at least *manage* it. Identifying marketplace demand patterns, making well-thought-out projections, and taking a realistic look at the market may not alter demand, but these activities allow a company to respond more effectively to customer demand than a company that doesn't do as effective a job in each of these areas. The classic example is a financially managed company that starts off with a target number for earnings per share. It then uses this number to calculate a target for profits, and finally translates this back into the sales numbers. This entire process takes place in a vacuum, without a focus on the marketplace.

Of course, this is not to say that financial goals aren't important— they are. But so is the marketplace. One of the overwhelming objectives for any company is to meet its customer service objectives. A customer-driven company will see demand management as a tool for satisfying its customers—a way to provide higher levels of customer service and increased customer responsiveness.

John Lewis, plant manager at Continental Can Co., found that his company's work on demand management provided a set of questions to ask the salespeople and the customers. "For example," explains Lewis, " 'You said you were going to sell 500,000 units and you only sold 410,000. Are the other 90,000 units going into the next month, or are they dropping out completely?' With the data, the salespeople seem more comfortable sitting down with the customers. They say, 'You told me you were going to take 500,000 of this, and you only took 410,000. This is the pattern. You're always overestimating what you'll need. Is there a reason for this?' Many times the customer will respond, 'I didn't know whether you were really going to be able to make them. I was buying from XYZ Company, and the only way I could get 400,000 from XYZ was to say I needed 600,000.' "

WHY IS DEMAND MANAGEMENT IMPORTANT?

If you can stabilize the top-level plans (production plan and master production schedule) through demand management, the effects will be felt throughout the entire organization. Well-managed companies have found that stabilizing the top-level plans creates enormous productivity improvements; all functions operate more smoothly and effectively. For example, when customer orders are promised on an existing schedule that meets the customer's needs, salespeople make better use of their time than they do when they must constantly act as go-betweens in negotiating deliveries. Manufacturing people focus on hitting the plans rather than frantically trying to deal with the latest changes to the schedule. The plant can better use equipment and labor, and supplier delivery performance improves because suppliers aren't chasing moving targets. Finally, quality improves because the company is not trying to push most of the month's shipments out the door at the last minute.

Demand management is not a panacea. No one has a crystal ball that can perfectly anticipate the "zigs and zags" of the marketplace—there will always be surprises. But demand management can help you better serve your customers and make life easier for everyone in your company.

With this as background, let's look at the different subjects in demand management:

- sales planning/forecasting

- order promising

- distribution center demands (or branch warehouse demands)

- interplant demands

- service or spare parts demands

SALES PLANNING/FORECASTING

The difference between sales planning and forecasting is like the difference between "Sic 'em" and "C'mere." With sales planning, the "Sic 'em" questions are: "What is our action plan to make the desired sales happen?" "What are our advertising and direct mail programs?" "Who are the customers we'll call on?" "What's our pricing?" In short, it's a proactive stance. For most people, forecasting is a passive exercise. People take a guess at the future and hope for the best.

A proactive sales plan is more likely to happen, and if it doesn't, an analysis quickly shows what worked and what didn't. Perhaps the sales promotion was more successful than planned, but the dealer program was less effective. With this information, salespeople can formulate a new set of plans and go back to the marketplace.

Tom Soccio, supervisor of planning and scheduling at Krautkramer-Branson, explains the kind of progress his company has made. "Our forecast accuracy has gone from 62 percent to 84 percent. In the feedback from field salespeople, it's evident that our customer service has increased, in terms of both our ability to turn product around and our ability to respond to upsides in the business. It's enabled us to get back market share that we once lost, and we're actually getting market share in some new areas. It's mostly just discipline, pulling in sales, project management, creating the environment to have a lot of open communication, formalized meetings, formalized schedules for turning in forecasts.

"We were a typical operation, getting forecasts on an irregular basis. The production manager would review the forecasts and scale them down because he didn't believe them. In all likelihood, the sales group had increased the forecasts, knowing he would reduce them. There was no forward vision—everything was extremely short term. We were also caught in a fiscal-year-planning trap. Early in the fiscal year things were fine, but as we went into the ninth, tenth, and eleventh months we still had no forecast for the first months of the next fiscal year. Now we've expanded that horizon to a rolling twelve-month forecast."

The approach that Tom referred to is shown in Figure 5.1. While the approach is somewhat different in every company, there are six common elements:

Figure 5.1   Sales Planning Process

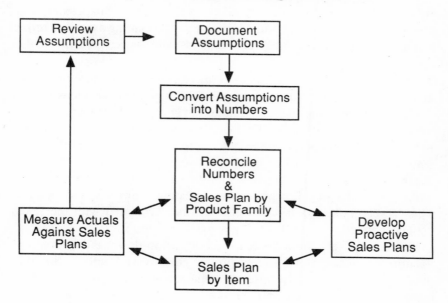

1. *Document the assumptions.* The process of sales planning starts with documenting assumptions. Unfortunately, many organizations fail to separate the assumptions and the numbers. Typical assumptions are the answers to such questions as: "What do we think the economy is going to do?" "What's happening with housing starts, oil prices, interest rates, exchange rates, and the like?" They can be very specific, such as "What do we think our competitors will do in terms of new product introduction, pricing, advertising, sales activity, and so on?" They can also be internal: "What are we going to do in terms of pricing, advertising, and so on?"

2. *Convert assumptions into numbers.* The assumptions are typically documented by experienced people in the company, generally top-level managers and sales management. Someone, typically called the demand manager or demand planner, then takes these assumptions and turns them into numbers—i.e., the sales plan. The demand planning position is new to many organizations. Typically, the demand manager or planner is located in the marketing department.

Once a company's approach changes from "C'mere" to "Sic 'em," there's a lot of work to be done in all areas of demand management. The demand planner's responsibilities involve sales planning as well as order promising, distribution, interplant demands, and service parts demands.

3. *Reconcile numbers to create a sales plan by product family.* In the area of sales planning, the demand manager or planner is responsible for working with both the sales and marketing groups to help them develop their proactive plans to make the sales plan happen as well as to reconcile their numbers. The sales organization is looking at the sales plan and how to make it happen: "What activities are needed?" "What are the potential pitfalls and how would we avoid them?" Marketing is looking at total demand, market shares, product life cycles, and the like. This larger market perspective needs to be reconciled with the sales plans generated by the sales and management groups.

As you can see, the sales plan is both a top-down and bottom-up document; a number of different groups get involved with putting the plan together. Each has a different perspective and makes a valuable contribution. And in the end, the process of consensus has to be reached for the sales plan to be a *company* plan.

4. *Break down the sales plan by item.* Once those questions are answered, the sales plan, still at the family level, must be broken down by product. Sometimes this is done with historical information, such as "In the past, this product has had 5 percent of family sales." For example, 12.5 horsepower lawn tractors account for 25 percent of all lawn tractor sales. But again, some assumptions come into play—"Why would it be the same? Why would it be different from last year? Has anything changed in the market that would mean this percentage ought to be different?"

At this point, the sales plan can be calculated for individual items. One way this can be done is to take the sales plan for the family of items and multiply it by the expected percentage for each item in the family. If the sales plan anticipates sales of 1,600 lawn tractors and the 12.5 horsepower tractor accounts for 25 percent of sales, then the forecast for this model should be 400.

A number of companies rely on software that forecasts an item's future sales from its sales history. Forecasts developed this way need to be verified in two ways. First, the future may not be like the past (it rarely is)—do these differences mean the forecast for this item should be changed? Also, how does the historical forecast compare with the sales plan for the family or item? If there is a significant disagreement, the differences need to be reconciled. It may be that the historical forecast is reconciled to the total forecast for the family of products because the future is expected to be different from the past. On the other hand, a historical forecast that adds up to more or less than the sales plan may open some eyes and cause the sales plan to be revised.

5. *Measure actual sales against the sales plan.* "We just started measuring the forecast," explains Ed Wohlwender, manager of inventory control/central planning at Hillshire Farm & Kahn's. "Everybody had an opinion. Fred Miller of Industrial Engineering has a saying: 'Without data you're just another person with an opinion.' Once we started looking at the data, some things were obvious just from looking at the graphs."

Since a forecast is never "right," meaningful measurement of a sales plan requires a tolerance. Let's say a sales plan calls for sales of 1,000 units per month and actual sales last month were 1,090. This might represent a statistical fluke, and no action is needed on this sales plan. However, if the actual sales were 1,500, then something is clearly happening. It could be a statistical peak, in which case we'd expect a corresponding valley, and over time the sales would average around 1,000 per month. On the other hand, this difference could mean something is happening in the marketplace, and the sales and marketing people should zero in on this and find out what has changed. A tolerance is needed to focus attention on those differences that should be reviewed and to distinguish them from minor deviations.

Forecasting has few if any absolutes. The best way to look at forecasting is to consider it a process in which you take the difference between what you predicted would happen and what actually happened, then make it smaller. Forecasting spare parts demands for large generators, for example, is mostly a matter of mathematics. Every so many hours the bearings need to be replaced. Based on the number of machines in the field, the age, and usage, a forecast for parts can be calculated with a reasonable degree of accuracy. On a monthly or quarterly basis, forecast accuracies of 80 or 90 percent might be possible.

High-fashion items, on the other hand, are anyone's guess. The first guess is whether or not an item will catch on in the marketplace. If it does, the next guess is to what degree, and, finally, when will the popularity fade? Both the rise and fall can be dramatic, and the period in between is like walking a tightrope. Sales forecasts for these items are far less accurate than those for the bearings mentioned above.

Consequently, the primary measurement of sales planning is an improvement in the accuracy with which the sales plan predicted actual sales. Did the difference between the plan and what actually happened get smaller? For the turbine bearings, did the accuracy rise from 80 percent to 88 percent? For fashion earrings, did the accuracy change from 55 to 60 percent? If so, then some new goals should be set.

Most companies measure sales plan accuracy by family and by individual item. Generally, the accuracy of the forecast for the family of items is better than for the individual items. It's easier to forecast the number of tires that people will buy than the number of specific *types* of tires (snow tires, all-season tires, tires of different widths, and so on). While it's important to measure both, in the end a manufacturing company makes specific items, not families. If the sales plan for the family is fairly accurate, but the mix is off significantly (for example, you've sold 200 percent of plan for product #2 and 50 percent of plan for product #3), then it's likely that you've bought the wrong materials and may have the wrong capacity.

6. *Review assumptions.* A difference between actual sales and the sales plan may indicate a change in the marketplace. It may be necessary to reforecast the item or family. The first step in this process is to reexamine the assumptions that were used to develop the sales plan. Is the economy recovering faster than expected? Are housing starts increasing? Was our promotion more successful than we predicted? The assumptions may need to be revised, and new sales plan numbers calculated.

The marketing group needs to look at these situations from an overall perspective. Is the product going through its life cycle faster than anticipated? Is the product being replaced by another technology? Is its market share slipping?

The sales group should also look at any sales plan that is out of tolerance—its members are in a good position to answer questions like "What's happening with our major customers?" "In competitive situations, are we experiencing more losses than expected?" "Are we doing better than anticipated?"

In any of these instances, the most fundamental issue is to understand the situation and revise the numbers accordingly. In short, it's a problem-solving activity that seeks to find the root cause by updating the assumptions. Consensus may not be easy to reach, but each of the groups plays an important role, and each brings key information to the process.

In many companies, an impediment to this is the tendency to "shoot" the forecaster. Whenever anything goes wrong, someone can always point to the forecast and say, "If only we had an accurate forecast. . . ." In some cases, manufacturing people have unrealistic expectations about forecast accuracy.

Sales people, having been shot at before, develop their own ways to present a smaller target. One sales manager's fatherly advice to a new salesman was "Son, give 'em a date or a number, but never both." In other situations, the forecast can be the flash point for conflict between manufacturing and sales. Each is convinced that the other group is the problem. This leads to a losing situation and nonproductive rounds of finger pointing that generate more heat than light. A better approach is to create realistic expectations and work together as a team to make improved forecasts.

A fundamental principle of forecasting is that the further out into the future you forecast, the less accurate your forecast will be. This only makes sense, because more things can change the further out you go in time. Yet many companies have long lead times for material and capacity, and this often means significant commitments are made for material and capacity based on their forecasts. When companies implement Just-in-Time, their total lead times drop significantly. This in turn means that instead of making commitments on what they think is going to happen in week 40, they make commitments for what they think is going to happen in week 20, or even week 2. The forecast for week 20 or week 2 is going to be more accurate than the forecast for week 40, and so more accurate commitments are made. These help to reduce excess material and capacity, and also take some of the pressure off the forecasters to be accurate so far into the future. So, unlikely as it may seem at first, Just-in-Time is a significant help in the sales planning process.

ORDER PROMISING

The second major subject in demand management is order promising. Many companies promise customer orders based on standard lead times—for example, a piece of capital equipment such as a shear is promised for delivery to new customers in six weeks, bottles of vitamin C are said to be available "off the shelf," and so on. The problem is, a desired lead time of 6 weeks may be pushed out to 10 weeks by a flood of orders.

Likewise, if you say that bottles of vitamin C are available off the shelf and you just used up all the stock, vitamin C is no longer off the shelf. It's just gone from being an off-the-shelf product to one like the shear that will be promised for some date in the future. Customers have shown repeatedly that they can snap up product faster than manufacturers can make it. Alternatively, if the standard lead time for the shear is six weeks, sales have been slow, and the product can be delivered in four weeks, why not take advantage of the situation?

Good customer service means telling the customer the truth, which in turn requires good information. While you will not always be in a position to be able to give customers what they want, you should (1) at least give customers dates that they can count on, even if they aren't the dates the customers want, and (2) consider changing the master production schedule if you're violating the customer service objectives you've agreed on. (Refer to Chapter 6 for an explanation of master production schedule changes.)

One crucial tool for making effective order promises is the available to promise (ATP) calculation. Available-to-promise is a very simple calculation that uses the master production schedule, the on-hand inventory, and existing customer orders to show precisely what you can promise to customers. Available-to-promise shows how much of a particular product is available to promise to customers, and when it can be safely promised. This seems remarkably simple, and you'd expect most companies to operate this way, but that's not the case.

Figure 5.2 is an example of an available-to-promise calculation showing:

1. *Customer orders that have already been promised.* In this case, 100 of this product have been promised to customers in week 2, 30 in week 3, and another 20 in week 4.

2. *On-hand inventory,* in this case 10 units of this product.

3. *Scheduled production of this product* by date. In this case, 200 are scheduled to be completed in week 2 and another 200 in week 4.

Figure 5.2   Available-to-Promise Calculation

On Hand = 10	Time Period				
	1	2	3	4	5
Customer Orders		100	30	20	
Scheduled Production		200		200	
ATP	10	80	80	260	260

The ATP calculation shows what's available by week for new customer orders. If a customer called today, it would be possible to ship 10 units right away. These are the 10 units on hand. The production of 200 scheduled to be completed in week 2 will be used to satisfy the customer orders for 100 in week 2 and 30 in week 3 (leaving 70 of the 200 available to promise to new customers). The production of 200 scheduled to be completed in week 4 will be used to satisfy the customer orders for 20 in week 4 (leaving 180 of the 200 available to promise to new customers).

The calculation shown in Figure 5.2 is called a *cumulative available-to-promise calculation*. This is because the 10 on hand are added to the 70 available in week 2 to give a total of 80 available-to-promise units in weeks 2 and 3. Likewise, the 80 available in week 3 are added to the 180 available in week 4 to give a total of 260 available-to-promise units in weeks 4 and 5.

While ATP arithmetic is simple, it is nonetheless quite powerful. ATP answers the question "When can I promise a customer order?" If a customer calls and says, "I need 10 as soon as possible. When can they be shipped?" the answer is "Right away." If a customer calls and says, "I need 80 as soon as possible. When can they be shipped?" the answer is, "Next week." And if a customer calls and says, "I need 260 as soon as possible. When can they be shipped?" the answer is, "Week 4. But we can give you 10 right away, 80 next week, and the remainder in week 4."

Today, with technologies that provide accurate on-hand balances and on-line ATP calculations, sales, marketing, scheduling, or production people can easily perform order promising. Salespeople generally do the order promising if the customer expects a delivery date immediately. If the nature of the business is such that some engineering work is required before a promise date can be given to the customer, then order promising might be done by another group.

Some companies have additional features in their order promising systems. For example, they will take an entire order and look at the earliest date when they can ship all of the items in the order. They may be able to ship the first item next week, the second in two weeks, and the third in three weeks. Depending on the type of business and product, the company might choose to break the order into separate shipments or ship everything in week 3. The same logic is used with a product with many options, say, a car. If a customer wants a car with a V-6 engine, an AM/FM/CD player, and an interior trim package, the order promising logic identifies the earliest date when all three options are available and promises the delivery at that time.

In many organizations, available-to-promise is an on-line function, so that as customer orders are taken, the ATP is immediately updated and the system gives a clear, up-to-date picture of when delivery can be promised. If the ATP for a particular item is outside the customer service objectives (the next order cannot be promised until week 8, and six weeks is the objective), the order entry people should notify the master scheduler and request a change to the master production schedule. The objective of the change would be to make the master production schedule consistent with the customer service objectives. This might mean increasing the master production schedule, or moving scheduled production up to an earlier date.

If the master production schedule cannot be changed, then it's necessary to influence demand. In the long term, a company wants to make what it can sell, but there are times when, in the short term, it may be necessary to sell what can be made. There are a number of ways to influence demand in these situations, such as running a promotion on the products for which the company can handle the demand.

Setting these customer service objectives isn't always as simple as it sounds. A common problem is setting objectives for high levels of customer service, but not being willing to do what it takes to achieve them. If a product is to be delivered off the shelf, then it's necessary to invest in inventory. If the delivery objective is 24 hours, then it may be necessary to improve your manufacturing process so you can make the product quickly, and/or to invest in some inventory. It's necessary to define customer service objectives in terms of lead time to the customer, which will determine finished goods and work-in-process inventory levels using the current manufacturing processes. Either accept these levels, change the manufacturing processes, or revise the customer service objectives.

Improving the manufacturing process is what Just-in-Time is all about. Companies that used to promise customer orders eight weeks in the future can, using Just-in-Time, manufacture and deliver a product in a few days. Companies that were stocking hundreds of different products have eliminated their finished goods inventory and can now manufacture to the customer order in 24 hours. This is an integration issue that needs to be examined in a company contemplating a Just-in-Time implementation.

Most companies measure order promising by tracking how well they do in meeting their customer service targets. This is different from the kinds of external measurements that all companies should be doing. These external measurements look at how well the company is doing in meeting customers' expectations. For example, a company's customer service objective may be delivery in four to eight weeks. An internal measurement would determine how many orders were actually delivered in more than eight weeks or less than four. The results may indicate the need to revise the production plan or master production schedule. The results may also indicate that a significant number of orders are being expedited for special delivery (which generates significant chaos). The external measurement would detail how many customers expect delivery in less than four weeks. The results may indicate a need to revise the customer service objectives. For example, it may be necessary to revise the customer service objectives to delivery in three to five weeks.

DISTRIBUTION CENTER/BRANCH WAREHOUSE DEMANDS

"We used to sit and wait for the inevitable wave at the end of each quarter," explains Bob Magner, distribution manager for Digital Equipment Corporation's Westminster distribution center. "We didn't know how big it was, but we knew it was coming and couldn't take any chances. So we'd bring in an army of temporary workers to move material—at great expense, of course. Sometimes it paid off, but other times the wave wasn't as big as we expected, and a lot of the money was wasted."

"We had to do the same thing with the trucking companies," adds Dick McGee, Business group manager of OBU/CSMD (Options Business Unit/Computer Systems Manufacturing Distribution) at Digital. "We couldn't tell these vendors exactly how many trucks we'd need or when we'd need them, so we'd just shoot for the maximum. Of course, when we went to negotiate contracts with them we were at a serious disadvantage—they knew that whatever we told them would be wrong."

All this was before DEC adopted distribution resource planning (DRP). "The search for a system like DRP was born out of a crisis," says Paul Mantos, DEC's senior manufacturing consultant. "We didn't make our earnings one quarter because we missed the revenues by a day—the informal system couldn't keep up. So we had our own market crash—DEC's stock slipped 53 points. This was not only an embarrassment to management and a scare to employees, many of whom own stock in the company, but it was like the heart attack that saved the patient. We knew we had to do something, and do it soon."

Two years later, DEC realized the following benefits as a result of DRP, during a period when order growth averaged 15–20 percent per year:

1. Inventory turns improved by 61 percent.

2. Overtime was reduced by 90 percent.

3. Revenue shipments were 33 percent higher than in the previous year.

4. Freight was reduced by 16 percent.

5. Operating expenses were reduced by $8.5 million.

Distribution resource planning also works at Mass Merchandisers, Inc., which does not have its own manufacturing operations, but purchases products and then distributes them.

Ronnie Williams, senior buyer of health and beauty aids at Mass Merchandisers, recalls what things were like before DRP: "We were basing purchase orders on five-week averages. Seasonality can bite you real quick. For example, when we get a spot of cold weather we know that we will need a huge amount of cold remedy products from the warehouse. Using a five-week sales average, you don't pick up on those situations. You quickly get behind. Going out of season, you don't pick up on the slowdown. So, with a five-week average, you are always faced with very quickly being out of stock or very quickly being overstocked. DRP levels that out."

Steve Nelson, director of inventory management systems at Mass Merchandisers, credits DRP with helping the company to achieve significant improvements in customer service levels. "Prior to DRP, we would drop to the 85–88 percent level and it would take six weeks to recover. Today we have valid information that allows us to react before a problem becomes critical."

And Bob Dickson, executive vice-president and vice-president for purchasing at Mass Merchandisers, relates what happened to inventories: "We used to get pressure because inventory levels were too high, so we would work on reducing them, but there would be a big dip in the service levels. Now we have had new business brought on board along with many marketplace changes, but inventory levels have remained stable. Today our turns are consistent. Although we have added some 10,000 slow-moving SKUs (up 30 percent) over the last four years, our overall turns have improved."

Like DEC and Mass Merchandisers before DRP, many companies plan by using averages for distribution center (DC) demands (also called branch warehouse demands). Say, for example, that on average a distribution network uses 3,000 cases per week of notebook paper. On average, that's correct. But what happens if the New York, Los Angeles, and Chicago DCs all need to be resupplied this week? The shipping quantity to each of these locations is several weeks' supply. So 9,000 cases of notebook paper are needed this week. Suddenly, the average is off by a factor of three. In general, peaks and valleys create customer service problems. You may have a week with demand as high as 6,000 or

7,000 cases, and other weeks with demands of 0, depending on how frequently you supply the DCs and what quantities are shipped.

DRP is a planning and scheduling system for distribution networks. By using DRP, a company can accurately predict when distribution centers need to be resupplied, and accurately show the peaks and valleys in the demand pattern from the distribution network. If next week there is a demand of 7,000 cases, you can see that demand 5, 10, or even 20 weeks into the future and plan for it. If a distribution planner is able to see a peak demand some weeks in the future, the planner can have the inventory to support it, either by making sure there is enough production or by decreasing the shipping quantities to the DCs.

For example, instead of shipping 2,000 cases to the DC in Houston and 2,000 cases to the DC in Chicago this week, then being unable to meet the demand for 5,000 from Los Angeles next week, a planner could choose to increase the master production schedule to cover the peak demands. Or, the planner could cut the shipping quantities so that all the distribution centers would have some inventory (ship 1,000 cases to the DC in Houston, 1,000 to the DC in Chicago, and 2,000 to the DC in Los Angeles), and then resupply them in a week or two when more inventory is available.

The point is, there's no reason to subject your company to surprises in demand. With DRP, the demands of the distribution network are visible and can be managed.

Distribution resource planning is the logic of MRP (material requirements planning—see Chapter 7) applied to a distribution network. This logic is generalized network scheduling logic, and it works equally well for a distribution network. Figure 5.3 shows an example of DRP for a distribution center.

The Forecast is what is expected to be sold from this distribution center during a time period (in this case each week). The forecast for this type of notebook paper is 800 cases per week, except in weeks 4 through 6, when it increases to 900 per week.

In Transit are the quantities of product in transit from the central supply facility to this distribution center. The quantity is shown for the date when arrival at the distribution center is expected. In this case, 2,000 cases are expected to arrive in week 1.

Projected On Hand is an inventory projection out into the future. There are currently 1,200 cases in inventory, 800 cases are expected to be sold this week, and 2,000 cases are expected to arrive, giving a

Figure 5.3 DRP Example, Chicago, Notebook Paper

On Hand = 1200 Cases   Transit Time = 2 Weeks

Safety Stock = 1000   Shipping Quantity = 2000

		Weeks						
	1	2	3	4	5	6	7	8
Forecast	800	800	800	900	900	900	800	800
In Transit	2,000							
Projected On Hand	2,400	1,600	2,800	1,900	1,000	2,100	1,300	2,500
Planned Shipments	2,000			2,000		2,000		

projected on-hand balance of 2,400 cases at the end of the week. This drops to 1,600 in week 2, and will go to 800 in week 3 if nothing is done. But 800 is below the safety stock level of 1,000 cases, so the logic in the DRP software plans a shipment to arrive in week 3, uses the specified shipping quantity of 2,000 cases, and uses the specified in-transit time of two weeks.

The result appears on the Planned Shipment line. The plan is to ship 2,000 cases from the central supply facility to the Chicago distribution center in week 1, to arrive in week 3. Similarly, shipments are planned in week 4 to arrive in week 6, and in week 6 to arrive in week 8. These planned shipments are the key to providing visibility into the distribution network.

The planned shipments for each of the different distribution centers in the network can be summarized as in Figure 5.4.

Notice how the combined demands of the distribution centers can have significant peaks and valleys. The people who do the planning for the central supply facility will find this information invaluable. In week 4, for example, a number of the big distribution centers require shipments. If the planners can see the peak demand for 8,500 ahead of time, they are in a better position to have the inventory available. If they cannot see this coming, they probably will not have enough inventory to cover a peak demand of this size.

Figure 5.4   Total Distribution Demands (Planned Shipments)

Notebook Paper

	1	2	3	4	5	6	7	8
Chicago	2,000			2,000		2,000		
New York		2,000		2,000			2,000	
Los Angeles	3,000			3,000				3,000
Houston		1,500		1,500			1,500	
Toronto			1,500			1,500		

	1	2	3	4	5	6	7	8
Total	5,000	3,500	1,500	8,500	0	3,500	3,500	3,000

In a nutshell, DRP takes the forecast by item for each distribution center, the inventory, and the item data (shipping quantity, shipping schedule, transportation lead time) and calculates the planned shipments from the central supply facility to the distribution centers. These planned shipments are then accumulated and represented as demands to the master scheduler (see Chapter 6 for an example of how the distribution demands are shown on the master schedule report). The central supply facility could be a manufacturing plant, several plants, or a purchasing operation in the case of a pure distributor (like Mass Merchandisers) that does no manufacturing.

Plugging DRP into the master scheduling system involves more than just creating a technical interface. DRP makes the distribution network transparent in the sense that people can now see into the network and manage it globally. Excess inventory in one location can be transferred to another. Peak demands from the distribution network are visible at the plant weeks in advance, instead of being surprises, as before.

All this means that distribution and manufacturing people need to develop a new working relationship. Andre Martin, a pioneer in the field of DRP, says, "In the past, distribution was responsible for distributing inventory, and the unstated assumption was that inventory was there for the taking. In reality, the inventory wasn't always there, and distribution and manufacturing were put into adversarial roles." Distribution people would say, "If manufacturing could just supply the inventory, there wouldn't be stockouts." Manufacturing people's response, on the other hand, was "If distribution wouldn't keep surprising manufacturing with peak demands, we could run the plant efficiently." The information provided by DRP allows these groups to see the constraints each has to deal with, and to work effectively as a team.

The planned shipments from the central supply facility to the distribution centers can also be used for transportation planning. The distribution planning system is capable of generating a transportation planning report, which shows the weight and cube of the items to be shipped from a central supply facility to each DC each day or week. This enables a transportation planner to take best advantage of freight rates. For example, in Figure 5.5, 3.5 railcars need to be shipped to the Chicago DC this week and 1.5 railcars need to be shipped next week. The planner might consider moving half a railcar up from next week to this week and shipping early, or taking half a railcar and moving it out to ship later.

The planner is also responsible for efficiently using the railcar or truck. If a railcar is reaching its weight limit but hasn't used its cube, the planner might choose to change the mix. If the railcar for next week uses the cube but not the weight, one way to solve the problem would be for

Figure 5.5 Transportation Planning Report

From: Central Supply

To: Chicago DC

Week	1	2	3	4	5
Weight	1,360,108	550,126	705,010	420,106	750,206
Cube	34,086	13,080	18,065	8,015	7,583

1 Railcar = 400,000 Pounds
10,000 Cubic Feet

the planner to pull some of the lighter products into the current week and use the heavier ones next week.

For a complete explanation of DRP, see *Distribution Resource Planning: Distribution Management's Most Powerful Tool* by Andre Martin (Oliver Wight Publications).

INTERPLANT DEMANDS

Interplant demands (i.e., demands for a plant's product from another plant in the company) are a continuing source of frustration in many manufacturing companies. The supplying plant is usually convinced that the "customer" plant makes unrealistic demands and does not allow enough time. The customer plant, on the other hand, typically considers the supplying plant to be rigid and inflexible.

For the most part, all of this is unnecessary. The planning system at the customer plant can be plugged into the planning system at the supplying plant, and the most up-to-date picture of demand can be communicated rapidly and efficiently between the two locations. If something changes and the demand picture is different, then the two plants can work it out by determining whether they can make the plan happen or by deciding what changes, if any, need to be made.

This doesn't prevent customers from changing at a rate faster than the two plants can keep up with, but that's life in manufacturing. When customers do change their demands, however, two plants with connected planning systems can get accurate information quickly. With this information, they can then decide whether a change can or cannot be realistically made.

Formerly, the three plants of the General Dynamics Land Systems Division, manufacturer of the M1A1 tank, did not have a common master production schedule. Each plant would maximize its own schedule and build up its own inventory, resulting in production that was at one time thirty tanks behind schedule. Today, the integration and visibility provided by MRP II have allowed the different plants to tie into a division master production schedule for tanks, so that all three plants are working from a common game plan.

Managing interplant demand as the General Dynamics Land Systems Division has done involves connecting two planning and scheduling systems; what flows out of one goes into the other, as illustrated in Figure 5.6.

Figure 5.6   Interplant Demand

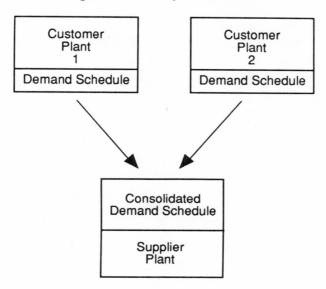

The planning system for the customer plant provides a schedule of what's needed and when it must arrive. For purchased items, this is a purchasing schedule. For items sourced from another plant, this schedule is represented as interplant demands. These demands are sent to the supplier plant, and are shown as demand on the master production schedule report (see Chapter 6 for an example of how interplant demands are represented). In effect, these are customer orders from the customer plant. This schedule of demand from the customer plant takes the place of the forecast—an application of MRP pioneer Joe Orlicky's idea, "Don't forecast what you can calculate." In terms of interplant demand, that means there's no reason for a supplying plant to be forecasting when it can simply plug into the planning system of the customer plant and accurately predict what's needed.

Once the interplant demands have been communicated from the customer plant to the supplier plant, the work begins. The work in this case is the cooperation between the two plants. On the one hand, the customer plant may need the supplier plant to change schedules more quickly than the supplier would like. The supplier plant, on the other hand, may need to stabilize its schedules because of material or capacity limitations, and the ever-present demands to run the plant efficiently.

Consequently, it's a process of cooperative negotiation—give-and-take, knowing what's realistic, knowing what needs to be done, and knowing how to make the plan happen.

In most cases, the two plants working together can devise a plan that meets both their needs. Figure 5.7 illustrates this process.

Let's say that the customer plant makes a change in its master production schedule to meet changing customer demand. This "explodes" down through the customer plant's planning system and creates a series of changed demands. These changes are transmitted to the supplier plant, and the planners there see these changes in demand.

It may not be necessary for the supplier plant to change its master production schedule in response to these changed demands. The supplier plant may have inventory that could be used to meet the demands. For example, it may have 500 bearing housings on hand, enough to meet an increase in demand of 100. Or it might be planning to manufacture a quantity greater than the immediate need, and this might allow the new demands to be covered without any changes to the master production schedule.

Perhaps neither is the case, and the supplying plant needs to make a

Figure 5.7   Changes in Interplant Demand

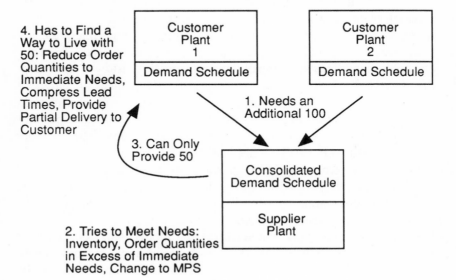

change to its schedule. Let's further assume some limitations in capacity, so the full amount of the change cannot be made. It may, however, be possible to make a partial change—perhaps half the change can be accommodated (the supplying plant can provide an additional 50), but the customer plant will have to find a way to do without the other half. The company may have to reduce some order quantities, compress some lead times, or, in the end, provide only a partial delivery to the customer. In any case, there needs to be a cooperative effort on the part of both the customer and the supplying plant.

Credibility can be a significant issue in making this process work. If the supplying plant says the customer plant never really knows what it needs and when it needs it, or if the customer plant says it can never get the supplier to deliver on time so it must always ask for more than it really needs, then the process breaks down. So it's the responsibility of the planners in each of the plants to maintain accurate information and credible systems, and to work honestly with each other.

Unfortunately, in some organizations there's a disincentive to work together. It may be to one plant's advantage to "stick" another plant with inventory. ("The end of the year is coming up, we're going to have a physical inventory, so let *them* keep it on *their* books.") Or let's say that the supplier plant supplies outside customers in addition to other divisions of the company. In such a case, it's usually more profitable to ship to the outside customers and let the customer plant suffer. In the end this hurts the total profitability of the organization. If these kinds of negative incentives are in place, it's important to dismantle them so people can work together as members of the same team.

SERVICE PARTS DEMANDS

All equipment manufacturers have service or spare parts demands that need to be managed well. Not only are service parts typically an extremely profitable part of business, but companies get a reputation for either having or not having service parts available. If their reputation in this regard is poor, they can have a difficult time selling their products. Finally, if service parts are not managed well, it may be necessary to cannibalize equipment being assembled for shipment. This not only affects shipments, profits, and new customer promises, but is extremely inefficient.

Service part demands can be difficult to manage because in many companies it's fairly typical to have unrealistic customer service objectives for service parts. For example, one capital equipment manufacturer's policy was to deliver service parts off the shelf or within two weeks—yet its customers could order service parts for a piece of equipment that hadn't been made in ten years! These items were not in inventory, and in many cases the manufacturer would have to buy the raw material and fabricate the parts. In such a situation, it was impossible to provide these parts in two weeks.

A solution is to establish categories for service parts. For example, the first category might be items that are typically ordered as service parts for equipment built in the last five years; these items would be available out of stock. Another category might be items that are not typically required to service equipment, or parts for equipment more than five years old. These items would be promised based on the lead time necessary to make the parts, including raw material purchase. If a part happened to be in stock, then it would be promised right away; if the material needed to make the part was available, then the part would be promised at the lead time necessary to fabricate it; and so on. Finally, a third category might be service parts for equipment older than ten years. In this case, some decisions would need to be made on the cost of supplying the parts and the possible advantages of upgrading or even completely replacing the equipment. Both manufacturing and sales would get involved in these situations.

Once these categories have been established, forecasts are needed only for the first category—those service parts that will be supplied from stock or raw materials to be used to make service parts. The remaining categories do not require any forecasting, since they will be manufactured to order.

The forecasts for service parts are then entered directly into material requirements planning as requirements for the items. Material planning (see Chapter 7) takes into account the total demands for the item—the demands for finished products plus the demands for service.

If all the demands cannot be met, the planner has the best picture of the situation and can either make or recommend a decision. Many times, the decision is whether to use a part on equipment that has been promised to a customer or ship the part to another customer for service. As always, the objective is to do everything possible to meet both demands. When that is not realistic, however, the decision will have to be made based on the company's customer service policy.

These situations will become visible when the available-to-promise calculation is used for service parts. The same types of ATP information can be displayed for service parts as for finished products, and the process described above can be used.

SUMMARY/CHECKUP

1. The days of accepting marketplace demand are over. That passive approach has been discarded in favor of a more active stance called demand management. Companies can control a number of influencing factors, and when they can't influence demand, they can at least plan for it. People are making the transition from "C'mere" to "Sic 'em." Where is your company on a scale of 1 to 10, with 1 being "C'mere" and 10 being "Sic 'em"? Where should you be?

2. Once a company makes the transition from the passive approach to the more active process of demand management, someone needs to fulfill the role of demand manager or demand planner. Do you have a demand manager or demand planner responsible for managing the demand stream feeding your planning and control system?

3. The process of sales planning is somewhat different for each company, but the fundamentals are the same for all:
   a. Document the assumptions.
   b. Convert assumptions into numbers.
   c. Reconcile numbers to create a sales plan by product family.
   d. Break down the sales plan by item.
   e. Measure actual sales against the sales plan.
   f. Review assumptions where actuals are out of tolerance.

How well does your company do each of these activities?

4. Companies no longer promise customer orders based on a standard lead time or an off-the-shelf assumption. Order promising should be done using an available-to-promise (ATP) calculation. Is such a calculation used in your company?

5. Distribution resource planning (DRP) should be used to plan the demands from distribution centers where such centers exist. The

accumulated demand from the distribution network is shown on the master production schedule report. If you have distribution centers in your company, is DRP being used in this way?

6. Where products are shipped between plants, the planning system for the customer plant should be feeding its demands to the planning system at the supplier plant. These interplant demands should appear on the master production schedule report. If you have interplant shipments in your company, is the demand being handled in this way?

7. Equipment manufacturers have to plan for service parts demands. These should be forecast only for ship-from-stock items or raw materials used to make service parts, and should be promised using an available-to-promise calculation.

Each element of demand management is important, although not all elements apply to every company. The result of demand management is a valid and well-managed demand stream. This demand stream feeds the remainder of the planning and control system, specifically the master production schedule, which is the subject of the next chapter.

SPECIAL ACKNOWLEDGMENTS

Richard Ling and George Palmatier for their contributions to the field of demand management, and Andre Martin for his original thinking on DRP.

Chapter Six

Master Production Scheduling

"The toughest thing is *not* to master-schedule," explains Frank Wetzel, director of materials and systems at Sealed Power, a manufacturer of piston rings and other combustion chamber components, "but to have management *respect* the master schedule. In the past, as in most companies, if our management got a call from a high-level officer at a customer's firm, the first reaction was to violate the master schedule and do whatever needed to be done to satisfy that customer, rather than try to manage the master schedule. That's changed. We still deliver 98 percent on time, almost across the board. But we don't see upper management whiplashing the factories anymore.

"I can think of one incident in which the owner of one of our customer companies called our president about delivery. It was a delivery that would have seriously violated our master schedule. Our company management was off site, and I was with the president. He was hot after he hung up the phone. As he was calling the plant to make sure it expedited the order, I told him, 'If you do this, you become the division expediter. Is that what you want?' Rather than expediting it, he put the problem in the hands of the plant management and the materials group. And instead of telling them to just do it, he asked them what they *could* do. In the past, it would have been 'You'll make it happen—I don't care if you're over capacity.' The plant, at the time, happened to *be* over capacity. It then negotiated directly with the customer. We didn't give the customer exactly what he was demanding, but we did give him what he needed for his business. I think from that day forward things changed."

The master production schedule (MPS) is best defined as an "anticipated manufacturing schedule"—*anticipated* because it represents what you expect to make in the future; *manufacturing* because it determines what you are going to make, as opposed to what you're going to sell; *schedule* because it is stated in terms of specific product configurations to be built in specific quantities on specific dates—for example, 500 large-bore piston rings on July 31.

If the production plan describes "what we are going to make" at the product family level, the master production schedule describes "what we are going to make" at the specific product level.

THE BALANCING ACT

The master scheduler creates a master production schedule on an item-by-item basis, attempting to balance the demands of the marketplace with the limitations that exist in manufacturing. Figure 6.1 illustrates this, showing both the demands and the limitations. The challenge to the master scheduler is to balance these two opposing forces.

Demand-Side Forces

The Sales Plan/Forecast
Most companies need to master-schedule prior to the receipt of customer orders. In other words, they must forecast demand and create a sales plan. If a company has a long backlog of orders, long enough to extend out beyond its lead times for material, sales planning may not be necessary. A company manufacturing for a government defense contract will typically not order material in advance of receiving the contract. But even in these situations, some sales planning is typically done beyond the backlog of customer contracts in order to calculate capacity. For these reasons, the sales plan is a key input to the MPS in almost every company.

Figure 6.1

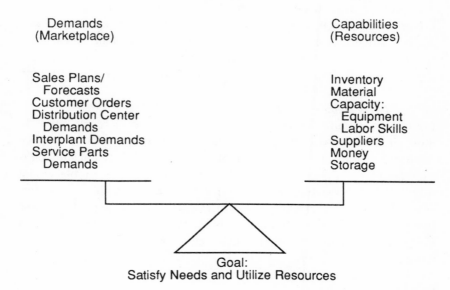

| Demands | Capabilities |
| (Marketplace) | (Resources) |

Goal:
Satisfy Needs and Utilize Resources

Customer Orders

Customer orders are demands that have been received and are yet to be satisfied. The total of customer orders that have been booked and not yet shipped is called the *backlog of customer orders.* Since customer service is a primary objective for every organization, customer orders are also key inputs to the master production schedule.

There may not be an appreciable backlog of customer orders for products delivered off the shelf, since turnaround time from receipt of order to shipment may be less than a day. A make-to-stock product, however, can quickly become a make-to-order product when the product is out of stock. For this reason, the backlog of customer orders can become an important input to the MPS, even for a make-to-stock company.

Distribution Center/Branch Warehouse Demands

As explained in Chapter 5, the planned shipments to the different distribution centers are calculated by the logic of distribution resource planning. These planned shipments are then summarized and represented as a demand stream (that is, the demands of the distribution network for product).

Interplant Demands

The planning system at the customer plant provides a schedule of what's needed and when it must arrive, and this schedule is represented as a demand stream. The demands are sent to the supplier plant, and accordingly appear on the master production schedule report. In effect, the supplier plant is simply plugging into the planning system of its customer.

Service Parts Demands

Equipment manufacturers generally supply service or repair parts. In most situations, these service demands are for components or supplies rather than for master-scheduled items. Examples include consumables, such as ink for a printing press, or spare parts, such as a replacement roller. It is also possible, however, to have service demands for a master-scheduled item. For example, a V-8 engine may fail in the field and have to be replaced. This engine not only is a master-scheduled item, but also has a service demand. Where such demands exist, they need to be represented in the MPS.

Supply-Side Forces

Inventory

On-hand inventory for a make-to-stock product should be represented in the master production schedule, since it will be used as one of the factors in determining when to make more. For example, if six weeks of inventory is on hand, then the next master schedule order isn't needed for another six weeks. If, however, the goal of the sales and operations planning meeting is to build inventory in anticipation of a peak selling season or a plant shutdown, then it may make sense to schedule production somewhat earlier.

Material and Capacity Limitations

These items are constraints on the master production schedule:

Material Availability. If the material is not available, the schedule won't happen on time. One major manufacturer, for example, was limited in its production of turbines by the availability of steel forgings from the primary supplier. The primary supplier was doing everything it could to increase capacity to the required levels, and the company was working to locate additional suppliers. In the meantime, though, the

MPS was limited to ten turbines per month, a quantity that reflected what the company could get in forgings.

In the long term, with enough dedication and money, the material availability constraint can be eliminated. But in the short term, it can have a significant effect on the master production schedule and must therefore be considered.

CAPACITY. In the same way that the turbine company was limited by material availability, companies can be limited by capacity. Consider the case of a machine tool manufacturer limited by its milling capacity. The company knew from its capacity planning system that it faced an overload situation. Unfortunately, solving the capacity problems would have required an investment of more than $1 million. The general manager and staff spent considerable time discussing whether or not to make the investment and, in the end, chose to postpone the purchase of additional capacity. In doing so, they restricted the MPS until it was clear where the business was going.

Both material and capacity constraints must be used as inputs to the process of master scheduling. They are not, however, generally presented in the master schedule report or display. Instead, they are usually handled as memos or, many times, just identified during the analysis of a particular plan.

When the demands of the marketplace are satisfied and the manufacturing resources are utilized at the same time, the master production schedule has achieved the best balance. The end result isn't a manufacturing schedule or a marketing schedule—it's a *company* schedule that helps the business achieve its objectives.

As you can see, master production scheduling is a challenging process that involves constant analysis and reaction in an attempt to balance the demands of the marketplace with the resources of the company. There is rarely a perfect or optimal MPS, only one that represents the best balance of responsiveness to customers and resource utilization. And while there is no "right" answer, some choices are clearly better than others, and some are so close that, when you weigh the pros and cons, you can only flip a coin in the end. The outcome is many times the least-worst choice. For these reasons, master scheduling is both frustrating and highly rewarding.

Many of the inputs to the master production schedule can be represented on a computer report or screen display. The most common master production schedule format is shown in Figure 6.2.

Figure 6.2   Master Production Schedule

On Hand =   Lead Time =   Cumulative Lead Time =

Order Quantity =

Safety Stock =

	Weeks							
	1	2	3	4	5	6	7	8
Sales Plan								
Production Forecast								
Distribution Requirements								
Interplant Demands								
Actual Demand								
Projected On-Hand Balance								
ATP								
MPS (Receipt)								

On Hand. Starting inventory position.

Order Quantity. Also called lot size or batch size.

Safety Stock. Stock used as a buffer against forecast errors or unreliable supply sources.

Lead Time. The time required to produce an item (rather than build the whole product from scratch).

Cumulative Lead Time. The time required to build the entire product from scratch. This is the longest path, in terms of time, from the top to the very bottom of the product structure. Changes in the master production schedule beyond the cumulative lead time can be made quickly by the master scheduler, because theoretically there's enough time to buy or make everything in the product. Within the cumulative lead time, though, changes to the master production schedule must be investigated before being approved because there may not be sufficient time to make or buy some of the items.

Time Periods for Display. The display shown in Figure 6.2 shows eight time periods. Most master scheduling systems work in terms of days. For purposes of display, however, most systems show weekly time periods because daily time periods are too cumbersome to use beyond a week or two. If a company needs to show daily time periods, it generally does so for a week or two, and then shifts to weekly time periods.

A related issue is how far into the future to master-schedule. Typically, a company will schedule beyond the cumulative lead times for the product that requires the longest time to manufacture. This makes it possible to do more effective capacity planning (equipment and skills procurement) and supplier scheduling (working with suppliers out beyond the quoted lead times).

Sales Plan. The sales plan or forecast for the item.

Production Forecast. Demand for the item required by higher-level schedules. To understand the importance of this function, consider Instron Corporation in Canton, Massachusetts, a manufacturer of strain measuring equipment. Instron's customers order the basic machine and then order a number of options or accessories. For example, a customer might order a special grip to hold the sample that will be measured, or might order an option to have the equipment automatically log the results into a computer. Instron master-schedules not only the strain measuring machines, but also the grips, computer logging options, and so on. The demand for these options coming from the scheduled production of the measurement machines would appear in the production forecast line.

The term *production forecast* is confusing to many people. It's a forecast because it's a guess. Instron schedules the production of machines and forecasts, or guesses, how many of its customers are going to want special grips, computer logging, and so on. For example, if Instron forecasts a demand for 10 machines and also forecasts a demand that 30 percent be built with the computer logging function, the production forecast for the computer logging option will be 3. Because it's a forecast based on a rate of production, it's called a production forecast. Once the actual customer orders are received, the production forecasts are removed, and the company does its planning based on what the customers actually ordered.

Distribution Requirements. The expected shipments from the central supply facility to the distribution centers, as explained above.

Interplant Demands. The expected shipments from one plant to another.

Not all companies have production forecasts, distribution requirements, or interplant demands. Where appropriate, these lines would appear on the master production schedule. Where they are not needed, they would typically not appear on the spreadsheet.

Actual Demand. The backlog of customer orders; that is, orders booked but not yet shipped. Typically, these orders are displayed at the promise date (i.e., the date the order has been promised for shipment to the customer).

In many master scheduling systems, the customer orders on the actual demand line are deducted from, or reduce, the forecast. For example, if the forecast is 100 in a particular week, and customer orders for 75 have been received, the forecast is reduced to 25. If the forecast is for 100 and an order is received for 200, two weeks of forecast are reduced to zero. Most software programs have some safeguards so that a single large order doesn't clear out the next six months of forecast. Most software can also indicate that a particular customer order is in excess of the forecast (called "abnormal demand") and should not reduce the forecast. This would be indicated, for example, when a new distributor starts operation and needs to create an initial stock of product.

Projected On-Hand Balance. A projection of on-hand inventory week by week. For a make-to-order product, inventory would typically not be on hand. In this case, the calculation can be thought of as a comparison of supply and demand. Negative numbers mean there is not enough supply to meet the demands. For a make-to-stock product, a continuing increase in this projection indicates an inventory buildup. In a situation in which a stockpile of material is being built up to cover a plant shutdown, this projection can be compared to the stockpile target, and corrections can be made to the master schedule as necessary.

Available-to-Promise (ATP). Provides the sales department with a reliable answer to the question "When can you ship?" This number is critical to customer service, as explained in Chapter 5.

Master Production Schedule (MPS). The anticipated manufacturing schedule for a particular item. There are two conventions for the MPS line: displayed at receipt date or displayed at start date. Most people use the receipt date because it makes the calculations easier to understand.

WHY IS MASTER PRODUCTION SCHEDULING IMPORTANT?

The master production schedule provides a tremendous amount of control over other schedules. It truly is the "master" of all the lower-level schedules. In a complex assemble-to-order product, one master schedule can control the schedules for 20,000 or 30,000 individual item numbers. Not all products are this complex, but the basics of master scheduling still apply—master scheduling is a highly leveraged activity.

Because it is a leveraged activity, the idea is to pick the point in the product structure that gives the maximum control with the fewest items to master-schedule. If you can control the schedules of 20,000 items with 500 master schedule items, that makes more sense than having to manage 3,000 master schedule items.

In order to pick the most effective point for master scheduling, it's helpful to visualize the entire product structure. This allows a company to select the point that requires the minimum number of items to provide the maximum amount of control, *control* being defined as setting a master schedule for one item and then determining the schedule for many other items. Figure 6.3 shows the patterns that are characteristic for most companies.

Pyramid

The pyramid pattern reflects the fact that the product has few end items but a great many lower-level items. In this case, it's desirable to master-schedule at the top of the pyramid—the end-item level—which

Figure 6.3   Master Scheduling Choices

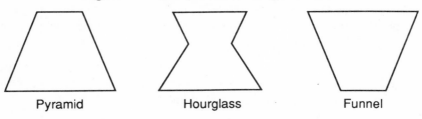

Pyramid   Hourglass   Funnel

represents the fewest items. The end-item level offers maximum control because everything is underneath the master schedule in the product structure. Electric motors that are shipped from stock are an example of a product for which the pyramid pattern is applicable.

Hourglass

Here there are many different end items, then a "choke point," then an increasing number of items. For example, a make-to-order product with many options, such as the strain measuring equipment manufactured by Instron, fits this pattern. At the level of the options (the choke point), there might only be 16 choices to worry about—the basic model plus 15 options, such as special grips and computer logging. Below the choke point, there are literally thousands of item numbers that need to be controlled. Above the choke point, there are potentially thousands of combinations of options. Therefore, the best place to master-schedule a product like this is at the level of the 16 choices, where the fewest item numbers will give the greatest amount of control.

The hourglass pattern doesn't apply only to make-to-order products with options. Consider Abbott Laboratories in Montreal, Canada, a pharmaceutical manufacturer. The choke point for Abbott is the unpackaged (or bulk) tablets. Below that level, there are a number of raw materials that are used to make the product. Above the choke point, there are a variety of different packaging configurations (e.g., bottles with 100, 250, 500, and 1,000 tablets). Master-scheduling the unpackaged tablets provides the greatest control with the minimum number of items.

Funnel

In this pattern, a small number of raw materials are common to a wide variety of individual products. An example would be bushings; when you go back far enough in the manufacturing process, every bushing starts as a slug of material. In such cases, a limited number of raw materials produce a wide variety of end items.

It might therefore seem logical to master-schedule at the level of raw material. But this is impractical in most situations because there are no items below the level of the master schedule, which means that the master schedule doesn't determine any other schedules. In short, the master production schedule provides very limited control. Consequently, it is usually necessary to master-schedule in the middle or at the top of the product structure in many of these situations. For example, a company might master-schedule 20 generic types of cabinets, and then replace them with the actual customer configurations when orders are received. In addition, at many companies, master scheduling and order promising are done in terms of hours of capacity. Upon receipt of a customer order, they schedule the configuration the customer requested—specific material and manufacturing operations. The master schedule display shows the number of hours booked, which are subtracted from the available-to-promise hours for new customer orders.

Combinations

Any or all of the previous shapes can be combined, and regardless of the combination, the objective is the same: to master-schedule the minimum number of items and get the maximum amount of control. Some companies have all of these different shapes because they have different products, each of which may have a different shape.

THE MYTH OF THE AUTOMATIC MPS

On the surface, master production scheduling looks like an ideal candidate for automation. After all, feed it forecasts, customer orders, inventories, and a few decision rules and . . . presto, out comes the MPS! Would that it were so simple. Companies have discovered, sometimes painfully, that master scheduling requires judgment, creativity, and product knowledge—things that computers don't do well and people do better.

The master scheduler should create and maintain the MPS. Once the schedule has been created, the computer is an invaluable tool for storing the information and displaying it as it is needed. Ideally, whenever the master scheduler needs information, it is on call. Decision making is reserved for the master scheduler because it involves identifying options (creativity), evaluating the options (judgment), and selecting and implementing the options (responsibility and accountability). The computer can be a powerful tool for helping to analyze the options, by "critiquing" decisions and by directing the master scheduler to look at certain items and suggesting, arithmetically, what to do with those items. But accountability must ultimately rest with a human being; the master scheduler must be responsible for creating and maintaining a valid MPS.

CHARACTERISTICS OF A GOOD MASTER SCHEDULER

Walter Goddard, CEO of Oliver Wight Companies, lists the characteristics of the ideal master scheduler:

- *Five years as a manufacturing supervisor.* As a manufacturing supervisor, the person knows how the products are built and has knowledge and an appreciation of how difficult it is to start and stop the factory on a dime.

- *Five years' experience in sales.* This gives the master scheduler an understanding of the customer, the marketplace, the need for high levels of customer service, the value of an order, and the need for responsiveness.

- *Good communication skills.* Master scheduling sometimes involves making the least-worst choice. This won't be the best choice for everybody, so it's essential that the master scheduler be able to communicate the situation so compromises can be reached.

- *Credibility within the company.* Reaching consensus within a group of people from different departments with different objectives is an essential, but difficult, task. The master scheduler must therefore be able to command respect from all organizations within the company.

THE CHALLENGE OF MANAGING CHANGE

The life of the master scheduler is ruled by change. For that reason, "master *re*scheduler" would actually be a more accurate job title. There are two types of changes the master scheduler will encounter: those within the company and those outside it. Examples of changes outside the company include

- *Demand from customers.* Selling more or less than forecast. The customer wants his order moved up to an earlier date or back to a later date. The customer goes on credit hold, wants the quantity changed, wants one item substituted for another, and so on.

- *Supplier problems.* A supplier calls and says he can't deliver all or part of an order. The reasons: equipment breakdown, quality problem, wildcat strike, suppliers who have failed to deliver to him on time, engineering change, process problems, and so on.

Given this steady stream of changes that bombard the master scheduler, the task is to constantly ask: "Do we have an attainable MPS?"

Many general managers want an "aggressive" MPS so they can go after as much business as possible. Another way of saying the same thing is that they want an ambitious MPS to stretch resources as much as possible. While this seems like a reasonable goal, the plan must be *attainable* by the company, and must be one that people will be *accountable* for hitting. If the plan isn't attainable, who will be accountable for it? Not sales, not manufacturing, not engineering. And without accountability you lose the measurement system and the ability to manage effectively.

THE TEST

The reality test of the MPS requires the master scheduler to say that as far as he or she knows, you'll have the material and capacity available when they're needed. If one or both can't be provided, then the MPS represents what you'd *like* to do rather than what you *can* do. In other words, it becomes a wish list rather than a company schedule.

A related issue concerns attitudes. The master scheduler can't simply be the "master eraser" who, at the drop of a dime, goes in and changes the plan to reflect the outside world. In fact, if the changes encountered turn out to be problems, the last choice is to change the MPS. The real objective is to make the schedule happen; companies that are particularly effective in their use of MRP II put a tremendous amount of effort into solving the problems that the system identifies.

The measurement of how well the MPS is doing involves three issues:

1. *Validity. Valid* means "doable"; if people follow the plans, there will be no surprises and they will achieve their goal, whether it's shipping product to the customer on time or sending finished goods into inventory on time.

2. *On-time deliveries.* Everyone in a manufacturing company is both a customer and a supplier. If you're the buyer in a company, the supplier is the vendor, but the customer is the factory. If fabrication is the first operation of the factory, and the second is subassembly, then the fabrication supervisor has a customer—the subassembly operation. The fabrication supervisor in turn needs materials from purchasing. Likewise, engineering or R&D has several customers—marketing and manufacturing. Everyone, as you can see, is involved in on-time deliveries, so the "buyers" should therefore be measured every week regarding on-time delivery to their customers.

3. *Hot lists versus schedules.* The acid test of whether the master scheduler is doing a good job is whether the plant can work to schedules and meet them without hot lists. A veteran of the factory floor will sweat buckets and experience heart palpitations at the prospect of losing a hot list. Yet in a company with a valid scheduling system, there's no need for a hot list, because the system provides better information. This is a difficult measure to achieve, because the informal system is always waiting for the formal system to break down. Therefore, if anything in the formal system *does* break down, the hot list will reappear. No hot list means that there are no breakdowns in the formal system, and the MPS is valid.

MASTER SCHEDULING ACTIVITIES

The work in master scheduling is managing the master production schedule. This work involves one or more of the following activities:

- adding to and deleting from the master schedule
- responding to action messages
- evaluating marketing requests for early delivery
- responding to sales plan changes

- responding to manufacturing or supplier problems

- verifying the master schedule against the production plan

Let's take a look at each of these.

Adding to and Deleting from the Master Schedule

As time passes, the master schedule needs to be updated. At the end of this week, the current week drops off the master production schedule. In addition, a new week is added to the master production schedule at the end of the planning horizon.

Dropping the current week starts with releasing master schedule orders into production. In many companies, when the master schedule reaches the lead time to make the product, the master schedule order is converted into a manufacturing order. When the manufacturing order is completed, products are either put into stock or shipped to the customer. This closes out the manufacturing order and removes it from the system. In process, high-volume, or Just-in-Time manufacturing, the master schedule orders are not always converted to scheduled receipts. Many times, these master schedule orders are simply authorized for production. This information goes out to the plant as a schedule, and when the schedule is completed, the master schedule orders are removed.

The typical company periodically adds to its master schedule at the end of its planning horizon. For example, at the end of every month it adds another month. If it plans a year into the future, at the end of every month it adds a thirteenth month to the schedule. Some companies wait and add to the master schedule once a quarter; others add every week, depending on the type of business. A production plan this far into the future is a requirement for adding to the master schedule—if there is no production plan for month 13, it's hard to have a master schedule for month 13.

Responding to Action Messages

Much of the master scheduler's day is spent responding to action messages. This is because of the volatility of the marketplace and the ever-changing nature of manufacturing. Also, customer orders come in at rates different from the forecast, and problems inevitably occur in the plant. So what looked like a wonderful master schedule last week looks like a total disaster this week. Most master scheduling software points out exception conditions, so the master scheduler can manage more effectively; it's much easier to deal with the exceptions than to plow through tons of "normal" data. Typical action messages include:

• Reschedule a master schedule to an earlier or later date.

• Add to the master schedule.

• Past due in the master schedule.

• Overpromised customer orders.

The master scheduler looks at the situation for the item, then works with people in the plant or with sales and marketing to resolve the problem. For example, the report may recommend moving a master schedule order to an earlier time period—perhaps the product is selling faster than expected. The master scheduler verifies that the recommendation makes sense, then decides on a course of action—making sure that the situation is happening consistently before looking for a remedy. Sometimes the best course of action is to sit tight and see what happens after a week. If a change is in order, the master scheduler asks whether the material and capacity will be available earlier. He or she will also explore various alternatives. Perhaps a product that uses many of the same materials is not selling as well and can be moved out three weeks. If so, it might be an easy trade-off.

In any case, the situation is not likely to be black or white; compromises and trade-offs between manufacturing and sales will likely be needed to arrive at the best decision. Ultimately, someone must make a decision, and that person is the master scheduler. If this decision is unpopular—and sometimes it will be—the manufacturing supervisor or the sales manager can appeal it through the chain of command.

One of the master scheduler's best approaches for dealing with these types of requests is simply never to say no. Instead, the master scheduler must say what it would take to honor the request. Now, it may turn out that the cost of the change or the disruption it will cause means that people will decide against it. For example, making the change may cost $5,000 and may mean missing another customer promise. That may not be worth it. The point is, most companies find it better to work from the positive position ("What would it take to make the change happen?") than to work from the negative ("We can't do it").

Evaluating Marketing Requests for Early Delivery

When the customer or sales group does not agree with the ATP-developed promise date for a customer order, the master scheduler usually gets involved. Perhaps the customer needs or wants the order earlier than the promise date, or expects it earlier because the delivery violates the company's established objectives for customer service.

Most often, the master scheduler is asked to add to the MPS or pull up an MPS order to an earlier date. This is the same as responding to an action message. In such cases, the master scheduler must look at the material and capacity constraints and work with manufacturing and sales people to understand the problem.

Even when the problems are understood, several constraints should be kept in mind when responding to requests for early delivery. First, it's easy to get overwhelmed; every request requires research and analysis—sometimes a considerable amount. And in some cases, there just isn't enough time to do the work. In that case, a company must do one of the following:

- Limit requests for rescheduling to earlier dates (so many per week).

- Add additional people in the master scheduling function to handle these requests.

- Reexamine customer service issues ("What should our delivery time be to customers?"). Maybe the reason for so many requests is that the customers are not happy with the stated customer delivery policies.

- Examine on-time performance issues ("Are we delivering on time?"). Maybe the reason for so many requests is that the customers don't have confidence in the delivery promises.

There is another alternative for dealing with customers who want an earlier promise date: repromise existing customer orders. Let's say the necessary material or capacity is not available to allow a change to the MPS. One option is to take a customer order promised in, say, week 3 and move it to week 6, then promise the new customer order in week 3. This decision would be made by someone in sales. For obvious reasons, this is an unpopular approach. Yet it is still done, on either a conscious or an unconscious basis. It's done unconsciously when companies expedite one customer order and fail to expedite another, allowing it to go late. The net effect is that new customer orders get shipped ahead of previous orders. It's best to make these decisions after looking at the alternatives, rather than letting the decisions happen by default and then dealing with the resulting problems.

Whatever your policy, it's important to recognize that a manufacturing company can stand only so much change to its master schedule. In theory, it's possible to work twenty-four hours a day, seven days a week without shipping anything. Here's how this would happen. The factory works to one schedule and gets about half the materials, parts, intermediates, and so on completed. The VP of sales or general manager comes out to the factory, meets with the manufacturing managers, and says, "Stop, I have a new schedule. Work on this, ignore the old one." The factory then switches to the new schedule, ignoring what was partially completed for the first schedule, and starting over again to get the materials, parts, intermediates, and so on for the new schedule. The same thing happens again, and now a third schedule comes into play. Meanwhile, inventory rises dramatically as half-completed products back up, and customer service takes a nosedive because nothing is complete enough to ship.

Most companies control this problem through a master scheduling policy that includes *time fences*. The master scheduling policy spells out how the master scheduler will respond to changes. The time fences determine the response.

"We have to be able to maintain the master schedule so that we have a two-week time fence, so we can say we will not change our master schedule for two weeks out," explains John Lewis, plant manager at Continental Can Co. "We say, 'For the next two weeks, this is what we're going to do, and the only person who's going to change it is the salesperson or me. Period.' And that has worked well. It has been a change because we used to bounce back and forth and do anything we wanted to."

Figure 6.4 shows typical time fences. Before the first time fence, few changes are made. This corresponds to the final assembly for assembled products or packaging time for soft goods—it's the fence Lewis just

Figure 6.4 MPS Time Fences

Emergency Changes	Trading Area	Adding and Changing

Stabilize	Material Ordered, Capacity in Place	Future Planning

described. Quality or process problems may mean reducing the master schedule. It's unlikely that anything could be added to the master schedule this close to the current date, although there is a possibility that similar products could be swapped—for example, eight-ounce brand-name cans of peaches could be swapped for private-label eight-ounce cans.

Beyond the second time fence, the situation is fairly flexible. This corresponds to the cumulative lead time for most products. For the most part, additions or changes to the master schedule can be done easily.

Most of the attention focuses on the area between the two fences, where changes can be made but trade-offs come into play. You may be able to make a change, but it will cost you; perhaps you'll have to reduce production on another product, resulting in longer lead times to customers.

The master scheduling policy would identify these time fences. In addition, it would specify how the master scheduler would respond in the area of trade-offs. For example, the master scheduler must:

1. investigate each change

2. answer in the positive (what it would take to make the change)

3. get back to the person requesting the change within two days

As with any situation in which there is likely to be conflict, the objective is to minimize the emotions, get the facts out, and have a group of people work on what's best for the company and the customer.

Responding to Sales Plan Changes

Most companies measure their sales plan accuracy by using some kind of tolerance. When a sales plan exceeds the tolerance, one of two things happens: Either they develop a new sales plan, or they reconfirm that the old sales plan is still valid and the deviation represents a "statistical fluctuation."

In the event that a company reforecasts a particular item, a series of action messages is likely to appear the next time the master schedule is run. These action messages will suggest moving the master schedule orders up to earlier dates or out to later dates, depending on the type of change to the sales plan. The master scheduler deals with a sales plan change in the same way as any other action or exception message (as explained above under "Responding to Action Messages").

Responding to Manufacturing or Supplier Problems

The objective is to make the master production schedule happen, not to change it. But when problems arise in manufacturing or with suppliers that threaten the master production schedule, there is a point at which the master production schedule must be changed, to preserve credibility and to accurately represent what will be manufactured.

The master scheduler is responsible for assuring that both of these activities happen, that the people in manufacturing and purchasing have done everything they can to make the schedule happen, and that if the schedule is not going to happen, it gets changed. Steelcase, Tennant, Black and Decker and other experienced companies all demonstrate an excellent balance. The similarities are striking: They all put enormous creative effort into making the master production schedule happen, but if in the end it's just not possible, they change it.

Verifying the Master Schedule Against the Production Plan

Since the master production schedule for a particular product is developed on an item-by-item basis, by looking at the sales plan for each item, the inventory, and the actual customer orders, the obvious question is "How does this match with the production plan for the family of products agreed upon in the sales and operations planning meeting?" It would be coincidental if master schedules, when developed individually for each item and added together, equaled the production plan for the family of items. In many situations, the two will be relatively close, since the aggregate sales plan by product family is used in the sales and operations planning process to develop the production plan. This same aggregate sales plan is reconciled with the sales plans for individual items. In situations in which inventory is being stockpiled in anticipation of a peak selling season, however, or in which a decision has been made to produce more than the marketplace demands to reduce the backlog, the MPS could exceed the immediate needs of the marketplace.

Consequently, what most people do is create the master production schedule on an item-by-item basis, then verify it, in total, against the production plan. This is done by adding up the master production schedule quantities for all items in a sales and operations planning family. Most master scheduling software has the capability to add up the master schedules for a family of products. This total is then compared to the production plan for this family that came out of the S&OP meeting. If they are in agreement (within some agreed-upon tolerance, say plus or minus 5 percent), no further work is necessary for that family of master schedule items. If they are out of agreement, the master scheduler is responsible for either changing the individual master production schedules, so that when added together they equal the master production plan, or asking to have the production plan changed.

What is not acceptable is for the master scheduler to "unplug" top management from the system—that is, to allow top managers to think that they're driving the system when in fact they're not. For example, in the sales and operations planning meeting, the general manager and staff may have made a decision to build or deplete inventory or to stabilize schedules in a volatile marketplace. These decisions resulted in an agreed-upon production plan. If the MPS is developed only by looking at the customer orders and the sales plan, while ignoring the production plan, then top management's decisions are being reversed or undone, without the approval of the team that developed the sales and operations plans.

MASTER SCHEDULING AND JUST-IN-TIME

With increasing frequency, corporations are saying to their divisions, "We want you to eliminate your finished goods inventory. We want you to change from a make-to-stock to a make-to-order business. We want you to quickly manufacture items and ship them." In a JIT environment, companies are making plans to manufacture only what is needed, eliminating the "waste" of excess inventory. Ideally, if customers were to buy a little of every product every day, then companies would manufacture a little of every product every day—an approach called mixed-model master scheduling (see Figure 6.5).

Figure 6.5   Mixed-Model Master Scheduling

	Weeks					
	1	2	3	4	5	6
Product A	12			12		
Product B		10		10		10
Product C			5			

	Weeks					
	1	2	3	4	5	6
Product A	4	4	4	4	4	4
Product B	5	5	5	5	5	5
Product C	1	1	1	1	1	1

Mixed-model master scheduling has a number of advantages. It's more responsive to the needs of the customer than batch master scheduling. If you can build a little of everything every day, then you can make what the customers need, and they don't have to wait. In addition, inventory drops because there is no need to stock each of the different products when you can quickly make what is needed. Finally, mixed-model master scheduling creates a more uniform demand for raw materials, components, and capacity. It's easier, simpler, and more efficient to schedule a plant when the flow is uniform than to deal with large peaks and valleys.

To accomplish mixed-model master scheduling, a number of process changes must take place so that small quantities can be produced economically. These changes include setup reductions, kanban, and good supplier relationships. In addition to these process changes, the master scheduler needs special tools to handle the mixed-model MPS. The extra transactions needed to master-schedule numerous products every day could become a tremendous clerical burden. Most JIT companies therefore use a tool called a *rate generator.* A rate generator automatically creates a series of master schedule transactions. For example, if the master schedule for personal computers is 500 per day from June 5 through August 21, the master scheduler enters the item number, the quantity, and the two dates. The rate generator creates master schedule orders for 500 in each of the days from June 5 through August 21 (78 days). This is much simpler than doing 78 separate transactions.

Tellabs, Inc., a manufacturer of advanced telecommunications products such as digital multiplexers in Lisle, Illinois, uses MRP II to plan what is to be built and what materials are needed. However, kanbans serve as Tellabs' authorized execution mechanism, signaling when work is to be done. When a box is empty, it is a signal to those cells upstream to produce more boards in lots of 10. The kanban, then, is an authorization to build.

The operation at Tellabs is typical of Just-in-Time manufacturing. Tellabs schedules a forecasted mix of products, but manufactures its products based on what customers actually buy. For every ten products, it might plan to make four "A's," five "B's," and one "C," which is how the master schedule would appear. This is the schedule that's used to plan for material and capacity. However, products are built based on the actual orders received, not the forecasted mix. If, for example, Tellabs receives orders for 5 "A's," five "B's," and no "C's," then that's what will be built. Over several days or weeks, the average mix will come out as expected. But for an individual day, the mix of customer orders is all that matters.

Most companies use kanban to trigger the production of components or intermediates, which in turn triggers kanbans for the purchased materials. The entire system is designed to be lean and efficient, and to respond quickly to changes.

MEASUREMENTS

The primary measurement of an effective master schedule is a minimum of 95 percent on-time performance by item, to the due date, within the specified tolerance. For example, if four of five items in the master production schedule are completed within tolerance, but one is outside the limits, the master schedule performance is 80 percent.

The tolerance used will depend on the company. A company that manufactures large, complex assembled products might have plus or minus 2 or 3 days as a tolerance; a company that produces 5,000 flashlights a day in a high-volume repetitive line might have a tolerance of plus or minus 0 days.

While the primary measurement is percentage of products that are on time, another critical element of master scheduling is what's called the *bow wave*. Figure 6.6 is an example of such a bow wave. If the master schedule builds a wave shaped like the bow of a ship in the current or past-due time period, it's not a realistic depiction of what is going to be manufactured. In fact, it typically indicates that the formal scheduling system has broken down and the informal system is setting the priorities. The fact that more is scheduled in a given week than can be produced means people can't believe the formal scheduling system, in which case they'll turn to some other system to learn what is really going on in the plant. Consequently, a second measurement of master scheduling effectiveness is the absence of a bow wave.

A third measurement of master schedule effectiveness is the number and types of changes being made to the master schedule. If a good deal of rescheduling takes place close to today's date, it's an indication of a poorly managed master schedule. Most often this happens because there is too much in the MPS, and when it's apparent that the dates will not be met, the schedule is moved out. Much close-in rescheduling can also be

Figure 6.6   Bow Wave

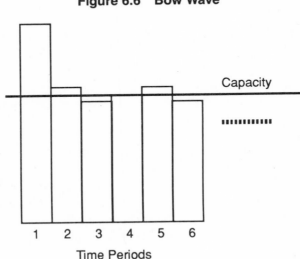

caused by a master scheduler who's agreeing to master schedule changes without investigating whether they're realistic. Often, a company in trouble with its customers will dictate to the master scheduler that he or she *will* move a customer up to an earlier date, regardless of whether it's realistic.

The solutions to these situations are not difficult to identify, but they can be painful to implement. The MPS has to be made realistic. That means eliminating the bow wave, stabilizing the schedule, and re-promising customer orders on dates that are realistic. Typically, these things need to be done in an environment in which actual shipments are below budget, customers are complaining, and frustration is the order of the day. It's a tough job, to say the least!

SUMMARY/CHECKUP

1. Master production scheduling is a balancing act, with the ever-changing forces of the marketplace bumping into some very real limitations in manufacturing. No company will claim that its MPS is "right." Some will say it's managed well, many will say it's managed poorly. How would you describe your master production schedule?

2. The following are inputs to the master production schedule:

- the sales plan/forecast
- customer orders
- distribution center/branch warehouse demands
- interplant demands
- service parts demands
- inventory
- material and capacity limitations

Are those inputs that are appropriate to your company included in your master scheduling process? Have any been left out?

3. Because master scheduling is a leveraged activity, it's important to do it at the most effective level in the product structure. The pyramid, hourglass, and funnel shapes help companies determine where to do their master scheduling. Which shapes apply to your products, and where will each be master-scheduled?

4. The test of a good master production schedule is validity. Do people believe the schedule? If hot lists existed before, have they disappeared? Do people work hard to meet the schedule? Is the master production schedule changed when it cannot be met?

5. The objective in managing the master production schedule is to provide a valid "anticipated manufacturing schedule." Doing this includes the following activities:

- adding to and deleting from the master schedule
- responding to action messages
- evaluating marketing requests for early delivery
- responding to sales plan changes
- responding to manufacturing or supplier problems
- verifying the master schedule against the production plan

Is each of these done in your company? If so, how well do people work together to deal with difficult issues as they come up during these activities?

6. In Just-in-Time environments, mixed-model master scheduling is becoming the norm. The mixed-model master schedule is used to plan the materials and capacity, and kanbans are used to authorize production. Does your company used mixed-model master scheduling?

7. An effectively managed master production schedule should yield at least 95 percent on-time performance by item, to the due date, within the specified tolerance. What is the on-time performance measurement in your company?

Master scheduling is one of the most challenging activities in a manufacturing business. It's "where the rubber meets the road" in reconciling the needs of the marketplace and the capabilities of manufacturing. Once set, the master schedule has leverage over the individual item schedules, as we'll see in the next chapter.

Special Acknowledgments

Richard Ling, Walter Goddard, and Al Stevens, pioneers in the MPS field.

Chapter Seven

Material Requirements Planning (MRP)

WHAT IS MRP?

On May 5, Carl Sandhurst was transferred from accounting manager to material planning manager. Carl's boss suggested this transfer, and either he had an odd sense of humor or he felt Carl needed to be thrown off balance. In accounting, things worked according to the book of procedures. Debits, credits, accounts, ledgers—these established procedures have existed in accounting since before Carl's grandfather was born.

Material planning in Carl's company, on the other hand, did not work according to the book of procedures; hot lists and expediting were the order of the day. It took Carl about a month to get to the point at which he questioned his sanity. "I can't believe that manufacturing really runs this way," he would say to himself over and over. While he didn't have a solution, he was still the manager of the area, and so he called a meeting to discuss the problem.

"How do we figure out what we need and when we need it?" he asked. (His company desperately needed schedules for raw materials, packaging supplies, intermediates, and bulk product.) Tim, who had been a material planner for years, volunteered, "We first need to know the requirements for each item, and this is not as straightforward as it seems." Tim explained that there was a complication involved in determining what materials were needed: While most people assumed the requirements were uniform day to day or week to week, in their company, as in many companies, uniform requirements were the exception rather than the rule. "For a particular purchased material, we may use 600 pounds in one week and none in another week," Tim said. So the first step in planning the material was to establish the requirements by week, although in some companies planning is done for each day.

At this point, for reasons no one was able to comprehend at the time, Frank stood up and began to draw on the flip chart, making a grid like the one in Figure 7.1.

"You also need to know what's in inventory, and whether any material is on order or in process," Tim explained. "For example, you might have a purchase order for 1,000 pounds of raw material to be delivered in three weeks. If the item is bulk product, you might have a manufacturing order being produced in the plant. It's important to know the quantity of the order and when it will be delivered." Frank added the inventory and the purchase or manufacturing orders to the grid.

"OK, now how do we know what's required and what's on hand? How do we know the schedule is valid?" Carl asked. Silence filled the room. Larry, who everyone knew could spend every cent he made and then some, ventured a suggestion. "Well, I can tell you what I do to calculate the projected cash balance in my personal checkbook. I look at the checkbook balance, look at when I need to pay certain bills, look at when I get paid, and do a projected balance. It's simple and it tells me whether I'll be able to cover my financial demands." There was an uproar because if the company

Figure 7.1   Requirements

Salicylic Acid

	Weeks							
	1	2	3	4	5	6	7	8
Requirements		200		400		900	400	300

Figure 7.2   Scheduled Deliveries

Salicylic Acid

On-Hand = 50 Lead Time = 4 Weeks	Weeks							
	1	2	3	4	5	6	7	8
Requirements		200		400		900	400	300
Scheduled Deliveries			1,000		1,000			

managed inventory the way Larry managed cash, they'd all be looking for work. Everyone, however, had to agree that the same method would work. Frank made this simple calculation on the flip chart to see how well the requirements matched up with the inventory and the manufacturing or purchasing schedule.

The projection in week 2 showed that there wouldn't be enough material on hand to satisfy the total requirements. "That means we'll need to expedite the existing delivery scheduled for week 3 and get it moved up to week 2," said Tim. Years of taking the blame for work stoppages had made him especially sensitive to anything that looked like a shortage. "And look at week 8. We don't have anything scheduled to cover those requirements."

"How much more will we need? And when will we need it?"

Figure 7.3   On-Hand Balance Projections

Salicylic Acid

On-Hand = 50 Lead Time = 4 Weeks	Weeks							
	1	2	3	4	5	6	7	8
Requirements		200		400		900	400	300
Scheduled Deliveries			1,000		1,000			
Projected On-Hand Balance	50	-150	850	450	1,450	550	150	-150

asked Carl, feeling a glimmer of hope for the first time in over a month.

"We normally order this material in quantities of 1,000 pounds, and the lead time from the supplier is four weeks," said Tim. Frank then represented the future planned deliveries on the grid (Figure 7.4).

At this point, Frank spoke up. "Congratulations, Carl, you just reinvented MRP, material requirements planning."

Figure 7.4   Planned Deliveries

Salicylic Acid

On-Hand = 50

Lead Time = 4 Weeks

	Weeks							
	1	2	3	4	5	6	7	8
Requirements		200		400		900	400	300
Scheduled Deliveries			1,000		1,000			
Projected On-Hand Balance	50	-150	850	450	1,450	550	150	850
Planned Deliveries (Due)								1,000
Planned Deliveries (Start)				1,000				

As you can see, MRP consists of a very simple, straightforward set of calculations and a commonsense approach to planning material. "But if it's so simple and logical," you might ask, "why haven't people been using it for years?" The answer: Though MRP calculations may be simple, they need to be done for 40,000 or so items a year or more into the future, and changes happen every day. It was the development of high-speed digital computers that finally allowed people to carry out the calculations in a reasonable period of time (several hours) and keep their plans up to date.

Today, MRP is still a simple set of calculations used to create and maintain valid schedules that show what items are required and when they are needed. It answers the question "What do we need, and when do we need it?"

**Figure 7.5   Manufacturing Resource Planning
(MRP II)**

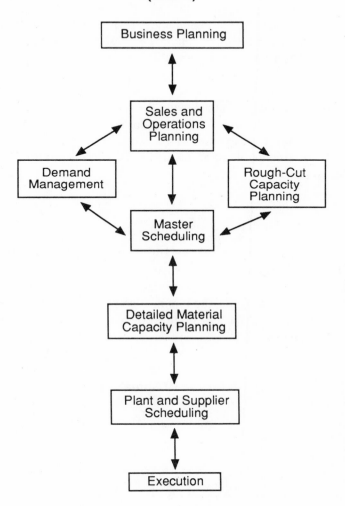

Looking "up," material planning is the way to make the MPS happen. The top end—business planning, sales and operations planning, demand planning, and master production scheduling—forms the top-level plans for the company. But if the top end isn't connected to anything, then there's no way to make the plans happen. If you can't take the top-level plans of the company and convert them into tasks that people can be held accountable for accomplishing, then it is scarcely better than making no plans at all. Material requirements planning translates these top-level plans into individual schedules for the 40,000 or so items that have to be manufactured or purchased in the typical company. These schedules are concrete enough that people can go out, make them happen, and be accountable for them.

Looking "down" from MRP, a number of other functions are dependent on the material plan. These include capacity requirements planning (which not all companies require) and the execution of the material and capacity plans. In addition, MRP provides much of the detailed information used to integrate the financial and operating systems. Therefore, material requirements planning forms a vital central link in the whole closed-loop process.

TYPICAL MRP SPREADSHEET

The format shown in Figure 7.6 is slightly different from the format in the previous example. Requirements are now Gross Requirements, Scheduled Deliveries are now Scheduled Receipts, Planned Deliveries are now Planned Orders, and the Planned Deliveries (Due) line has been deleted. The format shown in Figure 7.6 more closely resembles the typical MRP spreadsheet.

Figure 7.6   MRP Spread Sheet

Salicylic Acid

On-Hand = 50

Lead Time = 4 Weeks

	Weeks							
	1	2	3	4	5	6	7	8
Gross Requirements		200		400		900	400	300
Scheduled Receipts			1,000		1,000			
Projected On-Hand Balance	50	-150	850	450	1,450	550	150	850
Planned Orders (Start)				1,000				

RESCHEDULING

As Tim pointed out, there is a shortage projected in week 2. MRP warns of a shortage before it happens, so a planner can begin working on the problem today and resolve it in advance. How can it be resolved? If the delivery in week 3 can be moved up to week 2, the planner will have eliminated the shortage. If the delivery cannot be moved up, the planner must change the schedule so there are no unsatisfied requirements in week 2. There are a number of ways to do this, one being to change the MPS. Other ways include reducing lot sizes, compressing lead times, and making use of material substitutions. Each of these needs to be examined on a case-by-case basis.

Another highly significant feature of time-phased MRP is that it not only tells the planner when to expedite, it tells him or her when to "de-expedite"—that is, call a supplier or the plant and ask that the delivery of an item be moved to a later date. An example of this is the scheduled receipt for 1,000 that is due in week 5, even though it's not needed until week 6. It's interesting, but not unusual, that Tim didn't even mention this when he saw Frank's time-phased spreadsheet—he may not have even noticed it. Most informal systems are run by expediters who have been trained to focus on shortages. Manufacturing teaches a number of lessons, and one is that if you have too much inventory, the boss will chew you out from time to time. If, however, you shut the plant down once too often, you'll be out of a job. Most people sort out their priorities with regard to this situation fairly quickly. They also need very little time to realize that suppliers and the plant will typically be late in their deliveries.

If Tim had been asked about the scheduled receipt in week 5, his response would probably have been "Why not leave it alone? The material may be delivered on the due date, which means it will come in before it's needed, but getting it early is better than running out. Anyhow, since most suppliers are late, including the plant, asking for something before it's really needed just makes good sense. The supplier will be late, and things will work out about right. Moving deliveries out just seems to be asking for trouble."

What Tim and most people schooled in the informal system don't realize is that the most powerful expediting technique of all is "unexpediting." Why? Imagine a list of purchased or manufactured items that are due for delivery (due today, due this week, or past due). Figure 7.7a represents this situation.

Figure 7.7a
List of Items Due for Delivery

Entire List

1. _____
2. _____
3. _____
. _____
. _____
. _____
. _____
. _____
. _____
. _____
20. _____

a

Figure 7.7b
Supplier's Random Choice of Items to Be Completed

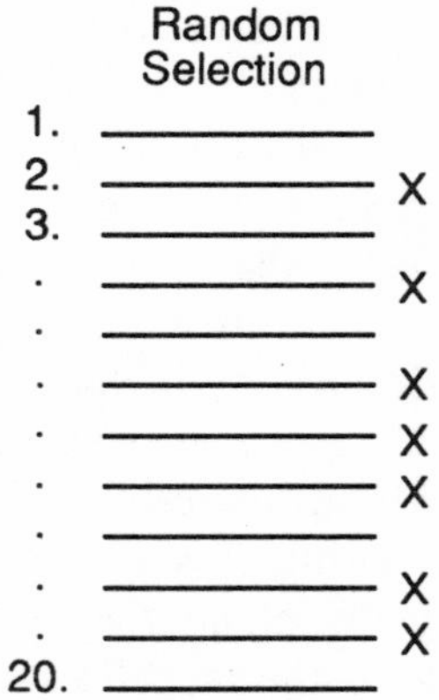

Random Selection

1. _____
2. _____ X
3. _____
. _____ X
. _____
. _____ X
. _____ X
. _____ X
. _____
. _____ X
. _____ X
20. _____

b

Figure 7.7c
List of Items After Rescheduling

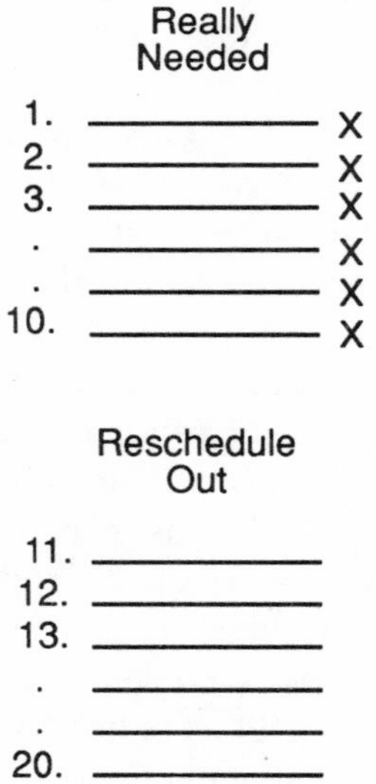

Really Needed

1. _____ X
2. _____ X
3. _____ X
. _____ X
. _____ X
10. _____ X

Reschedule Out

11. _____
12. _____
13. _____
. _____
. _____
20. _____

c

Are they all really needed now? In most companies, the answer is no. If the suppliers and plant know what is really needed today, they can focus all their efforts on producing those items. In most companies, there is so much overdue work that what gets completed is decided randomly. If a supplier has the schedule shown in Figure 7.7a, 20 items are due this week or past due, but the supplier can only make 10. Therefore, 50 percent of the items on the list will be completed. The question is "Which 50 percent?" If the list in Figure 7.7a is all the supplier gets, then the supplier makes the choice, and it's unlikely that the supplier has better knowledge of what you need than you do. So, the odds are that the supplier will deliver about 50 percent of the items you need. This is represented in Figure 7.7b.

On the other hand, if the 10 items that are not needed this week are moved out, the supplier can work on the remaining 10 items, rather than expending limited material and capacity on the 10 that are not needed (see Figure 7.7c).

The result of this situation is that supplier performance goes from 50 percent to close to 100 percent, and you get what you need to manufacture and ship products. This illustrates how a company has tremendous influence over the on-time performance of its suppliers, based on the quality of information provided to the suppliers (the accuracy of their schedules). The same thing is true for a company's own plant: The quality of the company's schedules is a significant contributor to the factory's on-time delivery performance.

Some people question this illustration. They say, "I need them all—give me all 20 items." There are two problems in this approach: Most companies don't really need all 20, and most suppliers don't have the material and capacity to produce all 20.

As Tim illustrated, most expediters will expedite deliveries but will not de-expedite them. Consequently, what happens in most companies is a false or phony backlog of work that is really not needed. Figures 7.8a and 7.8b illustrate the phony backlog.

In Figure 7.8a deliveries are scheduled, but over time things change, and some are needed earlier than originally scheduled. Expediters pull these deliveries up to earlier dates. Typically, however, they do not take the items that are not needed and move them out to later dates. Consequently, three categories of items appear in the past-due and current time periods:

Figures 7.8a and 7.8b   Phony Backlog

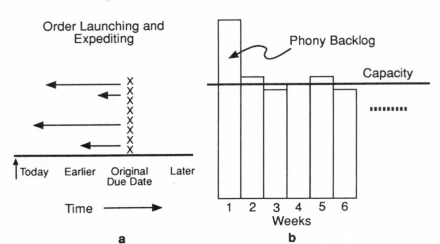

a

b

a. items that have been expedited and are now needed this week

b. items that were originally scheduled for delivery this week and are still needed this week

c. items that were originally scheduled for delivery this week but are no longer needed this week and were not moved out

This third category of items constitutes the phony backlog, shown in Figure 7.8b. The reason this category is so big is that it accumulates over time. If 20 percent of the schedule should be moved out and is not, that adds 20 percent to the phony backlog. Next week, another 20 percent is added, and so on. It simply makes no sense to insist that suppliers or the plant produce these items—they're not needed!

In addition, most suppliers and plants do not have the material or capacity to manufacture at the rate shown in Figure 7.8b. This level of production is significantly higher than the level in future weeks. If they did get the resources to make it happen, what would they do with them in future weeks? The manpower and equipment would sit idle. Insisting on performance to a schedule like that shown in Figure 7.8b is the scheduling equivalent of sticking your head in the sand.

To illustrate this, consider a run-in Carl Sandhurst had with one of the supervisors.

Mat Barnett was a skeptic of schedules, but having been a supervisor for almost twenty years, he knew enough not to say what he thought. Carl, as the new material planning manager, was also chief expediter, since the informal system was alive and well. If there was one thing that really irritated Mat, it was the constant stream of "hot" items that came from Carl and the other material planners. They were always out of breath and highly agitated, and they always had to have whatever it was yesterday. How could you run an efficient department when the people who gave you the schedules were bouncing off the walls and ceiling? "Do they know what they're doing up there?" Mat would mutter almost every hour.

And Mat did understand the importance of running an efficient department. Ron Drake, the VP of manufacturing, was a numbers man. He looked at reports on efficiency and the indirect-to-direct-labor ratio every day. In fact, he had charts on the wall for both. The fact that these two quantities were *easy* to measure but not *important* to measure never occurred to either Mat or Ron. Manufacturing had always run this way.

Finally, the opportunity Mat had been waiting for presented itself. Carl and several of the material planners came out to the plant, obviously distressed, and proceeded to explain to Mat that if they didn't have 2,000 pounds of bulk tablets done by Friday all hell would break loose. Carl had expected a fight. This would mean running the tablets on one of the older, less efficient machines. It would also mean lots of overtime. So Carl was surprised when Mat said, "OK, we'll have them for you on Friday," and the meeting was over.

Mat ran the older equipment, he put in the overtime, and an exhausted group of people delivered 2,000 pounds of bulk tablets on schedule Friday afternoon.

But that wasn't the end of the episode. Over the weekend, someone discovered another 1,000 pounds of bulk tablets that had been put away in the wrong location and had not been showing up in inventory. In addition, on the same day that Carl had met with Mat to request the 2,000 pounds of tablets, Jim Raymond, the CEO, had put out a memo to each of the distribution centers instructing them to reduce their inventories. So, on Monday morning, five of the seven distribution centers called to move scheduled deliveries of product out by several weeks.

All this meant that the 2,000 pounds of tablets Mat and his people made *weren't really needed for another four weeks!* Schedules were changed, and the tablets sat just outside the tablet-making department for seven days. Then they were moved to the stockroom, where they sat for another week and a half.

Two and a half weeks after Mat delivered the tablets, Carl needed another favor. If they didn't have 500 pounds of another type of bulk tablets, the world would come to an end. Salespeople were calling every hour demanding more of this product to meet their customers' needs. Unfortunately, the inventory reduction ordered by the CEO several weeks before had backfired. Inventory was lower, but so was customer service. Mat realized this was the time to spring his trap. "Follow me, Carl. I'd like to show you something," he said as he led Carl to the stockroom. "Aren't these the 2,000 pounds of tablets that you absolutely had to have over two weeks ago? Well, why are they still sitting here? I ruined my efficiency and I cost the company a lot of money in overtime, and it doesn't look like any of it was necessary. I'll make your 500 pounds of bulk tablets, Carl, but I'll make them on my terms, not yours."

Mat was simply reaffirming the pecking order. There was no way he could maintain his efficiency if people were always changing the schedule around. But for Carl, it was an important lesson. He realized that you can't hold people accountable for meeting schedules if they're not perceived to be valid. A schedule with a huge phony past-due backlog is not a valid schedule, and everyone knows it.

PLANNED ORDER RELEASES

The concept of planned orders can be difficult for people who haven't worked with an MRP system. Planned orders don't exist in most other planning and scheduling systems, so many people have no experience with them. Basically, a planned order is a purchase order or manufacturing order that hasn't been released yet. It's still too far out in the future.

In an order point system, for example, there are no planned orders because there are no orders beyond the current ordering cycle. An order point system requires that more of an item be reordered when the on-hand balance is low. In effect, the system's horizon is one ordering cycle or one lead time only, and there's no information about what will happen beyond the current order.

The planned order release is a very powerful part of an MRP system. Planned orders generate material requirements at the lower levels. A planned order is a plan to make something—a fabricated item, an intermediate, a bulk product, a subassembly or an assembly—on a particular date. That means the raw materials or components are needed on the start date. As a result, planned orders for a parent item create gross requirements for the raw materials or components used to make this item. Figure 7.9 illustrates this for one of the components used to manufacture a subassembly.

In addition to generating component gross requirements, these planned orders are automatically changed as requirements for the item change. This in turn causes the gross requirements for the component items and raw materials to be updated to reflect the changes. For example, if the master schedule is changed in week 50, the planned orders for the subassemblies, intermediates, bulk products, components, raw materials, and/or purchased parts are all updated. If the master schedule is increased, the planned orders are increased to meet the additional demand. If a master schedule order is moved up from week 50 to week 45, the planned orders for everything below it in the product structure are adjusted accordingly.

Planned orders are also used in capacity requirements planning (which is not required by all companies), in supplier schedules, in purchasing negotiation reports, and in financial interfaces between the financial and manufacturing systems.

Figure 7.9   Planned Orders/Gross Requirements

Parent	1	2	3	4	5	6	7	8
Planned Orders		500			500			500

Component								
Gross Requirements		500			500			500

Replacing the Informal System

As you've probably figured out, MRP II is really just a formalization of the informal system. Consider a company making an assembled product. The expediter goes to the stockroom with the bill of material for a product that appears in the master schedule. He has the stockroom people pull material off the shelf and "accumulate" or "stage" it—that is, put it on a pallet and then make up a shortage list. He then expedites those items that appear on the shortage list.

The same thing happens in a process company: A planner takes the schedule for production and the formulas that tell how to make the product, and then determines what materials are needed and when. Next, the planner checks to see if the materials are on hand or on order. If not, he or she calls the suppliers and expedites the shortages.

In MRP, the computer, in effect, does the same thing. It takes a master schedule, looks up the bill of material or formula to find out what material is required to manufacture the product, then checks the inventory to see if the material is on hand. If the material is not on hand, it tells the planner to order it and tells him or her when it will be needed. If the material is already on order, the computer will evaluate the due dates on that material and tell the planner if the due dates need to be changed. So MRP is simply a formal system for predicting the shortages and simulating what the expediter was really trying to do all along.

There are, of course, some key differences between MRP and an expediter operating in an informal system. The MRP system replans regularly; in contrast, the expediter would find it extremely impractical to put the items back on the shelf and start over again each week. The MRP system also predicts shortages early enough so that something can be done to prevent them. The informal expediting system simply cannot keep priorities properly updated, and usually finds out about shortages too late. As a result, the informal system costs more and is less effective.

What Are the Key MRP Activities?

On a daily basis, the material planner, the manufacturing supervisor, and the capacity planner are most directly involved with MRP. The responsibilities of these people are described below. (Note: Your company might have people who have the listed responsibilities but not these exact titles. What counts is the function, not the title.)

Material Planner

The primary task of the material planner is to create and maintain valid plans. This is done by either:

- rescheduling delivery dates to meet the demands or
- changing demands to reflect the actual delivery situation.

In addition, the material planner is responsible for:

- authorizing production and
- maintaining the item data.

Let's look at each of these.

Rescheduling delivery dates
Most planners work by responding to the action messages generated by the material planning logic.

The typical action messages a material planner sees are:

a. Past-due scheduled receipt.

b. Reschedule to an earlier date.

c. Reschedule to a later date.

d. Cancel.

e. Planned order due for release.

PAST-DUE SCHEDULED RECEIPT. This is the most urgent of all the messages, because a scheduled receipt that is past due and really needed is a shortage that means something will not get manufactured on time. On the other hand, if the scheduled receipt is past due and not really needed for some time (in which case there will be another action message telling the planner to reschedule to a later date), then it's important to reschedule it as quickly as possible. This is because the past due scheduled receipt will occupy the highest priority for manufacturing, if it's a manufactured item, or for purchasing, if it's a purchased item. There's no point spending a tremendous amount of energy expediting something when it should really be moved out.

Reschedule to an Earlier Date—Manufactured Items. This message indicates a projected shortage at some point in the future. In other words, if the scheduled receipt cannot be moved to an earlier date, some requirements will not be met. This is where the power of MRP really shows itself; rather than waiting for a shortage to happen, it projects the situation weeks in advance, so corrective action can be taken.

To reschedule a delivery to an earlier date, the manufacturing people (in the case of a manufactured item) or the purchasing people (in the case of a purchased item) must agree to a new date. The reason is that they are now accountable for delivery on that date. The planner's job is to create schedules that other people will be held accountable for hitting. Consequently, if a delivery is being moved up to an earlier date, the planner must verify that the people affected by the change agree to be held accountable for meeting that date.

In the case of a manufactured item, that typically means checking with the people in the plant to verify that they can complete the item by the need date. In some cases, people in manufacturing may say that they can't complete the item by the date the planner needs it, although they may be able to move it up somewhat. In this case, the planner will have to deal with the requirements that cannot be met—a process described in the next section.

In some companies, the material planners and the manufacturing people set up guidelines so they don't have to check on every single item. For example, if a delivery is more than a month in the future, and the requested date change is only a week, the planners and manufacturing people may have a guideline that says the planner can reschedule without checking with manufacturing. The purpose of setting up these guidelines is to streamline communications and not waste time on requests for approvals that will always be granted.

Reschedule to an Earlier Date—Purchased Items. The supplier scheduler (or vendor scheduler, as this person is sometimes called) is the material planner for purchased items. The term *supplier scheduler* is used to differentiate this person from the purchasing agent or buyer. This distinction will be explained in more detail in Chapter 10, but basically the supplier scheduler deals with the timing and quantities for deliveries of purchased items, and the buyer deals with the negotiation of price, specifications, sourcing, and quality.

The supplier scheduler typically communicates with the suppliers, and is therefore responsible for verifying that a supplier can meet a new date. The process is basically the same as the one used for manufactured items, in which the planner verifies that the reschedule is realistic, the difference being that the supplier scheduler is dealing with an outside supplier.

In some cases, the supplier scheduler calls the supplier to reschedule a purchase order. In many cases, however, suppliers are issued supplier schedules that show the latest requirements and indicate any changes since the last schedule. For example, a supplier schedule might indicate that a particular quantity is now needed in week 2, whereas last time it was needed in week 5. In a situation like that, the responsibility rests with the supplier to get back to the supplier scheduler if there is a problem meeting the new date. The principle of "silence is approval" needs to be established and maintained. This means that if the supplier scheduler doesn't hear from the supplier, it is understood that the dates in the supplier schedule will be met.

RESCHEDULE TO A LATER DATE. As mentioned earlier, rescheduling deliveries out to a later date is one of the most important tools for achieving on-time performance—"de-expediting" really is as important as expediting. Not surprisingly, companies that get excellent results from planning and control systems tend to do a top-notch job in the rescheduling area. They've taught their suppliers and their plants that due dates mean something: The due dates are when they really need the items. This understanding usually takes time to develop because, with the informal system, both suppliers and the plant have been taught that due dates mean little, if anything—if an item is really needed, an expediter will call.

Companies change this attitude by providing valid schedules, follow-up, and delivery performance measurement. Providing valid schedules means rescheduling deliveries out to later dates so the suppliers and plant can see what's really needed and when.

Companies should also set up streamlined communications to handle the rescheduling of orders out to later dates. For example, a guideline may specify that a planner can reschedule deliveries to later dates without checking with the plant or suppliers. Even so, there still needs to be a notification of what's happened; because it may not be possible to move the delivery out—it may be too far along. This happens most often with suppliers who have put considerable material and labor into an item and would really like to get it out of their inventory.

When a planner reschedules a delivery out by 10 weeks, the supplier is being asked, in effect, to "eat" the inventory that results from planning mistakes. If a supplier objects, it might be wise to accept the shipment in the interest of maintaining good supplier relations.

In the case of manufactured items, the same thing can happen: An item may be nearly completed and the supervisors may want to get it out of their departments rather than leaving it semifinished for an extended period of time. Again, the best strategy is to work with the people involved.

Changing Demands

The first course of action for a material planner is to reschedule the manufacturing and purchasing deliveries to meet the demands coming from the master production schedule. If, however, the schedule can't be changed to meet the demands, then the demands will have to be changed to reflect reality. It's critical to show what will really happen in the future as feedback comes in from the plant and from suppliers.

If the demands aren't changed, then the schedules are no longer valid. People will quickly lose faith in the system and look for other ways to find out what is needed and when it must arrive. For example, if an eyepiece for a video camera will not be available in week 2, it makes no sense to expedite the other components for delivery in week 2. If the eyepiece won't be available until week 5, then the material planner should let everyone know about the situation.

You'll make few friends in manufacturing if, as a planner, you say nothing and people threaten suppliers, pay for premium freight, and stay late to make sure material gets received, only to realize that it isn't needed.

There are a number of ways to reduce the demand, the most obvious being to reduce the master schedule. Although adjustment of the master schedule may be the most obvious course of action, it is also the *last* thing that should be done. The first is to work through the product structure a step at a time, looking for solutions at each stage.

For example, Figure 7.10 shows a demand for 100 circuit boards in week 4. Manufacturing has a problem with its equipment and can produce some, but not all 100, in week 4. The immediate demand is for

Figure 7.10 Reduced Lot Size

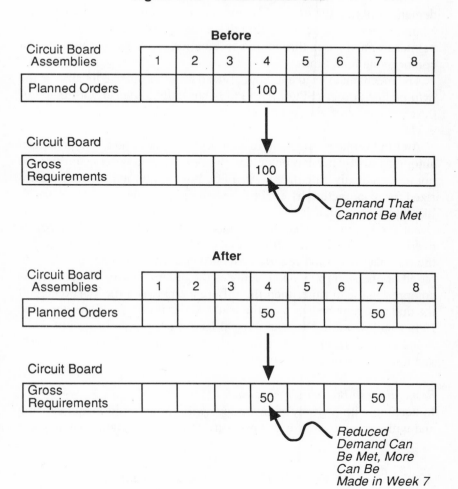

50 boards; the remaining 50 in the lot will be used to cover requirements three weeks later. In this case, the planner proposes manufacturing 50 boards now and then another 50 in three weeks. This would change the demand from 100 to 50 and create a new demand for 50 three weeks in the future. Manufacturing agrees to produce 50 boards in week 4 and another 50 by week 7, and the solution is implemented.

In other cases, it may be possible to compress lead times, moving the demands out into the future. It's fairly typical when dealing with a large, complex product structure to find that a requirement at a lower level can be met in most cases through a combination of changing lot sizes and compressing lead times.

The mechanism used to compress lead times or change lot sizes is the firm planned order (FPO). An FPO is basically a hybrid with many of the characteristics of a scheduled receipt and a planned order (see Figure 7.11).

An FPO is like a scheduled receipt because its due date is not changed automatically by the computer, and its start date and order quantities are not automatically calculated. An FPO, however, is not actually authorized for manufacture by either the plant or a supplier. In that sense, it's like a planned order.

An FPO is used to handle situations in which the planner needs to override the normal logic of material planning. The normal logic places the due date when the requirements are needed, calculates a start date based on the lead time, and calculates the order quantity. If a planner is compressing lead time, then the difference between the start date and the due date may be less than the lead time. It is also possible to use the FPO to allow more than the normal lead time in anticipation of additional delays, or when scheduling work early to smooth out overloads and underloads in a capacity plan.

Responding to Bottom-Up Feedback
In keeping with Murphy's Law, things will go wrong in manufacturing and with suppliers. When this happens, the material planner or supplier

Figure 7.11   Firm Planned Order

	Scheduled Receipt	Firm Planned Order	Planned Order
Action Messages	Yes	Yes	No
Automatically Changed	No	No	Yes
Released to Manufacturing	Yes	No	No

scheduler will be notified of a delivery that will miss its due date. This is handled in the same way as a requirement that can't be met. It may be possible to compress some lead times, split a lot size, or implement any of the other techniques described above. The important thing is to make sure there is feedback from suppliers and from the plant. As mentioned above for suppliers, the fundamental principle of "silence is approval" needs to be established and maintained. That means that if a planner doesn't hear from someone, he or she should assume that the schedule will be met.

In most manufacturing companies, there are years of history in which the opposite was true—people didn't trust the schedules, so the expediters had to ask people whether they could meet this or that delivery date, an extremely inefficient use of everyone's time. Under "silence is approval," it is the responsibility of the manufacturing departments, purchasing, and suppliers to meet the schedules, and if they can't they must get back to the material planners and discuss the problem.

Generally, if a company is having trouble making "silence is approval" work, it's typically because the company has unrealistic schedules with a large phony backlog. In a situation like this, a strict interpretation of "silence is approval" would mean reporting back on nearly all the items, since nearly all deliveries will be late—and repeating the same message day after day. Of course, people would correctly see this as an enormous waste of time, and focus on what items are needed to make shipments. That means they would give up on the schedule and, in no time at all, the company would be back to operating with the informal system. The solution in this situation is to fix the phony backlog by rescheduling deliveries to a time when they can realistically be made.

Dealing with Requests to Change the Schedule
As explained in Chapter 6, the master scheduler will be requested to make changes, such as moving a master schedule order up to an earlier date or increasing the master schedule. When this happens, the master scheduler will work with the material planner, manufacturing supervisors, supplier schedulers, and the capacity planner (if capacity requirements planning is applicable) to ensure that the change is realistic.

In a company that manufactures windows, if the request is to increase the master production schedule by 200 windows in week 15, the material planner will mark up the MRP reports in week 15 by adding 200 to the gross requirements for the items on the bill of material for windows. The planner will then recalculate the projected on-hand balance and note what changes, if any, will have to be made to meet the additional demand. If the planned orders change as a result of this calculation, the planner will go through the same process using the MRP reports for those items. Depending on the type of product, this can be a fairly involved process.

For the windows mentioned above, there might be 10 or 20 items the planner needs to check. In a complex product structure with 10 to 20 levels, a change to the master production schedule may require that a planner examine hundreds of items. Verification that the new schedule is realistic can take quite a few hours of dedicated effort spread over several days, especially considering the time necessary to contact suppliers and people in the plant. Consequently, every organization has a limit to the number of change requests it can deal with on a daily or weekly basis.

One way to deal with the large volume of change in complex products is to look at only the critical items. The planner may do this analysis on the 20 percent of the items that account for 80 percent of the difficulty in producing the product. These are typically the long-lead-time items. The master scheduler and material planners are normally familiar with these items, and they check them first. This simplifies the checking process, and if the items look good, the master scheduler typically makes the change and lets the computer do the number crunching for all the other items. If one of the other items turns out to be a problem that can't be fixed, then the master scheduler reverses the change. Other companies, however, insist that all items be checked before allowing the master scheduler to make a change.

A number of companies have simulation capability in their software. This automates the process of recalculating numbers, so a planner no longer has to mark up hard-copy reports. What can't be automated, however, is the approval process for determining whether the plant and suppliers can meet the new dates. So while simulation capabilities are a help, the majority of the work still has to be done, and there's still a limit to the number of changes that can be dealt with on a daily or weekly basis.

One approach that has been tried, but is not recommended, is simply making the master schedule change and then seeing what happens. If it turns out not to be realistic, the master scheduler can backtrack and undo the change. The problem with this approach is that people may already be making changes with suppliers and the plant based on the new schedule. When the schedule change is rescinded, these people will have to contact the plant and suppliers and reverse the changes. Not only is this more work than investigating the change properly before implementing it, but it undermines the credibility of the schedules.

Each organization should look at its capacity in the planning area and match it up with demand. If the sales and marketing group requests 10 changes per day and the planning department can't keep up, then the company must increase the planning staff, decrease the number of requests for changes, or both.

All this boils down to where a company strategically needs to place its resources. If there are numerous requests for changes, it's important to respond to them. But at the same time, the company must check to see that these are not "self-inflicted wounds." If the planning department is constantly trying to move deliveries to earlier dates because customers are unhappy with the dates they've been promised, the root problem needs to be identified and addressed.

Are the promised lead times too long because the production plan is too low? If so, the S&OP process is the way to deal with the problem. Are the customer lead times too long because it takes too long to manufacture the product? If so, it may be necessary to carry inventory of semifinished products that can be quickly completed and shipped. Another solution is to shorten the lead times using Just-in-Time approaches.

Similarly, if the company is missing promised dates, and that is what is causing all the requests for change, then this problem needs to be addressed. Is there a problem with the execution side of the business, in either manufacturing or purchasing?

In each of these situations, hiring more resources in the planning department to investigate master schedule changes would only be treating a symptom, not the cause. Some of the best-run companies with the most effective use of MRP II maintain fairly stable production plans and master production schedules, yet are most responsive to customers, because they do an excellent job of managing the other issues listed above.

Authorizing Production
In addition to making supply equal demand, the material planner is responsible for authorizing production either in the plant or from

suppliers. As planned and firm planned orders come due for release, an action message will be generated by the system. The material planner must verify that the production is needed. The reason for having the material planner authorize production is accountability. Before authorizing manufacturing or a purchase commitment, someone should verify that it makes sense to do so. If it does, two choices are available for each: The choices for manufacturing are:

1. Release the planned or firm planned order into a manufacturing work order.

2. Authorize the planned or firm planned order, but do so without creating a manufacturing work order. This is done most often in process or Just-in-Time manufacturing.

The choices for purchasing are:

1. Release the planned or firm planned order into a purchase order.

2. Authorize the planned or firm planned order on the supplier schedule. This changes the status of the delivery on the supplier schedule from planning information for the supplier to a commitment.

For manufacturing work orders, the planner's responsibility is to verify that the company has all the material or components, using what is called a *component availability check,* before actually releasing the order. There's no point in issuing manufacturing orders if the components or raw materials aren't on hand.

In theory, a component availability check should not be required— everything should arrive on the date needed. But few companies operate with 100 percent on-time performance to the due date, so there will be situations in which purchasing or manufacturing deliveries have gone past due.

In some environments, a component availability check may be unnecessary. Consider a chemical plant. Chemicals are not put in a stockroom and then issued to a manufacturing order; they are pumped from one tank to another. The same is true for continuous-flow or assembly-line manufacturing, in which material will be available at the next step based on the previous step's output. In these situations, items are manufactured and immediately consumed without being stocked in between. Consequently, these items appear in the on-hand balance briefly, or not at all. In such an environment a component availability check would show shortages when in fact there may not be a problem at all. So a component check is typically not used in these situations.

Similarly, in a JIT environment, where there's a continuous flow or kanban, a component availability check is typically not used. Kanban controls the specific movements of material on the plant floor, and work orders are not used.

In addition to the normal release of orders, the material planner will need to deal with situations in which orders have to be released short (in terms of both materials and lead time). For example, the nameplate for a garden tractor may be short, but assembly can begin and the nameplate can be put on near the end of the production. An example of a short-lead-time release would be a situation in which a turbine blade that normally takes three weeks to manufacture is needed in two weeks. In such a situation, the planner must check with the people in the plant and gain their agreement. Are they able to shorten move and queue times, work overtime, add additional equipment, and so on, to finish the item in two weeks? These are the people who will be held accountable for on-time delivery, so they must agree to the short-lead-time release.

For purchased items the process is similar, but there is no component availability check. The supplier scheduler works with the suppliers to make sure the items can be delivered on time. In most situations, a supplier schedule has been showing the planning information to the suppliers for some time. As a delivery comes within the commitment period, the supplier scheduler authorizes this commitment. This should be no surprise to the supplier, and if the supplier has a problem in meeting the delivery date, that problem should have been raised some time ago. In situations in which the requirements change and the supplier is surprised by a new schedule, the supplier scheduler and the supplier should work together to agree on realistic dates that the supplier is able to meet.

Maintaining the Item Data

Finally, the material planner maintains the item information. While companies can store a tremendous amount of information for an item, the material planner is typically responsible for the planning data: information on lead time, ordering rules, and safety stock. The approach most companies take is to use the current order quantities and lot sizes, and put their energies into reducing those numbers, rather than attempting to scientifically and precisely define them. If the quantities seem reasonable, there's little point in deciding whether the order quantity should really be 537 or 450. In keeping with the JIT philosophy, the most effective use of time and energy would be to concentrate on shrinking the lot size from 500 to 400 to 300, and so on.

The same approach holds for lead times. If the current lead time for an item is seven weeks, but the item can be manufactured in five, then five weeks should be used in the planning system. It's typical in many companies to add some "fat" to the lead time in the hope that this will make it easier to meet the due date. Problems in meeting due dates are typically capacity problems, supplier problems, or process problems. Adding lead time only hides these problems and delays their correction. In addition, lead times with "fat" reduce the credibility of the planning system. If everyone knows that there is a week of extra lead time for every level in the product structure, the supplier scheduler and the suppliers are never sure when the material is really needed. "Is it five levels from the top or seven? If the supplier is three weeks late, is this really a problem? Should I even feed back that there is a delay?"

In addition, padding the lead times makes more items overdue with both the supplier and the plant. When a company has trouble meeting schedules, one of the best things to do is to cut the lead times down to only what's really needed to make the product, and see what the real priorities are. The idea is to start with lead times that are reasonable and work on reducing them.

A similar line of thinking applies to another piece of item data: safety stock. In the informal system, the name of the game is "never run out," and so safety stock seems like a good idea. However, if you set an unnecessarily high safety stock level, it's hard to distinguish what's really needed from what's not. "What happens if we don't meet the due date on this manufactured or purchased item? Do we miss shipments to customers? Or do we just have a little less inventory?" As mentioned above in the section on rescheduling deliveries to later dates, honesty is an important characteristic of a good scheduler. If you need something, then you should let someone know. If you don't really need it, then you don't want to use up scarce capacity or materials.

This is not to say that safety stock is always unnecessary. There are some very legitimate reasons to have it: uncertainty of supply or uncertainty of demand. Uncertainty of supply means the planner can't count on a supplier to deliver on time or in the right quantity. If one of the company's main products uses bearings that are shipped from Germany by boat, a planner might want to carry some safety stock. If anything goes wrong at the supplier's plant, in transit, at customs, or within the plant, it will stop production on the product. This is a legitimate use for safety stock. Such situations are the exception, and companies that manage MRP II well have few, if any, items for which they carry safety stock to buffer what's available at the plant or from suppliers.

According to the Just-in-Time approach, this safety stock is "waste" and should be eliminated. To do this, solutions would have to be found for each of the different problems: how to make sure the supplier ships on time, how to make sure there aren't problems in transit, how to make sure the bearings clear customs, and so on. It's important to expose the problems and fix them rather than continue covering them with safety stock.

The other reason to have safety stock is uncertainty of demand in a marketplace that is fairly volatile. For example, sales of a particular cosmetic average 100 per week, but occasionally a customer requests 200. A safety stock of 100 can cushion against these demand fluctuations. But again, in the spirit of JIT, someone needs to ask, "What can we do to eliminate this unnecessary inventory? Can we understand our customers better and eliminate some of the surprises? Can we shorten lead time so that instead of making product in a matter of weeks, we can turn it around in a matter of hours?" These are the types of questions that need to be answered when maintaining the item data.

Manufacturing Supervisor

The manufacturing supervisor plays an important role in material planning, with responsibility to meet both delivery due dates and the capacity plan. With respect to material planning, the manufacturing supervisor works with the material planner in the following activities:

- approving the requested reschedules from material planners

- feeding back information if it appears that an item will not be completed by the delivery due date

- approving or rejecting short-order releases

Approving the Requested Reschedules from Material Planners

As explained earlier under the material planner's responsibilities, master schedule changes, engineering changes, customer requests for earlier delivery, and so on will all cause the material planner to ask the manufacturing supervisor to reschedule manufacturing deliveries to earlier dates.

In many cases, the material planner talks directly with the manufacturing supervisor and asks if the new need date can be met. In other situations, the material planner works through the capacity planner. In many companies, the material planner has a regular meeting with the manufacturing supervisor and capacity planner (where such a job exists) to review the reschedules.

If the manufacturing supervisor agrees to the new date, the material planner will make the reschedule and the manufacturing supervisor will be responsible for hitting the date. If the manufacturing supervisor decides that the date isn't realistic, he or she will negotiate an attainable date with the material planner that balances the needs of the customer against the capabilities of the manufacturing environment. As with all decisions, if either party is unhappy with the results, that person can appeal to his or her manager, who in turn can go up the chain of command, although this rarely happens.

Feeding Back Information If It Appears That an Item Will Not Be Completed by the Delivery Due Date

Occasionally, a delivery will be delayed, perhaps because of a quality or process problem, or equipment that's down. For instance, a pump motor may burn out, and nothing can be packaged for another week until it's replaced. At that point the manufacturing supervisor is responsible for advising the material planner of the problem and the expected completion dates for the items that will not meet their current delivery dates.

The material planner is responsible for working to minimize the impact on customers and trying to find a way to meet the master schedule despite the problem. Again, if the company has a capacity planner, that person will most likely be involved in the discussion. The capacity planner might be the one to feed back the information to the material planner. Regardless of who does it, this feedback is necessary. As mentioned before, the principle of "silence is approval" is in effect—everyone in the company assumes that the manufacturing supervisor can meet the dates unless told otherwise.

Approving or Rejecting Short-order Releases

As mentioned above, the material planner may request a short-order release—short in terms of material, or short in terms of lead time. Since the manufacturing supervisor will be held accountable for completing the order by the due date, the manufacturing supervisor must agree to the short-order release. Typically, this means starting to build the product without all the components, or compressing the normal lead times. This may or may not be practical. If the delivery date is not feasible, the manufacturing supervisor is expected to negotiate a more acceptable one. Once this is done, the material planner is responsible for minimizing the impact on the master production schedule. As mentioned before, both the manufacturing supervisor and the material planner can appeal the decision up the chain of command, if necessary.

MRP INTEGRATION ISSUES

Just-in-Time

As companies implement Just-in-Time, their material planning becomes easier. This happens for two reasons: The master schedule becomes more linear, and the number of levels in the bills of material decreases.

MRP can deal with any type of manufacturing schedule, whether it's highly repetitive with the same quantity every day, or extremely lumpy (zero demand for a couple of weeks, then a demand for several hundred, then three months of no demand, then a demand for a hundred, and so on). As companies do more and more work with Just-in-Time, they tend to smooth the flow of work through the plant, so the demand for materials is smoother, with fewer peaks and valleys.

Linearity measures the smoothness or evenness of the master production schedule and the planned orders in MRP. Completely linear flow would mean that the same amount is produced every day, or maybe every hour. As the flow becomes more linear, the order quantities decrease to meet the immediate needs, suppliers can plan on repetitive schedules, and utilization of equipment in the plant is easier to plan.

Most companies also reduce the number of levels in their bills of material, which is similar to what many process companies do. Tennant Company, a manufacturer of riding sweepers, is a good example of this. For years, the company manufactured its sweepers in a "traditional" mode, issuing material from the stockroom for the subassemblies, building the subassemblies, and then putting them back in the stockroom. Next, it would issue the subassemblies plus other material for the final assembly, build the final assembly, and ship the product.

With Just-in-Time, Tennant was able to collapse the bill of material so it had fewer levels. It now issues the subassembly material along with the final assembly materials, builds the subassemblies "in line" as the first step of the final assembly, and uses them immediately. The benefits of this approach are the elimination of the "waste" of moving the subassemblies back to the stockroom, picking the subassemblies, moving them to the final assembly area, and cutting the work orders for subassemblies. Tennant cut the combined subassembly and assembly lead times by more than half, making the company more responsive to its customers and gaining a competitive advantage.

Tennant's material planning system handled this change by coding the subassemblies as phantom levels in the bills of material. Phantoms are "blow-through" assemblies that appear in the bills of material but are not actually stocked. When the work orders were created for the final assemblies, all the materials needed for the subassemblies as well as the assemblies were on the picking list.

Concurrent Engineering

As companies do more concurrent or simultaneous engineering, they have a greater need to integrate the engineering or development activities with the manufacturing and purchasing activities. Manufacturing and purchasing are dependent on the completion of development activities like design and the creation of drawings, methods, and specifications in order to meet their delivery commitments. In some companies these are called R&D activities, and they can include clinical trials, FDA approvals, chemical stability tests, corrosion testing, and so on.

In the days when engineering or product development would design a product and "throw it over the wall" to manufacturing and purchasing, it was less critical to have the various buying and production activities integrated. Today, most development is happening at the same time that purchasing is buying materials and manufacturing is carrying out early manufacturing operations. And schedules are so tight that neither engineering nor purchasing nor manufacturing can afford to be placed in a situation in which it cannot meet its delivery commitments because another group did not support it.

One company that has done excellent work in this area is Martin Marietta Astronautics Group, Special Products Division, which has linked its manufacturing and development schedules. "The manufacturing operation had fairly good control of its schedules once it had product in its door. But engineering had difficulty in getting product to manufacturing's door when originally promised," explained Jim Kemp, manager of program control.

Where was the breakdown? "It all had to do with engineering not being able to plan from a scheduling standpoint and a capacity standpoint. If that front-end activity could not be controlled, it was fruitless to try to control the manufacturing and test operations," Kemp says.

The result of this integrated effort is less unplanned overtime in manufacturing and Special Products. Overall, there's also less anxiety, says Kemp. "People are now more relaxed in their responses and more creative in their thinking."

Many companies use a PERT-type system to manage their development activities. They interface this system with MRP—which schedules the manufacturing activities at the detailed item level, as illustrated in Figure 7.12.

Figure 7.12   MRP/PERT

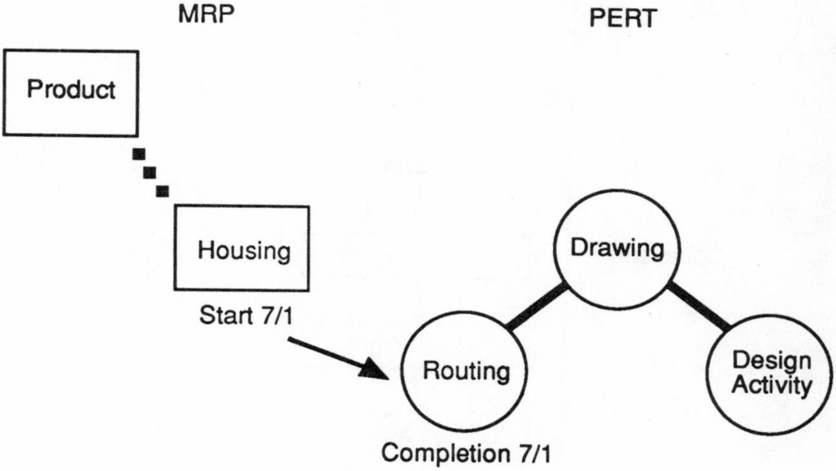

In such an arrangement, if the date of the housing in MRP moves out by two weeks, then the new start date for the housing will be passed to the PERT system. This changes the date the routing for the housing needs to be completed. Similarly, if something happens in the engineering area and the drawing ends up being behind schedule by three weeks, then that information is passed back to MRP. It takes the form of feedback from engineering indicating that the housing can't start for another twenty-one days. This is similar to the feedback from purchasing or manufacturing on items that will not meet their scheduled due dates. In a company with an R&D center, the activities would have different names, but the concepts are the same.

Typically, a company must write its own interface for passing the dates from the MRP system to the PERT system in engineering or R&D. The interface is fairly simple, identifying the items in the engineering schedule that are affected by the dates in MRP and transferring those dates from MRP to the engineering system.

Another less popular approach to the integration of MRP and the development schedules is to use the MRP system to plan and schedule both the manufacturing and nonmanufacturing operations. This is illustrated in Figure 7.13.

Figure 7.13   MRP

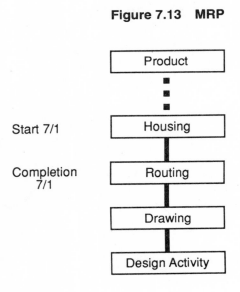

The nonmanufacturing activities are given item numbers. They are represented in the bills of material and are scheduled using the MRP planning system. This way, the development schedule is integrated with the manufacturing schedule. If the due date for a housing moves out by two weeks, then that information is passed down through the MRP system and the date the routing is needed for the housing moves out by two weeks. This happens in the same way that the need dates for components are adjusted when the date for the parent product changes. The housing and the routing for the housing are linked through a bill of material.

The Elliott Company, a manufacturer of custom-built steam turbines and compressors, uses this second method. Elliott has developed a special piece of software that does its scheduling for both manufacturing and nonmanufacturing activities.

Either of the two methods explained above is workable. In many companies, the engineering group has its own PERT system already in place. So, rather than ask engineering to replace its system with a different one, it makes more sense just to integrate the two. It is, however, important to verify that the PERT system being used is capable of capacity planning and dispatching, since some of the older systems do not contain these features.

MEASUREMENTS

The primary responsibility of the people in the planning department is to make plans and schedules that people can be held accountable for achieving. Specifically, the people who will be accountable for meeting schedules are manufacturing supervisors, supplier schedulers, engineering or product development people, and suppliers. The question then becomes, "How do you measure the validity of a plan?" The best answer is "By determining whether the people who will be held accountable for hitting the plan agree that it's valid." So the way companies measure material plans is to ask the people in the plant, in engineering or product development, and in purchasing whether they have a valid schedule. This means that the results are largely subjective. As mentioned before, it is more difficult to measure these types of things, but not impossible. Questions to help in this assessment are: Do you believe the schedules? Are they realistic? What happens if you don't think a schedule is realistic?

SUMMARY/CHECKUP

1. Material requirements planning (MRP) is now accepted as the most effective way to plan for material in any type of manufacturing business, including hard goods, chemicals, food, electronics, and textiles. It's a simple, straightforward set of calculations that answers the question "What do we need and when do we need it?" Is your company using MRP to plan for material?

2. MRP not only shows when to order material, but also keeps the due dates for material up to date as things change. This up-to-date information provides valid schedules—schedules people believe and can be held accountable for meeting. Does your company maintain valid schedules? Do the people in the plant and in purchasing believe the schedules?

3. Rescheduling manufacturing and purchasing deliveries to later dates ("unexpediting") is one of the most powerful tools for assuring on-time deliveries from both the plant and outside suppliers. How well does your company "unexpedite"?

4. The objective in managing MRP is to provide a valid set of material plans that others can be held accountable for meeting. Doing this includes the following activities:

   a. rescheduling delivery dates to meet the demands
   b. changing demands to reflect the actual delivery situation
   c. authorizing production
   d. maintaining the item data
   e. feeding back information if it appears that a delivery due date will not be met

Is each of these done in your company? If so, how well do people work together to deal with difficult issues as they come up during these activities?

5. Concurrent engineering and concurrent development are becoming the norm, and, as a result, MRP and the engineering or development scheduling system must be integrated. The schedules for engineering or development activities should be linked to the schedules for manufactur-

ing and purchasing. If there are significant engineering or development activities in your company, are they linked and kept up to date?

There is another equally important plan—the capacity plan. Some companies use rough-cut capacity planning only; others use rough-cut and capacity requirements planning. Whatever the approach, every manufacturing company needs some form of capacity plan. Without one, there is no assurance that the material plan can be achieved. For this reason, capacity planning is the subject of the next chapter.

Chapter Eight

Capacity Planning

Capacity planning answers the question "What do you need and when do you need it?" in terms of reusable resources such as equipment, manpower, cold storage, and tooling. On one level, capacity planning is relatively straightforward. Once you know what you're going to make and when you're going to make it, a simple calculation using a list of activities needed to complete the required items will determine the equipment and labor requirements. These capacity requirements are then summarized by equipment or labor skill and compared to the available capacity. This process, in a nutshell, is what capacity planning is all about.

There are two types of capacity planning: rough-cut capacity planning (RCCP) and capacity requirements planning (CRP).

ROUGH-CUT CAPACITY PLANNING

"We do rough-cut capacity planning, but we have not done detailed capacity planning," explains Frank Wetzel, director of materials and systems at Sealed Power. "Our focused factories produce a particular product line, size, and kind. Within these factories we deal with only two or three variations, so the process is pretty straightforward. Rough-cut capacity planning works well for us, so we have not moved to detailed capacity planning, and we really don't see a need to."

Frank Wetzel's experience is typical of the experience of many companies that use rough-cut capacity planning and find it is adequate to meet their capacity planning needs. Rough-cut capacity planning is the simpler of the two types of capacity planning. In rough-cut, the top-level plans are extended by a summarized resource profile for each product. The resource profile identifies the key resources required, the number of hours of resources required to make the product, and approximately when those resources are required relative to the completion of the product. Figure 8.1 is an example of a resource profile.

Figure 8.1   Resource Profile

Mix	9.0 Hours/1000 Gallons
Fill	3.5 Hours/1000 Gallons
Case Pack	3.0 Hours/1000 Gallons
Warehouse Space	12.0 Cubic Feet/1000 Gallons
Glass Supplier	50.0 Pounds/1000 Gallons

Notice that the resource requirements are mostly hours, but in the case of warehouse space and the glass supplier the requirements are stated in terms of space and weight.

The resource profile is extended by the top-level plan for each product, and the numbers are then summarized by piece of equipment. This results in a capacity plan, as shown in Figure 8.2.

Figure 8.2   Summary Rough-Cut Capacity Plan

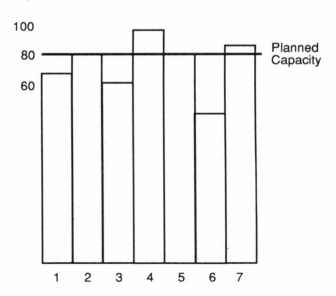

The report in Figure 8.2 shows the capacity requirements for a filling line by time period. These time periods are typically months, but could be weeks or even days in some companies. The report could be run monthly as part of the S&OP process, or more frequently as the master schedule changes. The report also shows the planned capacity of the filling line. This planned capacity is developed from the demonstrated capacity (what the line has historically been able to produce) and any changes that would cause this number to change (working additional hours, installing new equipment, etc.). The comparison of the required capacity and the planned capacity identifies overloads and underloads.

In week 4, for example, 100 hours of capacity are needed. Historically, the filling line has only been able to produce 80 hours per week. The difference, 20 hours, is the problem. How would a planner get the necessary hours to meet the plan? Fortunately, there are a number of choices, some of which are listed below:

- Run the filling line on a weekend—16 hours on Saturday and 4 on Sunday.

- Run the filling line overtime—4 hours of overtime for five days would give the extra 20 hours needed.

- Off-load work to other equipment in the plant.

- Subcontract the work out to another company with the same type of filling equipment.

When working on an under- or overload problem, the capacity planner needs more than the information on the summary report. Figure 8.3 shows a detailed report that reveals each of the items that make up the load. For example, the overload in time period 4 on the summary report is caused by 14 different products listed in Figure 8.3. This type of detail is necessary if the planner is to propose solutions, such as off-loading work to different equipment, running items in smaller batches, or changing the plan. In each case, the planner needs to look at the individual products and assess the situation.

But what if the plant is already running three shifts and there's no opportunity to add capacity? What if there are no subcontracting opportunities, and no other filling lines that could handle the work? One option is to change the top-level plan, although this is generally an undesirable

Figure 8.3   Detailed Rough-Cut Capacity Plan

Filling Line — Time Period 4

Item	Quantity	Hours
1. Grape Juice	500 Gallons	12
2. _____	_____	___
3. _____	_____	___
. _____	_____	___
. _____	_____	___
. _____	_____	___
. _____	_____	___
. _____	_____	___
14. _____	_____	___

Total Hours		100

solution. But for a make-to-stock product manufactured in quantities that exceed the immediate needs, it may make sense to run a quantity that is smaller than normal in order to reduce an overload. For example, rather than making 1,000 cases of apple juice in week 4, a solution may be to produce 500 cases in week 4 and then another 500 in week 8.

The right solution depends on many factors unique to each company and each situation. What are the costs of the different solutions, and the lengths to which you, as a company, are prepared to go in order to meet customer service objectives? Are you willing to spend $100 to deliver a customer's order on time? What about $1 million? These are questions regarding the value of customer service and the cost of overtime, subcontracting, off-loading work to another work center, retooling, new equipment, and so on.

Now let's look at the reverse situation—an underload. In this case, there is available capacity, but not enough capacity requirements to fill it. For instance, in time period 6 the filling line has capacity requirements of 60 hours and planned capacity of 80 hours. This creates an underload of 20 hours.

Again, the planner has a number of choices for solving the problem. One is to let the equipment sit idle. Another is to move work up from a different time period to fill the "valley." In some situations, in which equipment time is relatively inexpensive, idle time is not a problem, but in others it's a critical concern. Consider a paper mill. If the flow of pulp through the mill stops, the equipment requires an expensive and time consuming clean-out operation. Therefore, it's important to keep the equipment running, preferably at a constant rate.

The rough-cut capacity plan can be calculated from either the production plan or the master production schedule. The production plan would be used where the items in an S&OP family are fairly similar. For example, if different apple juice products all use about the same amount of key resources, then one resource profile will work for the entire family. The production plan for the apple juice family of products can be extended by the resource profile to produce the rough-cut capacity plan.

If, however, the number of hours required for filling or case packing is significantly different for the different apple juice products in the family, then there should be a resource profile for each apple juice product (master schedule item). Then the master production schedules for each product can be extended by the resource profiles to produce the rough-cut capacity plan.

When is rough-cut sufficient to run a business? Most companies with flow-type manufacturing use rough-cut capacity planning only. This includes most process manufacturers, and Just-in-Time companies that make extensive use of kanban to control the movement of material. There are exceptions, however. ICI Fine Chemicals in Huddersfield, England, is a chemical manufacturing company with a number of high-volume manufacturing plants on its grounds. This company found that it needed capacity requirements planning to effectively manage their capacity.

In addition, some companies have specialized requirements that require a more detailed approach to capacity planning. For example, in a number of companies the rough-cut plan is transferred to a personal computer for specific scheduling of number and size of crews, union restrictions on number of hours worked, and so forth.

CAPACITY REQUIREMENTS PLANNING

"We'd never really done detailed capacity planning," explains Stan Grubbs, MIS supervisor at Boeing Defense & Space. "Part of that omission stemmed from a lack of tools but it also came from a basic doubt on the part of both the production scheduling and shop-floor people. Frankly, they thought we couldn't do much about it, even if we identified our capacity problems."

"Once we began using CRP, it evolved into a very useful tool. All of our forward planning in the shop is done through our capacity planning reports. It took us about a year and a half to get to that point. And it took comparing the capacity tools with some of our old methods, like load reporting in the shop, to prove the validity of the tools—to get people to use them. At first, people just didn't want to deal with it. They didn't believe it would really work. Now, most of the people in the shop live and die by that information. And they really wouldn't run the shop any other way.

"We're part of a larger organization, and people felt that our schedules were dictated from above. Every time you had to deal with a capacity issue, you'd immediately have to change the master schedule. Management couldn't convince people otherwise; we tried to demonstrate that you could work up through the product structure within the lead times we had, that we could take some time out of queue, things like that. It all came down to getting in there and working through real cases. I consider it a success because we worked through our own doubts. We did something that is kind of unique for this place: We used the generic tools, took them on faith, and modified them to some extent to maximize their effectiveness. But we started with something that was plain vanilla and made it start working for us."

Grubbs' company is typical of a complex manufacturing environment. Rough-cut capacity planning is not sufficiently detailed to identify all the capacity problems in this environment, so it is used in such companies as a validity check on the top-level plans, after which capacity requirements planning (CRP) is used to do capacity planning for each work center.

The CRP calculations are nearly identical to the rough-cut capacity planning calculations. However, instead of using the production plan or master production schedule, as is done in rough-cut, CRP uses the material plan: the scheduled receipts and planned orders in MRP. And instead of using a resource profile, CRP uses the routing to identify the resources that are needed to make an item. Detailed capacity requirements are then calculated and accumulated by resource—work centers and labor skills—much as in rough-cut. The capacity requirements are displayed in a format similar to the one used in rough-cut capacity planning, and their use is nearly the same. Overloads and underloads are identified and planners work to resolve these. The primary difference is that rather than looking only at the key resources, as is done in rough-cut capacity planning, CRP looks at every work center, and on a detailed level.

To illustrate this we'll use a frame and a spot welder. Figures 8.4, 8.5, and 8.6 are examples of routings, CRP summary reports, and CRP detail reports.

Figure 8.4   Frame

Sequence	Description	Work Center	Setup	Hours/100
10	Clean	9002	.5	30.0
20	Spot Weld	9010	.3	20.0
30	Paint	8060		5.0
40	Drill	7015	.2	12.0

Figure 8.5   Capacity Requirements Planning Summary Report

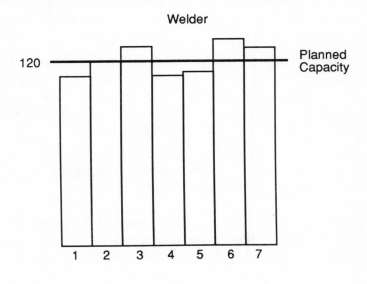

Figure 8.6   Detailed Capacity Requirements Planning Report

Welder — Week of March 27

Item	Quantity	Hours
1. Frame	50	10.3
2. _____	_____	____
3. _____	_____	____
. _____	_____	____
. _____	_____	____
. _____	_____	____
. _____	_____	____
. _____	_____	____
18. _____	_____	____
Total Hours		135

In this example, MRP has a planned order for 50 frames due March 27. The routing for the frame identifies the spot welder as one of the work centers. A work center is:

1. *A machine or group of machines that do similar work.* In the case of several machines, say, two spot welding machines, one work center would be created with a capacity equal to two spot welders.

2. *A cell.* A cell is a group of dissimilar machines that have been arranged together to speed the flow of work. For example, a cleaner, spot welder, paint gun, and drill might be arranged in a U shape. Frames would start at one end, and in a short time finished items would begin appearing out the other end.

3. *A process line.* An example of a process line would be mechanically connected flow equipment that fills and caps bottles, applies labels, and puts the bottles into cases.

Capacity requirements planning can be done for any of these different types of work centers, although for this example we'll use the first type. If the frame is due for completion on the 27th, then on the 27th the machining department needs to complete the last operation—drilling. On the 26th the paint area needs to complete the painting operation, on the 25th the spot welding needs to be done, and so forth.

Some companies would complete each operation on all 50 frames before moving the frames to the next operation. Others might overlap the operations by sending smaller quantities of frames—say, 10 at a time—from one operation to the next.

Let's take the spot welding operation, which is due to be completed on March 25. Fifty pieces times the standard (20 hours per 100) gives 10 hours of spot welding. This generates a capacity requirement for 10 hours of spot welding time on March 25. Similar calculations are done for all of the other operations on this item, and also for all other items in the material plan. These capacity requirements are then sorted by work center and date, and the result appears as the CRP summary report (Figure 8.5). The time periods on this report are typically in weeks, although some companies use days. Capacity requirements planning is generally run weekly, but it could be run more frequently if the plans change. The detailed capacity planning report shown in Figure 8.6 lists all the different items that are scheduled to pass through the spot welding work center during the week of March 27.

That's all there is to the CRP calculation. Although the calculation is simple, the power of the technique lies in the ability of computers to handle the large amounts of data. It's not uncommon in a typical manufacturing company to have hundreds of thousands of capacity requirements that must be generated and then organized by work center and date. Capacity requirements planning makes it possible to manage such volumes of information and produce meaningful reports that can be used to manage capacities effectively.

SHOULD I USE CRP?

In a job-shop, disconnected-flow environment, where complex assemblies are manufactured in batches, with hundreds of different work centers, rough-cut capacity is sufficient to tell whether the master schedule is in the ballpark—but detailed CRP is essential for verifying that capacity is in fact available on each of those hundreds of pieces of equipment, and for each of the different labor skills. Capacity requirements planning should be used, in addition to rough-cut capacity planning, where there are:

1. Many work centers that must be planned. Capacity requirements planning plans all work centers.

2. Many levels in the bills of material or formulas. Capacity requirements planning uses the item data: planned orders and scheduled receipts in MRP, order quantities, and routings. This accounts for the effects of on-hand balances, order quantities that are greater than immediate needs, and lead-time offsets based on the routing.

CONSIDERATIONS FOR ALL TYPES OF CAPACITY PLANNING

While every company has *some* form of capacity planning, many companies lack an *accurate* mechanism for calculating capacity requirements. This is because most companies lack credible plans, so people have never had confidence in the numbers used to generate capacity planning information. For example, consider a company with a massive phony backlog, say, six weeks' worth of work at the plastic molding machines, all of it either overdue or due this week. Capacity planning would simply extend the standard hours and end up with an absurd requirement—say, 600 hours of work to be done this week, when the capacity of the equipment is only 110 hours per week.

The point is, if the computer applies the math of capacity planning to a phony backlog, the manufacturing people will take one look at the resulting report and then toss it. Even if there isn't a phony backlog, some companies lack credible material plans. If the plans are changing so fast that no one believes them, then people won't believe the capacity plans derived from those material plans. Consequently, the information will not be used for decisions such as hiring people, putting on extra shifts, or buying new equipment.

The most obvious reason for CRP is that without a valid capacity plan, the material plan is also invalid. If the capacity is not there to support the material plan, the material plan will not happen either, and therefore it has little meaning. In a closed-loop MRP II system, all the functions work in concert with one another—sales and operations planning, master production scheduling, material planning, and now capacity planning. Each plays a necessary role.

This validation of the material plan is done by identifying overloads and underloads on critical pieces of equipment or for critical labor skills. These problems need to be identified as early as possible; it's far easier to solve a capacity problem that's 20 weeks in the future than one that needs to be fixed in four hours. Obviously, planners have far more options available when they can look 20 weeks into the future. For example, they can deal with a problem far out on the horizon by subcontracting, using new tooling, acquiring new equipment, or implementing a methods change. If they're trying to solve a problem this afternoon, their options list is reduced to overtime, extra shifts, or changing the master schedule, none of which may be desirable.

Finally, capacity planning is important because it allows people to deal with problems quantitatively. Too often, companies stop at the fact that they have an overload or underload. What's the size of the underload? Five hours? Five hundred hours? It's important to quantify the problem in order to develop practical, cost-effective solutions that can be implemented in the necessary time frame.

OTHER APPLICATIONS OF CAPACITY PLANNING

Where concurrent engineering is being done, capacity planning is used to plan for the skills of engineering or development workers—designers, CAD operators, methods people, testing people, and so on.

It is also possible to use capacity planning for other reusable resources such as cold storage. In a food processing company, cold storage is an expensive and important resource, and capacity planning can be used to effectively plan for it.

Many companies plan labor requirements at several levels. They might look at the labor skills individually, aggregate the requirements by department, and finally summarize all the departmental labor requirements into a total for the entire plant. This shows what labor skills are needed within each department, and what labor requirements are needed for the plant.

Such an analysis often shows there is enough capacity in total, but there are mismatches between skill sets. In such a case, capacity planning can assist in developing cross-training programs to deal with situations like having too many assemblers and not enough welders.

OTHER CONCEPTS

Even though capacity requirements planning has evolved significantly, a number of terms still linger in the vocabulary of the field, the two most prevalent being *finite loading* and *machine loading*.

Finite Loading

Finite loading is a technique in which the computer is allowed to make decisions and solve capacity problems. For instance, if an overload exists in week 4, the computer identifies the situation, evaluates some alternatives, and schedules a third shift or proposes some other solution.

The idea of letting a computer handle the analysis and decision making is irresistible to some people. Unfortunately, it's an idea with a poor track record for success. As mentioned before, computers are good at handling ones and zeros and manipulating massive amounts of data, but when given the opportunity to evaluate options and creatively make decisions, they don't fare well. Human beings do a much better job of applying creativity and making informed judgments.

Numerous companies can relate tales of buying finite loading systems because of the finite loading algorithms. They go on to say how they later disconnected the finite loading calculations and ran these systems as capacity requirements planning systems. Most finite loading systems have been discontinued, although a few remain. And some companies have even achieved operating improvements from using finite loading. These improvements, however, are due to Wight's 35th law: "When you change five things at once and things get better, credit will be given to the most complex thing you changed, when the improvements actually resulted from the simplest thing you changed." The benefits from finite loading have come from the basic capacity planning that is a part of the technique, rather than from the logic that allows the computer to solve problems.

What does seem to work well, however, is to use a finite scheduling system as a simulator. The planner allows the finite loading algorithm to run, then looks at the results. If the planner and the manufacturing supervisor like the solution—for example, adding two hours per day of overtime in the milling department for the next two weeks—then they implement this solution. The finite loading software does the arithmetic, but people evaluate the solutions, make the decisions, implement them, and are accountable for the results.

This approach is becoming more common in the scheduling of process manufacturing. Here, the master scheduler restricts the finite loading calculation to the top-level parts of the manufacturing process, like filling and packing. The finite loading calculation works as a simulator showing the master scheduler and manufacturing supervisors different alternatives for utilizing the filling and packing line, so they can discuss the alternatives and make a decision.

Machine Loading

Even though machine loading is outdated, it is occasionally still mentioned today in capacity planning discussions. Figure 8.7 is an example of a machine loading report. It provides capacity planning information based only on scheduled receipts. For most companies, the work to be done this week exists in the form of released orders. The work to be done 50 weeks in the future exists in the form of planned orders. Consequently, as you go further out in time, the machine loading report, which shows only the scheduled receipts, gives the picture of a diminishing work load over time. That, of course, is incorrect. The manufacturing supervisor will have work in week 20—it exists in the form of planned orders that have not been released into scheduled receipts yet. As a result, machine loading is not an effective way to do capacity planning, and few companies use it.

Figure 8.7   Machine Loading Report
Work Center #1065
Weekly Capacity—240 Standard Hours

Week	Load	Over/ Underload
Past Due	824	+584
1	286	+ 46
2	150	− 90
3	90	−150
4	39	−201

WHO DOES CRP? WHAT ARE THE ACTIVITIES?

While a number of different people can be involved in the process of solving a capacity problem, most of the work in capacity planning is done by the capacity planner and the manufacturing supervisor. Others in the process can include: the master scheduler (for changes to the master schedule), a buyer or supplier scheduler (for subcontracting to an outside supplier), a material planner (for changes in order quantity), an engineer or R&D person (for redesign, retooling, rerouting, and off-loading), sales or marketing people (for moving customer orders), and finance people (for the purchase of new equipment).

Capacity Planner

The capacity planner's primary responsibility is similar to that of the material planner: to create and maintain valid plans. In this case, the goal is to create valid capacity plans. This is done by either changing capacity to meet the demands or changing the capacity requirements to reflect the actual availability of capacity. While it would be possible to have someone in the role of capacity planner for rough-cut capacity planning, this is typically not done because there are so few key resources involved. Typical activities for the capacity planner include:

- reviewing the capacity planning report for under- and overloads and working with manufacturing supervisors to identify solutions

- dealing with requests to change the master schedule

- maintaining the work center data

Let's look at each of these.

Reviewing the Capacity Planning Report for Under- and Overloads and Working with Manufacturing Supervisors to Identify Solutions
The capacity planner uses the CRP summary report to identify overloads and underloads. Using the CRP detail report, the planner identifies possible solutions. These include such options as:

- increasing capacity by using overtime, weekends, and/or extra shifts

- off-loading work to another work center in the plant

- subcontracting work to an outside supplier

- changing the material plan to reduce the capacity requirements and relieve an overload

- changing the material plan (increasing quantities or doing work early) to relieve an underload

- changing the master production schedule to reduce the capacity requirements and relieve an overload

- working with engineering or development to redesign, retool, or develop new methods to relieve an overload

- acquiring new equipment and/or hiring new people

In each case, the capacity planner works with the manufacturing supervisor to develop plans the supervisor can be held accountable for meeting.

To illustrate the working relationship between the capacity planner and others in the company, imagine an overload in a manufacturing cell that does cleaning, welding, painting, and drilling. The overload is in week 5. The capacity planner would look at the options for increasing capacity, including overtime, running on Saturday or Sunday, or running the cell on a third shift. The capacity planner and manufacturing supervisors would look at the pros and cons of each alternative and then select the best one. The "best" alternative will depend in part on the timing of the problem.

The possible solutions to this overload problem include creating a new cell, which would mean purchasing new equipment and training people. Since the overload is in week 5, this is unlikely to work. But if the capacity planner is trying to solve a consistent overload, this might be the best choice, in combination with some short-term solutions.

If the capacity planner has done everything to increase capacity and none of the choices will work, the next step is to consider reducing the capacity requirements to match the available capacity. To do this, the capacity planner should review the CRP detail report, looking at the items that make up the load in week 5. With some detailed product knowledge and a good working relationship with the manufacturing supervisor, the capacity planner can look at individual items and identify alternatives.

For example, it may make sense to off-load some items to other work centers. Even if these items are done less efficiently at the other work centers, this option may still make sense because it's less expensive than subcontracting and certainly better than delaying a customer order. And if the other work centers have available capacity, there's no real out-of-pocket cost.

Sometimes subcontracting is the best option. A number of companies strategically use outside suppliers to stabilize their employment and to keep their equipment in use, rather than buy equipment and man to peak loads. Another option is to look at redesign, retooling, and new methods so that an item runs more efficiently. In such cases, the capacity planner, manufacturing supervisor, and engineering people should work together on developing the solution. Again, this might not happen fast enough to solve an overload problem in week 5, but for a continuing overload and in combination with some short-term solutions, it may make a great deal of sense.

There are a number of options available to the capacity planner in working with the material planner. It may be possible to cut order quantity, which reduces the load in one week but creates new capacity requirements in future weeks. If the future weeks have available capacity, this can be a good solution. If the future weeks are all overloaded, then this won't solve the problem, only delay it.

If the capacity planner has unsuccessfully tried to increase capacity and reduce the capacity requirements, but has failed to come up with a good solution, the last resort is to reduce the master schedule or reschedule it to a later date. While this is not a preferred course of action, occasionally it has to be done. As Stan Grubbs pointed out, there are often ways to change order quantities or compress lead times to deal with capacity problems and still meet the master production schedule.

Dealing with Requests to Change the Master Schedule

When investigating a change to the MPS, the master scheduler must ask: "Do we have the materials and capacity to make this change?" The capacity planner must provide an answer to the capacity question. There are two ways to check capacity: manually and by computer.

Manually, the material planner would identify the items that would change if the master schedule were changed (as explained in Chapter 6) and feed this information to the capacity planner. The capacity planner would then use this information and the routings to calculate the additional capacity requirements from these changes. Finally, the planner would mark up the capacity planning reports, noting where underloads and overloads appear.

For example, the master scheduler wants to move an MPS order for 300 air conditioners from week 7 to week 4. The material planner looks at the request and responds by identifying several fabrication and subassembly items that will have to be completed earlier than when they are currently scheduled. The material planner then feeds the item numbers and the new dates to the capacity planner, who performs a quick calculation using the routing and identifies another 20 hours that are needed in the stamping area next week, and 15 additional hours in the subassembly area in week 3. Since both of these work centers were already loaded to their capacity, the additional hours have created overloads in both work centers. The capacity planner now works with the manufacturing supervisors to solve the two overloads.

As is the case for the material planner, the best policy for the master scheduler is to never say no, but instead to identify what has to be done if the change is going to happen. For instance, the capacity planner working with the supervisors might determine that to accommodate the change they'll have to subcontract the stamping work and work two Sundays in the subassembly area. At that point, someone needs to evaluate the customer service issues associated with making the change and compare them to the cost and disruption of the solution. The company can then make an informed decision.

The computer approach would involve a simulation. Both the material plan and the capacity plan would be rerun, and the planners would evaluate the results. As explained for simulations of the material plan, the savings from simulation are in the calculation of the data. The problem resolution, which is usually most of the work, takes the same amount of time.

Maintaining the Work Center Data
Like the material planner, the capacity planner is responsible for the basic planning data. The material planner is responsible for the item data, and the capacity planner is responsible for the work center data. This includes the data on demonstrated and planned capacity, and, in companies with shop-floor control systems, it includes certain scheduling rules, such as move and queue rules for the work center and rules on the number of shifts the work center is operated. The capacity planner works with the manufacturing supervisor to develop these data, and then the capacity planner is responsible for maintaining them.

Manufacturing Supervisor

The manufacturing supervisor's responsibility is to meet both order due dates and the capacity plan. With respect to capacity planning, the manufacturing supervisor would:

- work with the capacity planner to develop capacity solutions

- meet the planned capacity numbers

Work with the Capacity Planner to Develop Capacity Solutions
In most companies, the capacity planner meets weekly with the manufacturing supervisor to review the CRP reports and identify possible solutions for work centers that have underloads or overloads. If they cannot agree on a solution, they can appeal to their respective managers for a decision, although this is rarely necessary.

The different options for solving these capacity problems have already been covered above in the section on the capacity planner's responsibilities. In a number of these cases, the capacity planner will be responsible for doing follow-up work, such as meeting with the material planner to see if an order quantity can be reduced, or meeting with engineering to discuss off-loading or new methods.

Meet the Planned Capacity Numbers
In the same way that the manufacturing supervisor is responsible for meeting the due dates, he or she is responsible for meeting the planned capacity numbers. Planned capacity is typically developed by looking at the demonstrated capacity (history) of a work center and then including any changes that would either increase or decrease the capacity. If an automatic insertion machine for electrical components is consistently producing 160 standard hours per week, then that would be its demonstrated capacity. If, however, the work center were to be operated more hours per week through overtime or extra shifts, then the planned capacity would be greater than the demonstrated capacity of 160 hours. Since the manufacturing supervisor will be accountable for meeting the planned capacity, the supervisor needs to agree to this number.

What happens if a work center is not achieving the planned capacity number? Is the problem an equipment breakdown? If so, the manufacturing supervisor should work with the maintenance people. Is it a process problem? If so, the supervisor should work with engineering. It could be that the problem is a lack of work coming into the work center. If the work center is only getting 50 standard hours of work per week, and there is little in queue, then it's unlikely that the work center will be able to put out 80 standard hours each week. Regardless of the reason, the manufacturing supervisor is responsible for bringing the work center up to its planned capacity, or getting the capacity changed to a more realistic number.

MEASUREMENTS

The measurements are similar to those described in the previous chapter on material planning—the goal is to create a plan to which people will agree to be held accountable, in this case a capacity plan. How do you measure the validity of a plan? As with the material plan, the best method is to ask the people in the plant whether they have a valid schedule. This means the results are largely subjective. As mentioned before, it is more difficult to measure these types of things, but not impossible. Questions to help in this assessment are: Do you believe the capacity plan? Are the capacity requirements and the planned capacities realistic? What happens if you don't think a capacity plan is realistic?

SUMMARY/CHECKUP

1. Capacity planning answers the question "What do you need and when do you need it?" in terms of reusable resources such as equipment, manpower, cold storage, and tooling. Every company needs rough-cut capacity planning (RCCP). In addition, some companies, typically job-shop environments with disconnected flow, require capacity requirements planning (CRP). Does your company use rough-cut capacity planning? Does it use capacity requirements planning?

2. Applying the math of capacity planning to a phony backlog or schedules that no one believes is a major reason companies fail to get results from capacity planning. Are you using a valid set of plans to drive capacity planning in your company?

3. Finite loading is a technique with a poor track record for success, and most finite loading systems have been disconnected. Finite loading programs, however, are being used successfully as simulators—to evaluate different options quickly, and also for line scheduling in process manufacturing.

4. The objective in capacity planning is to provide a valid set of capacity plans that others can be held accountable for meeting. Doing this includes the following activities:

a. changing capacity to meet the demands
b. changing the capacity requirements to reflect the actual availability of capacity
c. dealing with requests to change the master schedule
d. maintaining the work center data
e. meeting the planned capacity numbers

Is each of these done in your company? If so, how well do people work together to deal with difficult issues as they come up during these activities?

Once a company has a valid material plan and a valid capacity plan, the challenge is to make the plans happen. As mentioned before, people sometimes confuse planning with execution. Not only must a company develop a good set of plans, but it must execute them well. Communicating and executing these plans is the subject of the next two chapters.

SPECIAL ACKNOWLEDGMENT

James Correll for his definitive work in capacity requirements planning.

Chapter Nine

Plant Scheduling

Every day, infant food manufacturer Ross Laboratories, a division of Abbott Laboratories in Brockville, Ontario, provides its plants with a schedule of products to be made. The plant completes its schedule, then cleans out the equipment in preparation for the next day's production. That's plant scheduling at its simplest.

Three thousand miles away, Beckman Instruments in Fullerton, California, uses kanban to control the movement of centrifuge frames through its various manufacturing operations. There are no work orders, no time cards, and a number of the people on the plant floor order material from suppliers. The plant schedule is just the list of customer orders from a sister plant in Palo Alto. The schedule arrives via fax, and kanban is used to resupply the components from the fabrication and paint areas.

And 1,000 miles up the coast from Beckman, Comtek, formerly a division of Tektronics, a maker of frames, enclosures, and sheet-metal parts in Portland, Oregon, uses a shop-floor control system to communicate the operation scheduling information to its plant floor. In some cases, the work centers scheduled this way perform as cells. In other cases, Comtek's equipment operates as "functionally" grouped work centers, with all the stamping machines in one area, all the welding equipment in another, and so on.

The casual observer may wonder, "How would I decide among these different plant scheduling techniques? They all seem to work." Yes, they all do work, but only because *each is suited to the manufacturing environment in which it is deployed.* The objective of plant scheduling is the same for all companies: to effectively communicate the schedules, and to provide a sufficient degree of control to assist people in meeting their delivery commitments. The methods differ because the requirements differ.

PRODUCTION SCHEDULES

Heekin Can in Cincinnati, Ohio, produces almost a million cans per shift. With that kind of volume, there are no work orders, because the flow of material through the plant is so fast that the products would be gone before a work order could find its way out to the plant floor. Instead, a production schedule similar to the one shown in Figure 9.1 is used to communicate schedules.

This production schedule is often a listing of the master production schedule for the day. It specifies the items to be manufactured, the quantities, and the dates. Most companies limit the information on the production schedule to the next day or two. The distinguishing feature of this type of production schedule is that it is geared to an *item,* not an operation. In other words, individual operations are not scheduled.

At Heekin, and at ICI Fine Chemicals in Huddersfield, England, the master schedule orders are authorized in the computer. The orders are changed from planned to authorized, but no paperwork is created. When the product is completed at ICI, the master schedule order is reduced, and the order is ultimately closed out when the entire quantity

Figure 9.1   Production Schedule

Line #1	10/25/xx
Product 1042	75,000
Product 1089	15,000
Product 1042	27,000
■	■
■	■
■	■

has been reported. At Heekin, the master schedule orders are dropped at the end of the day. If, for some reason, the scheduled production was not completed, a separate decision is made on where this difference should go on the master schedule, or whether to drop it from the schedule (in the case of a make-to-stock product being built for inventory).

The production schedule is an efficient, effective way to meet the scheduling needs of the manufacturing environments just described. Once a product starts down the pipeline in a chemical reactor, it will come out the other end. There are no scheduling needs in between. The same is true for a packaging line, a bottle-filling line, and so on. Where individual operations do not need to be scheduled, the production schedule is usually the best tool for communicating the manufacturing schedule.

Using the Production Schedule

Since the production schedule usually comes directly from master schedule, the master scheduler typically sets the dates. In some situations, such as that of ICI, where the output of one process plant is the raw material for the next, the production schedule is derived from the material plan. In this case, the material planner sets the production schedule for the supplying process plants.

The manufacturing supervisor and/or the production operators use the production schedule to manage the work on the plant floor. Depending on the experience of the operators, the degree of participative management in the company, and the complexity of the scheduling decisions, the operators may use it and only check with the supervisor when a problem appears. In other cases, the supervisor makes most of the decisions.

The supervisor also gets involved in the use of the production schedule if there is insufficient capacity to make the schedule happen. Ideally, the capacity plan was worked out when the master schedule was set. The reality, of course, is that problems do appear, and several people may have to hold a short meeting to sort out the situation.

Measurement Against the Production Schedule

The primary measurement of the production schedule is 95 percent or better on-time performance to the delivery date within a specified tolerance. The tolerance will vary by company and industry, but for most process or repetitive manufacturers a typical tolerance is less than a day—the work needs to be completed on the day it was scheduled for completion.

Summary: Production Scheduling

In many types of industries, such as chemical manufacturing, food processing, or high-volume repetitive manufacturing, the need to track every operation is unnecessary, the cost is prohibitive, and the entire manufacturing process would actually slow down.

A production schedule is a simple and effective way to communicate the schedule in a manufacturing environment in which scheduling is done by item, not by operation. The advantages are that it's simple, easy to use, and provides sufficient control in these types of manufacturing environments.

KANBAN

The Beckman Instruments plant in Palo Alto, California, has developed an innovative application of kanban to schedule the production of motors for its laboratory centrifuge line. As the last motor of a particular type is lifted off the shelf, it releases a colored flag on the end of a long shaft. This flag is visible from the other side of the plant, where the motors are assembled. The color of the flag indicates the type of motor just used (Beckman uses several different motors for different centrifuge models), and the person making motors only has to look up from time to time to see which flags are up and know which motors to build.

As Beckman's system indicates, kanban is a visual control system used to govern the movement of material on the plant floor. In its most basic form, kanban is a work authorization that restricts the amount of work between two work centers by setting limits.

The simplest everyday example of kanban is the milkman (sadly, of yesterday). If you wanted two bottles of milk, you left two empty bottles in the milk box. The empty bottles were an authorization to provide more milk.

A manufacturing equivalent of the milk bottle is a container. When the container is empty, fill it up again. An empty container is an authorization to produce. There are no work orders for these items.

"We've defined which items we're going to manufacture discretely and which we're going to make repetitively," explains Al Gronlund, plant manager at Diamond Cabinets. "Those repetitive items are on kanban. They require no work orders. An example is a warehouse issue to our cutting department. It doesn't have to go through production control. If there are spikes in customer orders where the demand is more than anticipated, then the cutting cycles are more frequent. If there is no demand, then there is no cutting cycle. So I estimate that we've eliminated three or four steps of management approval–type activities."

Kanbans can take on an amazing variety of forms. Some examples include: squares on the floor, carts, boxes, colored flags, parts boards, clips, and cards. Figure 9.2 shows an example of squares on the floor. If a square is empty, work is authorized (Figure 9.2a). If it's full, work is not authorized (Figure 9.2b).

Figures 9.2a, 9.2b   Kanban Squares

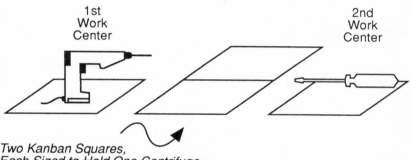

1st
Work
Center

2nd
Work
Center

Two Kanban Squares,
Each Sized to Hold One Centrifuge—
Both Are Now Empty, Work Is Authorized

a

1st
Work
Center

2nd
Work
Center

Both Squares Are Full,
Work Is Not Authorized at the 1st Work Center

b

For squares to work, the people in adjacent operations must be able to see one another. Containers like carts and boxes are popular as kanbans because they combine two functions: they protect the material inside, and they act as work authorizations. When containers are used, the adjacent operations don't have to be in visual contact with one another. One operation can be in one department and the next operation in another department, or even another building. When the empty container is returned to an operation, it serves as a work authorization to make more of that item.

Cards are also popular kanban signals. When a card returns to an operation, it is an authorization to make more product. The card itself indicates the quantity. When production of an item is complete, the card is sent along with the work to the next operation. When these recently manufactured items are used, the card is returned, authorizing a replacement of the items.

A variation on the use of cards is the use of labeled golf balls. These golf balls have been imprinted with the item number and quantity. They roll down a chute to the previous work center, authorizing production.

As you can see, the number of ways to signal that an operation should make more is only limited by the imagination. Anything that communicates the information from one work center to another can be used as a kanban.

Whatever the specific mechanism—containers, cards, spaces, golf balls, etc.—kanban limits the work-in-process. There are two squares in Figure 9.2, so the maximum amount of work-in-process is four items (centrifuges in this case). That's one in the first operation, two in the two squares between the first and second operations, and one in the second operation.

Despite the seemingly limitless number of kanbans you can create, all kanbans fall into two categories. Bill Sandras, in his book, *Just-in-Time: Making It Happen* (Oliver Wight Publications) identifies brand-name and generic kanbans. Brand-name kanbans mean "Replace what you used up." If you just made item number 347294, which is a circuit board for a telephone switch, then the kanban says, "Make more of the same item." Where there are limited numbers of items to be produced, such kanbans work well. For example, Figure 9.3a shows brand-name kanbans for two different circuit boards.

As the number of items increases, however, brand-name kanbans become increasingly more cumbersome. If there were a hundred differ-

Figure 9.3a   Brand-Name Kanbans

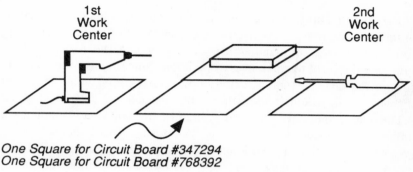

One Square for Circuit Board #347294
One Square for Circuit Board #768392

a

Figure 9.3b   Generic Kanbans

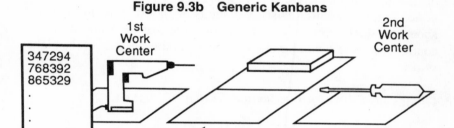

Two Squares, Both for Any Type of Circuit Board

b

ent items being manufactured, there could be hundreds of items between operations. This would create a large work-in-process, and consume a great deal of floor space. In the JIT framework, both work-in-process and floor space are considered waste, and should therefore be eliminated.

The way to eliminate that waste is to use generic kanbans. Figure 9.3b shows the same circuit board being manufactured, only this time with generic kanbans. When a kanban square is empty, work is authorized, but the item to be manufactured in this case is not necessarily what was used up. Instead, the item to be produced is based on the schedule. When a kanban square next opens up, the first item to be manufactured will be circuit board number 347294; when another kanban square opens up, circuit board number 768392 will be produced; and so on. With generic kanbans, the kanban square provides the signal to produce, and the schedule tells people *what* to produce.

Summary: Kanban

Where Just-in-Time is being implemented or used, kanbans are likely to be the primary tool for controlling the movement of work on the plant floor. The increased manufacturing velocity and the focus on flow eliminate the need to track every operation. Since items move quickly through the various manufacturing steps, such tracking would be a form of "waste"—it wouldn't add value to the product.

The degree of control provided by brand-name and generic kanbans is sufficient to run the business. Consider a turbine blade that takes five weeks to complete in a traditional manufacturing environment. If there are twenty manufacturing operations, operation completions are being posted every day or so. In a Just-in-Time environment, the same turbine blade may be manufactured in a few hours, or a day or two at most. The same degree of control exists; the status of the work is updated with about the same frequency. The difference is that the same degree of control is achieved with far fewer reporting points because of the higher velocity.

OPERATION SCHEDULING/SHOP-FLOOR CONTROL

"Shop-floor control is our best success," says Stan Grubbs, MIS supervisor at Boeing Defense & Space. "We were used to having a large amount of behind-schedule work in our shop. That was just the way we'd always operated. People felt it was always going to be that way. We had things coming in late, problems with vendors, all the normal sort of problems. People just didn't feel there was much we could do about it.

"We really started focusing our shop and scheduling people on the release of orders on time. Then we began measuring the MRP performance at each cost center. At the beginning, we were delivering about 20 to 30 percent of product on schedule. That was one reason people were so discouraged about working on this issue. It seemed as if the goal was unreachable.

"We actually put together a plan for attaining 95 percent on-time performance. It involved working out the global issues within manufacturing, scheduling, and process engineering. We predicted almost to plus or minus 5 percent how long it would take us to achieve 95 percent. It was based on getting issues resolved and continuing to focus on the measures. This year, we had better than 95 percent on-time delivery of product out of our shop. It was a real success story. It really came from continuing to challenge people to get at the root causes of our scheduling problems, and refusing to accept any excuses."

Stan's experience is typical of many companies using operation scheduling, or shop-floor control as it's commonly called. Operation scheduling originated in complex job-shop environments with disconnected flow—environments in which, for instance, a work order goes from one work center (say, a milling machine) to the next (say, a punch press), then on to another department for degreasing and painting, and is finally brought back for a final boring operation. At each work center there is a queue, and work is taken from the queue and run through the center, then moved to the next operation. Shop-floor control systems track a work order through every operation. They are usually updated when:

1. a work order is moved from one operation to the next

2. a setup is completed on a work order at a particular operation

3. pieces are completed at an operation

4. all pieces are complete through an operation

Figure 9.4 shows a work order using shop-floor control. As the report shows, the first operation has been completed and the work is waiting in queue at the second operation.

Figure 9.4a Work Order Status Rail

Sequence	Description	Work Center	Quantity Complete	Status
10	Mill	9013	30	Complete
20	Punch	8016		In Queue
30	Degrease	6002		
40	Paint	6150		
50	Bore	9021		

Today a number of companies are using bar codes to simplify the data entry for shop-floor control transactions. In addition, many are eliminating some of the transactions entirely.

"We have 20 or 30 routing steps," explains Frank Wetzel, director of materials and systems at Sealed Power. "Initially, we tried traditional shop-floor control reporting, in which people would report completion of each routing step. In many cases, product flowed so quickly through those steps that we couldn't collect it fast enough. In addition, we found that a dispatch list with 30 routing steps on it for many orders was an unmanageable tool. The shop foremen and shop superintendents could not use it.

"The system required a lot of additional reporting from our people, and for no good reason. We still needed a dispatch list. Our process at that point took three weeks; we're down to two weeks now for a plain piston ring, with 30 steps. So we needed to manage priorities, but we didn't need to manage priorities at each operation. So we took the shop people and identified milestones—key resources. It turned out that the same resources we used for rough-cut capacity planning became our milestone reporting resources. We reported flow through those resources only. That meant the dispatch was reduced to four or five work centers. The priorities could still be maintained because we had due dates through those work centers."

The issue here is degree of control. As with the production schedule and kanban, the question is "What level of control is needed?" Reporting transactions at a level of detail not needed to control the business is a form of waste, and therefore it should be eliminated.

Another solution to the problem of excessive reporting is to create cells. If five operations are done in a cell, the routing for the item will be reduced if all five operations are combined into a single routing step. Reporting for shop-floor control will happen only at the end of the cell, and a dispatch list will exist for the cell, not for the individual operations that happen within the cell.

Operation Scheduling

In addition to providing tracking capabilities, shop-floor control also provides important scheduling information to the people on the factory floor. It calculates when an operation should be started and completed to meet the scheduled due date. This is the same calculation used in capacity planning to determine the date for capacity requirements. It's done by taking the order due date and back-scheduling each operation using the scheduling rules, as illustrated in Figure 9.4b. If the order is to be completed on the 15th, then the boring operation (the last operation) needs to be started and completed on the 15th, the paint operation should be finished on the 14th, and so on.

Figure 9.4b   Work Order Status Rail

Sequence	Description	Work Center	Start Date	Due Date
10	Mill	9013	4/05	4/05
20	Punch	8016	4/07	4/11
30	Degrease	6002	4/13	4/13
40	Paint	6150	4/14	4/14
50	Bore	9021	4/15	4/15

Some companies create special scheduling rules. If extra time is needed for "curing" an epoxy compound, that could be part of the scheduling rules for the item.

Once these operation-start and operation-due dates have been calculated, they can be displayed for the people in the factory. Figure 9.5 is an example of a dispatch list produced by a shop-floor control system.

Notice in Figure 9.5 that the work orders are arranged by the start date of each operation. Also listed for each work order is the due date of the operation (when it should be completed at the work center) as well as the due date for the order (when all the operations for the item should be completed). This information enables the manufacturing supervisors to identify work orders that are behind schedule, so that they can work with the capacity planner to develop solutions. In the event that they are unable to develop solutions that would allow a work order to be completed by its due date, it is their responsibility to get back to the material planner.

This report also shows the work order number, order quantity, and the status of the order (in queue at this operation, the number of pieces completed at this operation, operation complete, on hold, and so on).

Figure 9.5 Vertical Mill

Today's Date: 4/12

Item	Quantity	Order Number	Operation Number	Operation Start	Operation Due	Order Due	Hours	Status
—Jobs at This Work Center—								
35378	500	52895	20	4/13	4/15	4/19	11	Queue
69359	250	69359	15	4/16	4/16	5/04	6	Queue
48571	140	48571	30	4/19	4/20	4/25	14	Queue
—Jobs Coming to This Work Center—								
65773	100	58741	40	4/10	4/10	4/20	6	Run
58741	800	69347	30	4/16	4/19	4/23	14	Setup
98321	225	28767	12	4/20	4/22	4/30	19	Hold

The dispatch list shows the jobs at each work center and lists the work orders in queue as well as those that are to arrive during the next few days.

Why Shop-Floor Control Is Important

The people on the factory floor are responsible for meeting the due dates—both the operation due dates and the order due dates. Shop-floor control is simply a tool to help make that happen. The tracking and monitoring aspect of shop-floor control shows the location and status of a job. The scheduling aspect indicates when each operation should be started and completed. Therefore, you can use shop-floor control to evaluate a job relative to the schedule. If it's behind schedule, this information motivates the manufacturing supervisor to look at the situation and think about how to get the job back on track and complete by its due date. "Do we need to add capacity? Cut the order quantity and run a partial lot? Speed up the process? Eliminate the move and queue by moving it quickly from one operation to the next and working on it immediately? Perhaps overlap operations?" Again, there are many choices for solving the problem. But each solution requires the manufacturing supervisors to be aware of the problem; shop-floor control makes the problem visible so the supervisors can go about choosing the best solution.

Operation Scheduling Activities

Shop-floor control is primarily a tool for the manufacturing supervisors and the machine operators on the manufacturing floor who actually perform the work. The most common use for the dispatch list is to identify which job to work on next. To illustrate this use, we'll refer to the dispatch list shown in Figure 9.5. We want to answer the question "Which is the next item that should be started at this work center?" Item number 35378 has the earliest operation start date, and it's physically in queue in front of the work center. This item, however, is not overdue to start. In the section of the dispatch list that shows the jobs coming to the work center over the next few days, item number 65773 is overdue to start, but it hasn't been moved to this work center and may not be available.

The person using the dispatch list should call the previous work center to learn where this job (item number 65773) is before starting a job that will tie up the work center for several days. It may mean a delay of an hour or so to wait for this late job to arrive, but waiting to find out the status of item number 65773 will eliminate several additional days of delay, which in turn could make a significant difference in getting the late order back on schedule.

The preceding example illustrates the fact that the people on the manufacturing floor are expected to use their experience to make decisions on which job to assign next. The decisions may be made by the manufacturing supervisors, the capacity planners, or the machine operators. The person using the dispatch list to make these decisions will vary from company to company, and even in different divisions or plants within the same company. In an organization in which the operators are highly experienced and are permitted by management to work with minimal supervision, they may be the ones who make the decisions. If a department is critically behind schedule, customer orders are being shipped late, and the work force is not as experienced in both the manufacturing processes and the company, then the supervisor or the supervisor working with the capacity planner may make the decisions.

Another important use for the dispatch list is to identify orders that are in danger of being late. Let's assume that the phone call to check on item number 65773 yields bad news: Not only is the item not ready, but it will not be ready for another two days. This means that item number 65773 is likely to miss the order due date. The manufacturing supervisor is expected to develop a solution, possibly working with other supervisors. The operation scheduling information gives clear and accurate warnings of jobs that are behind schedule so people can work on solutions to meet the due dates. Jobs that are significantly late to the operation-start and operation-due dates need to be reviewed. The review can be as simple as noting that the job will catch up because it will go to the top of the dispatch list at every operation, and there are 10 more operations over the next four weeks before the due date. It's also possible that some action is required—for example, if the job is authorized for 24-hour operation and move and queue times are to be minimized or eliminated.

Sometimes productivity savings can be achieved using the dispatch list. For example, in a situation in which the first work order on a list is an item made from aluminum, the second is made from brass, and the third is made from aluminum, it's necessary to clean out the chips in the machines each time the operator changes from one metal from another. For productivity reasons, it would make more sense to run the two aluminum jobs together, and the brass job before or after. If, according to the dispatch list, there's enough time for all the jobs to meet their due date and yet be grouped together in the most productive sequence, then the people using the dispatch list have the freedom to do such a grouping. Again, the dispatch list and the planning system in general are simply providing information that can be used to run the business more effectively.

Most companies provide some guidelines that are used to make scheduling decisions on the factory floor. Jim Correll, a leading authority on operation scheduling, suggests that companies set up a series of guidelines that contain the following elements:

1. The dispatch list is the only priority tool in the factory. If someone comes to you with a hot list, don't accept it. If there's some reason why the dispatch list isn't giving correct information, then fix the list—don't revert to the informal system.

2. If you're behind schedule, work in the sequence shown on the dispatch list. Productivity is a secondary issue at this point— the major objective is to meet the demands for production in the master schedule.

3. If you're on or ahead of schedule, and you can resequence work to do it more productively without missing any due dates, then do so.

4. If an item is going to miss its due date, that information needs to get back to the material planner.

Different organizations may expand on rules or add additional ones that are specific to themselves. Generally, though, guidelines like the ones above are in place at companies doing operation scheduling.

Integration with Kanban

In many situations, kanban eliminates or significantly reduces the need for a shop-floor control system. In the case of brand-name kanbans, for example, there is no need for shop-floor control. Where generic kanbans are being used, a dispatch list or a production schedule is used to tell the first operation what to make, and kanban controls some or all of the subsequent operations.

As companies move to greater uses of kanban, cells, and focused factories with flow-type layouts, the need for tools such as shop-floor control is likely to diminish. All of these approaches significantly speed the flow of material and simplify the scheduling.

Operation Scheduling Measurements

The primary measurement in shop-floor control is 95 percent or better on-time performance to the order due date within a specified tolerance. The tolerance will vary by company and industry. A typical tolerance would be plus or minus 2 days.

Another measurement is the number of past-due operations on the dispatch list. An easy way to assess performance in this area is to walk out onto the factory floor and pick up a dispatch list. If many of the operations are past due, the formal system has clearly broken down. If, on the other hand, the dispatch list for a work center has only one or two operations past due, then the schedules are valid and credible. While this is not as clearly quantifiable as, say, 95 percent on-time performance, it's a useful measurement in assessing the health of a shop-floor control system.

Summary: Operation Scheduling/Shop-Floor Control

Operation scheduling, or shop-floor control as it's more commonly called, is generally used in complex job-shop environments with disconnected flow. The level of control needed in this type of manufacturing requires scheduling by operation rather than just by item. Operation schedule dates are needed to assess where work is relative to its completion date, and status reporting on the different operations is needed to track the progress of the work.

Strategically, the manufacturing world is moving to flow. Faster throughput, less inventory, and reduced costs are all powerful incentives for change. As we see more companies adopting flow environments, there will be more and more use for kanban and production schedules, and less use of shop-floor control. It would be premature, however, to write the obituary for shop-floor control. It works well in the environment for which it was intended, and that environment is not likely to disappear altogether in the foreseeable future.

INPUT-OUTPUT CONTROL

Input-output control is the means of verifying that the capacity plan is being executed as planned. Input-output control is seen most often in job-shop, disconnected-flow environments in conjunction with capacity requirements planning and shop-floor control. It can, however, be applied to almost any situation in which capacity planning is being done.

Figure 9.6 shows the output side of input-output control for a particular work center, in this case a group of milling machines.

You can see in Figure 9.6 that the planned output is 112 standard hours per week, but the actual output is less than this amount, yielding a cumulative deviation over four weeks of minus 76 standard hours. In other words, the work center is not producing the expected hours of output. The first question to ask would be: "Is the work coming into the work center?" The input side of the input-output report provides this information to a planner (Figure 9.7).

This report shows that the planned input is 112 standard hours per week. The actual input is fairly close to that, as seen by the cumulative deviation of 4 standard hours. It's clear from these numbers that the work is flowing into the work center but not coming out. Therefore, this work center is the problem. If the work weren't coming into the work center, then the problem would be "upstream."

In a job-shop environment with jobs moving in a network fashion, it's sometimes difficult to identify the problem, especially when multiple work centers contribute to the situation. By looking at the input-output control reports, planners can clearly see which are the problem work centers, even in a complex network of interconnected work centers.

Figure 9.6   Input-Output Control—Output Side

Vertical Milling

	-4	-3	-2	-1	1	2	3	4
Planned Output	112	112	112	112	112	112	112	112
Actual Output	90	97	95	90				
Cumulative Deviation	-22	-37	-54	-76				

Today

Figure 9.7   Input-Output Control—Input Side

Vertical Milling

	-4	-3	-2	-1	1	2	3	4
Planned Output	112	112	112	112	112	112	112	112
Actual Output	114	115	116	107				
Cumulative Deviation	+2	+5	+9	+4				

Today

Planned Quantity = 40
Actual Quantity = 116
Tolerance = 30

Why Is Input-Output Control Important?

Many companies do capacity planning but never monitor the execution of the plan. Unfortunately, the cumulative effects of small capacity shortfalls can be significant, yet insidious. For example, assume a 10 percent shortfall in output at a milling work center when compared to the plan. At the end of 10 weeks, the work center is 1 week behind, and virtually every job is now late—based on a tolerance of 2 days. At the end of a year, the work center is *5 weeks behind!* Not many companies can afford to lose 5 weeks' production out of a year. So it's not the individual variations but the cumulative effect that takes a toll.

To identify problem work centers, and not respond to minor fluctuations in the numbers, companies establish tolerances. Whenever the cumulative deviation for either input or output exceeds a predetermined number of hours, action must be taken to correct the situation. Experience has shown that it's much easier to solve a problem if you know what the boundaries are ahead of time. In the case of the milling work center described above, the number is 30 hours. Since the cumulative deviation is out of tolerance, the manufacturing supervisor responsible for this work center must take action to correct the problem. A planning and control system doesn't solve problems—it simply identifies them so people can do something about them. This particular problem with the milling work center may be a quality problem, an equipment breakdown problem, a manpower problem, and so on.

The Lead Time Syndrome

The other reason why input-output control is important is the control of lead times. The largest and most variable component of lead times in a job-shop environment is the queue time. Figure 9.8a shows the buildup in queue for the milling work center, from 40 standard hours (a little less than two days in queue time) to 116 hours (over a week).

Unfortunately, when something like this occurs, people often launch a massive assault on the problem. If, for example, a particular department is behind schedule, the instinctive response is to allow more lead time for the items that go through that area. But if a capacity problem is the reason the department is behind schedule, this only aggravates the situation. If the lead times are increased, let's say by one week on the

Figures 9.8a and 9.8b   Queue at Milling Work Center

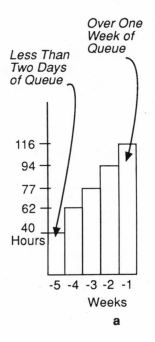

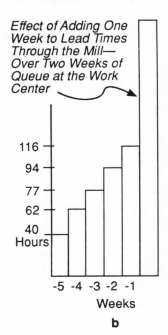

milling equipment because it's behind schedule, this only dumps more work into the work center. Instead of an average of 112 standard hours per week coming into the work center, an increase in lead times will temporarily increase the input rate to something like 224 standard hours the following week. This is because all 112 hours of work that would have been released next week are released now, in addition to the work for the week after that (112 hours now due for release because of the added lead time through the milling work center). Work in all the other weeks will also be shifted by a week, so work that was in week 5 will move to week 4 and so on. This is shown in Figure 9.8b.

The net effect of this action is to dump more work into the work center, but not get any more out. Remember, though, the problem with the mills wasn't a lack of work going into the work center, but a lack of output coming from the work center. Increasing the lead time therefore makes the problem worse, not better. The solution is to either increase the flow of work out of the work center or reduce the flow of work into the work center.

The Data for Input-Output Control

The data on the input-output report come from a number of different sources. Shop-floor control generates the actual input and output numbers, since it records the movement and completion of each operation.

The *actual output* line is based on the operation completion transactions. If an operation is finished and required 30 standard hours, then 30 standard hours are shown as the actual output in the specified time period (most people use time periods of weeks, although it is possible to use days).

The *planned output* line comes from the manufacturing supervisor. The manufacturing supervisor commits to a number of hours that can be produced from the work center. This is the planned capacity.

The *actual input* side of the input-output report results from the move transactions in the shop-floor control system, where move transactions are used. If move transactions are not used, then the actual input to a work center is based on the operation-complete transactions at the previous work center. If an operation is worth 30 standard hours and it gets moved into the work center today, then 30 standard hours get added to the actual input for the time period.

The *planned input* side is taken from capacity requirements planning.

If the CRP summary report for the work center shows 112 standard hours per week as capacity requirements, then 112 standard hours per week are shown as planned input for the time period.

The *cumulative deviations* are based on simple math: The calculation takes the planned input and the actual input and compares them. The same calculation is done with the output side.

The *tolerances* are numbers agreed to by the capacity planner and the manufacturing supervisor. When do you have a problem? If 10 hours of cumulative deviation is not a problem, but at 50 hours you'll begin to miss schedules, then the tolerance is somewhere between 10 and 50 hours. Most companies pick a number that seems reasonable—50 percent of the planned queue, for example—and revise it if necessary.

The *planned queue* is a target set by the capacity planner and manufacturing supervisors. It's the amount of work they want to put in front of the work center. The larger the queue, the longer the lead time and the larger the work-in-process. The objective should be to reduce the size of the queue. On the other hand, queues serve a useful purpose by evening out the uneven flow of work into work centers. If jobs of 20 and 30 hours are moved into a work center with a weekly capacity of 40 hours, then it makes sense to have some planned queue to even out the large peaks and valleys in work flow. In keeping with the Just-in-Time philosophy, however, it makes sense to ask why it's necessary to have these peaks and valleys. Why can't the flow of work be more uniform, more linear? If it were, then the queues could be reduced.

Who Does Input-Output Control?

The capacity planner meets with the manufacturing supervisors to review the input-output control report. This is done in the same meeting where the capacity requirements planning reports are reviewed. In the same way that overloads and underloads are discussed, work centers that have exceeded the tolerance on either input or output are identified. Working together, the manufacturing supervisors identify possible solutions. Again, if they cannot agree on a solution, they can appeal to their respective managers for a decision, although this is rarely necessary.

In some cases, any number of people may be brought into the problem-solving process. For example, if there's a tooling problem, then machine operators, manufacturing supervisors, toolmakers, and engineers may all get involved.

Input-Output Control Measurements

The primary measurement in input-output control is 95 percent or better conformance to planned output. In other words, if the planned output out of a particular work center was 75 standard hours per week, did the work center actually produce those hours?

In some companies there are situations in which the average hours agree with the plan but there are significant week-to-week variations. For example, a large, complex welded assembly might be worth 100 standard hours of welding. On the day the assembly is completed, the work center is credited with 100 standard hours as actual output. But in the prior week, while workers were welding the assembly, the work center wasn't credited with any output because no operations were completed. In that case, the actual output for the work center will be quite lumpy: 0 hours one week and 100 hours the next. If the planned output for the welding work center is 50 standard hours per week, then over a two-week period the work center has achieved the planned output. One solution is to report partial completion of the work—in this example, 50 hours the first week and the remainder the next week.

In other situations, it might not be acceptable for a work center to fall short of its target every day. For example, in a high-volume chemical plant there may not be enough storage to hold the raw materials and intermediates if one plant doesn't achieve its production rate for the day. In this case, if a plant doesn't achieve its rate, there is a problem and someone should look for solutions. Is it a quality problem? An equipment problem? A training problem? Whatever the nature, it must be tracked down and solved.

Summary: Input-Output Control

Like operation scheduling, input-output control is generally used in complex job-shop environments with disconnected flow. The networked movement of material makes it difficult to find problem work centers. In addition, problems are constantly shifting, with one work center being a problem today, and another a problem next week. For all these reasons, a tool is needed to clearly identify those work centers where solutions are needed.

Input-output control is this tool. It clearly identifies work centers that are not executing to the plan. Information on the status of the different work centers is up to date.

As the use of capacity requirements planning and shop-floor control decreases, so will the use of input-output control. But, as mentioned above, it would be premature to write the obituary for any of these techniques. They work well in the environment for which they are meant, and that environment will exist for some time to come.

SUMMARY/CHECKUP

1. Production schedules, kanban, and operation scheduling (shop-floor control) all work. This is because each is suited to the manufacturing environment in which it is deployed. The objective is the same: to effectively communicate the schedules, and to provide a sufficient degree of control to assist people in meeting their delivery commitments. The methods differ because the requirements are different.

2. The production schedule is a simple and effective way to communicate the schedule in a manufacturing environment in which scheduling is done by item, not by operation. Production schedules are used in industries such as chemical manufacturing and food processing, and in high-volume repetitive manufacturing, in which the need to track every operation is unnecessary and the cost is prohibitive. Should a production schedule be used to communicate the schedules in your company?

3. Where Just-in-Time is being implemented or used, kanbans are likely to be the primary tools for controlling the movement of work on the plant floor. The increased manufacturing velocity and the focus on flow eliminate the need to track every operation. Brand-name and generic kanbans provide the degree of control needed to run the business. Should kanban be used to control the movement of work in your company?

4. Operation scheduling, or shop-floor control as it's more commonly called, is generally used in complex job-shop environments with disconnected flow. The level of control needed in this type of manufacturing requires scheduling by operation, rather than just by item. Operation

schedule dates are used to assess where work is relative to its completion date, and status reporting on the different operations is used to track the progress of the work. Should shop-floor control be used to calculate operation schedule dates, communicate the schedules, and track progress in your company?

5. The primary measurement in plant scheduling is 95 percent or better on-time performance to the order due date within a specified tolerance. The tolerance will vary by company and industry, ranging from zero to several days. What is the level of on-time performance in your company? What are the tolerances?

It should be clear from this chapter that there are many reasons why plant scheduling is an important activity. All these reasons are valid for suppliers, since suppliers are plants just with different ownership and locations from your own plants. The next chapter explains supplier scheduling.

SPECIAL ACKNOWLEDGMENTS

James Correll for his work with operations scheduling, and William Sandras for his contributions on kanban.

Chapter Ten

Supplier Scheduling

"Probably our most significant effort in purchasing was supplier scheduling," explains Stan Grubbs, MIS supervisor at Boeing Defense & Space. "The results achieved with pilot vendors on supplier scheduling were just phenomenal. We had vendors perform at 100 percent delivery for several months. Once they understood the system, the vendors were really excited. One reason these results were significant was that many of our suppliers deliver hundreds of different parts. Some of the initial pilot vendors were our higher-volume vendors. Their results were just staggering, really overwhelming to people, as was the whole idea that you could initiate this type of long-term relationship with suppliers.

"Our material scheduling folks are working with suppliers to schedule deliveries," Grubbs continues. "We have some people delivering weekly or every other week now. That's been a real change for us. In the past, we would try to take delivery of three months of inventory at a time. It took a while for people to understand it. But once we moved to more frequent, incremental deliveries, the vendors were much more responsive."

This doesn't sound like the adversarial vendor relationships that exist in many companies. The conventional wisdom says, "Keep them in the dark, play them off against one another, and make sure they know you'll pull your business from them in an instant."

203

There is still plenty of work for those tough, crusty, men-of-few-words purchasing managers who have perfected the "big-stick" approach to dealing with suppliers, but there is less of it every day, because more and more companies have made their supplier relationships more team-oriented, with specific objectives and expected results. Teams work inside the plant—the entire company benefits when sales, manufacturing, engineering, and finance work as a team—and external teams work equally well. When a company and its suppliers work as a team, both organizations benefit.

PROVIDING SCHEDULING INFORMATION TO SUPPLIERS

One aspect of working *with* suppliers rather than *against* them is providing scheduling information. The supplier schedule is a document that gives your suppliers information about what you need and when you need it (to the best of your knowledge). That seems rather straightforward, doesn't it? Wouldn't everybody want to do it? Not necessarily, for several reasons.

As mentioned above, some people simply don't trust their suppliers. It's difficult to "keep them in the dark and play them off against each other" if they have your planned schedule of purchases.

Second, many companies don't have a valid material plan. If you don't know what you really need, your supplier won't either. By providing a valid material plan, however, you can tell the suppliers what you think you'll need and they won't have to guess about it. After all, who's more likely to be correct about your needs—you, or someone outside the company? Unless a company's schedules are completely out of control, its own estimates will be considerably better than those of an outsider who doesn't know the company's master production schedule or inventory. If you can help your suppliers to run their businesses better, everyone in the loop will operate more efficiently and enjoy the accrued cost savings.

Surveys have shown that companies using supplier scheduling consistently get much higher delivery performance and much lower purchase costs than companies that don't. In an Oliver Wight survey, companies using hard-copy purchase orders reported 76 percent on-time delivery performance and a 2 percent reduction in annual purchase costs. Companies using supplier schedules and supplier schedulers reported 95 percent on-time deliveries and an 11 percent decrease in annual purchase costs. In the average manufacturing company, these kind of results translate into significant dollar savings. (For a more detailed explanation of this subject, see *Purchasing in the 21st Century* by John Schorr, published by Oliver Wight Publications).

Where do these savings come from?

Bob Dickson, executive vice-president and vice-president for purchasing at Mass Merchandisers, Inc. (MMI), a distribution company that uses DRP to feed its supplier schedule, explains: "It used to take half a day to order an item from a vendor, from beginning to printed purchase order. This can now be done in three seconds. Buyers have more time today to manage and make better decisions."

Steve Nelson, director of inventory management systems at MMI, expands on what happens if buyers can spend more time doing professional purchasing and less on paperwork and expediting: "Today, a buyer of an unfamiliar product line can manage inventories as effectively as someone who has been in the business for years. For example, in 1986 we picked up a specialty food business, which added over 5,000 items to our product list. Within six weeks, we were managing the inventories more effectively than the original owners had ever been able to do and we had no expertise with this product line. The new superior level of information allows us to make scientific judgments about what we are trying to do in planning for the future rather than spend all our time reacting to what was killing us yesterday."

THE SUPPLIER SCHEDULE

Phil Presti, purchasing manager at Valleylab, describes his company's supplier scheduling system. "We download the schedule for seven or eight of our bigger suppliers off the main system. That gives us the demand by week for the first 10 weeks, and then we go into four-week buckets beyond that point. We go anywhere from six to nine months out with that schedule. A zone is set that locks in the requirement with a purchase order number. We assign a PO number to that release at a certain point—whatever we've negotiated with the supplier, 4 weeks or 10 or 12 weeks. Beyond that, there is another zone—we call it the raw material zone. We permit the supplier to go out and buy raw material in support of the requirements that fall within that zone. Beyond that zone, it's just information for planning purposes. Typically we set up one PO for the whole year, and just add releases to it.

"There was a lot of skepticism at first from our suppliers because we didn't have the best reputation for maintaining schedules and they wondered how we were going to be able to do this with any consistency," says Presti. "But it's gone great. There are very few phone calls. You mail the schedule out, parts come in. We negotiate a price at the beginning of the year—same price for every release—so that's fixed, and we don't have to talk about that.

"At first," Presti continues, "we stalled somewhat because we were concerned about having formal contracts in place with a lot of these suppliers. We felt the schedule didn't really contain it. As we've moved along, we haven't seen a major need for very complicated contracts. We went a little bit more slowly than we could have—it was something new to us."

Valleylab's experience with supplier scheduling is typical of the experience of many companies. The schedule itself, the zones, and the contracts are all issues that each company has to address.

At Valleylab, MIS creates a file on the main frame from the material plan and downloads it into a personal computer for printing by the purchasing people. Other companies generate the supplier schedule on their mainframe computers. Both methods work. Figure 10.1 is an example of a supplier schedule.

The quantities in the first three weeks indicate commitments, the next two weeks are in the material zone, and the remaining numbers are planning information for the supplier.

In the *committed zone,* the quantities in the supplier schedule are treated the same way as a purchase order. As Presti explained, Valleylabs attaches a purchase order number to each quantity.

In the *material zone,* the quantities in the supplier schedule constitute a commitment for material but not labor. This authorizes the supplier to purchase the material, but not to start work on the items—a useful approach in situations in which material can be difficult to get. Rather than have the supplier wait for a commitment, then order material, only to find that the needed material is not available and therefore the supplier will miss deliveries, the customer uses a different and more cooperative approach. With this approach, the supplier will not be stuck with the

Figure 10.1   Supplier Schedule and Zones

Weeks

	1	2	3	4	5	6	7	8
Tan Bracket				250				250
Black Bracket	300							
Clear Bracket								
Tan Housing			600					

■   ■

■   ■

■   ■

Red Housing						400		

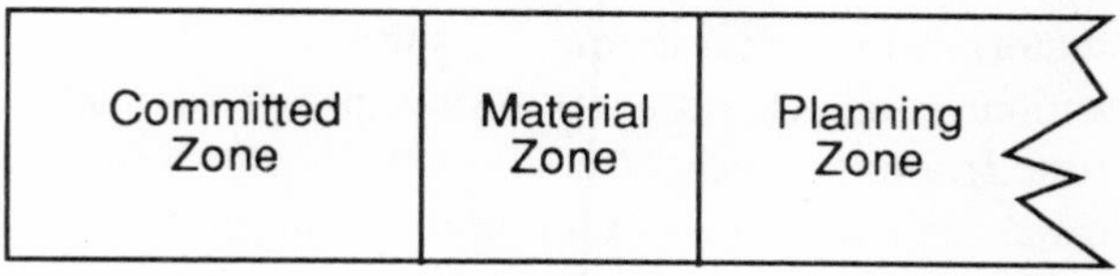

Committed Zone	Material Zone	Planning Zone

raw material inventory. If the schedule changes and the raw material will not be used, the supplier can bill for the inventory, which is now owned by the customer and can be used for future production. In exchange for this commitment, the supplier is expected to deliver on time.

This approach is also helpful in retaining flexibility on the mix of items being purchased. For example, one company purchased circuit breakers from a supplier that quoted 21 weeks for delivery. No amount of negotiation could budge this supplier, because it took 15 weeks for the supplier to get the raw material. The customer pointed out that the same raw material was used to make nearly all the circuit breakers, and it took only 2 weeks to manufacture a circuit breaker. The customer agreed to commit to the material costs 21 weeks out, but in exchange wanted the flexibility to change the type of circuit breaker up until 3 weeks before the scheduled delivery. In this case, the committed zone was 3 weeks, and the material zone was 21 weeks.

Finally, the quantities in the *planning zone* are for the supplier's planning purposes only. While this information does not constitute a commitment, it does provide a benefit to both the customer and the supplier. Rather than having to guess, the supplier gets excellent visibility into the customer's future demands. Rather than having to deal with lengthening lead times, the customer is "in the supplier's schedule" as far out into the future as the supplier schedule goes. This is because the supplier understands that if he cannot make the deliveries shown in the supplier schedule, he must get back to the customer.

JUST-IN-TIME SUPPLIER SCHEDULES

In a Just-in-Time environment, the supplier schedule typically has smaller time periods—days instead of weeks—and a more repetitive pattern to the quantities. Figure 10.2 is an example of such a schedule.

In a Just-in-Time supplier schedule, some of the zones may be eliminated. For example, some companies provide the supplier schedule as planning information only, and use kanban to authorize the delivery of material. In this situation, the supplier schedule is used for planning and kanban is used to create the commitment to produce. Notice also that the time frame for the zones is much shorter, reflecting the shortened lead times typical of Just-in-Time manufacturing.

There are a number of ways to communicate the supplier schedule, the most basic being to print out the schedule and put it in the mail or fax it. But more and more companies are using electronic data interchange (EDI) to communicate the schedules electronically. Any of these methods can work. The important thing is the communication, not the form it takes.

Another important aspect is the notification of changes. If suppliers have to compare the old and new schedules for changes, they're not likely to be too enthusiastic. For this reason, it's important to show the current schedule and highlight the changes so they're easy to see.

Presti's experience at Valleylabs points up the concerns many people have about purchasing contracts. A purchase order is a contract and a schedule rolled into one document. With supplier scheduling, the contract and the schedule are separated. The contract is arranged ahead of

Figure 10.2   Just-in-Time Supplier Schedule and Zones

Days

	1	2	3	4	5	6	7	8
Tan Bracket	30	30	30	30	30	30	30	30
Black Bracket	35	35	35	35	35	35	35	35
Clear Bracket	5	5	5	5	5	5	5	5
Tan Housing	75	75	75	75	75	75	75	75
Red Housing	50	50	50	50	50	50	50	50

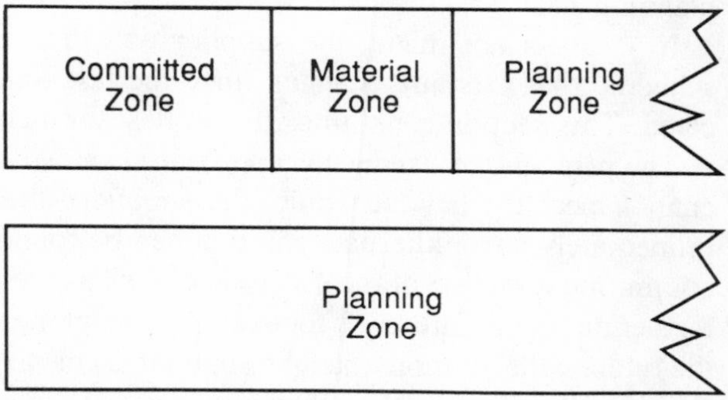

Committed Zone	Material Zone	Planning Zone

Planning Zone

time. In Presti's situation, the company and suppliers negotiate the contract once a year. The schedule, on the other hand, is constantly changing. As a result, supplier schedules are communicated frequently—at least weekly, and sometimes more often.

WHO DOES SUPPLIER SCHEDULING?

The supplier scheduler, buyer, and supplier are most directly involved with supplier scheduling. The responsibilities of these people are described below.

The supplier scheduler (or vendor scheduler, to use an older term) is responsible for managing the supplier schedule. The position of supplier scheduler is different from the position of buyer or purchasing agent.

The buyer is responsible for negotiating with the suppliers—defining the specifications, the quality levels, the price, and so on. In effect, the buyer sets up the buy, and the supplier scheduler works out the individual deliveries. The buyer typically doesn't come back into the process unless the supplier scheduler is having a serious problem with the supplier.

The supplier's role in using the supplier schedule is to meet the due dates or communicate any problems to the supplier scheduler. In the event of a significant change to the supplier schedule, the supplier scheduler will typically call the supplier to discuss the situation prior to sending a revised schedule. If the change is inside the committed zone, the supplier has made a commitment, and the supplier scheduler is asking for a new commitment. If the change is in the planning zone, the scheduler may or may not choose to call ahead of time. A call will typically not be made if the change is relatively minor or is out in the planning zone.

If a call is not made, the supplier will look at the section on the schedule that lists any changes since the last schedule was communicated. This section constitutes the request for a change.

The principle of "silence is approval" is at work here. If the supplier cannot meet the new schedule, the supplier scheduler needs to know immediately so an alternate solution can be found. This applies to the commitment section of the schedule as well as the planning information farther out in the future. If, for example, the planning information out in the future calls for more than the supplier is able to produce, the supplier should call and make the scheduler aware of the situation.

What if the scheduler thinks that the supplier is going to be late, but has said nothing? It's important to emphasize that supplier schedulers as well as suppliers are accountable for delivery on time. For example, the supplier scheduler cannot get off the hook by saying, "The supplier told me the shipment would go out on Thursday."

It's important to emphasize that the objective is to develop honest communications with suppliers. This is a process that can take time, from the perspective of both sides. The purchasing group may think a supplier will promise whatever date the customer wants to hear, regardless of what will really happen. The supplier may see the customer as unable to provide valid schedules. As Presti commented, Valleylabs' suppliers were skeptical that they could deliver consistent schedules.

An education day for suppliers is an important element in generating trust and opening channels of communication. It does not create credibility, but it does prepare both groups for the process of *building* credibility. Credibility comes from both groups performing as advertised: the purchasing group providing valid schedules, and the supplier meeting its delivery commitments on time.

The role of the buyer is to work with suppliers on quality, price, and delivery. Many companies today are also including suppliers in the initial design of products, and the buyer would be included in this process as well.

In setting up a contract with a supplier, the buyer would use a negotiation report, like the one shown in Figure 10.3.

The information on this report is extracted from MRP—it's the planned orders for future delivery. These deliveries are sorted by commodity, and presented for the buyer to use when negotiating with suppliers. Thus, the buyer has the best available information on what material will be needed, and in what quantities. As a result, the buyer is not negotiating for 500 sheets of fiberglass sheet needed on short delivery. Instead, the buyer is negotiating for $236,460 of fiberglass products over the course of the year. This allows the buyer to do what is most effective for the company: spend money well.

SUPPLIER SCHEDULING MEASUREMENTS

"One thing we've done in purchasing is to measure our suppliers' performance against their promised delivery dates as well as their performance against the MRP need date," explains Boeing's Stan Grubbs. "We weren't formally doing that before the MRP project. After some intense discussions with our purchasing managers, we convinced them to actually track delivery dates manually, before our software was available. Our suppliers started achieving some improvement, and recognize new opportunities for further improvement. This step was very significant because one of the critical issues with releasing orders to the floor on time was the overall performance of our vendors. Getting the measurements out there very quickly made it possible for the vendors to see their own performance improve over time. It was difficult to convince people that it was necessary to do some things manually, but the

Figure 10.3 Supplier Negotiation Report
Commodity: Fiberglass

Item	Usage				Annual Usage	Unit Cost	Annual $
	1 Quarter	2 Quarter	3 Quarter	4 Quarter			
Sheets—.25 × 5 × 7	400	500	500	400	1,800	9.35	16,830
Sheets—.50 × 5 × 7	700	800	900	600	3,000	13.25	39,750
Sheets—.25 × 3 × 12	200	200	300	350	1,050	6.70	7,035
Sheets—.50 × 3 × 12	400	500	400	600	1,900	11.27	21,413
							22,160
Totals ■ ■ ■					22,160		■ ■ ■
							$236,460

purchasing supervisor has told me that he now sees why it was important for us to take this approach."

As Stan indicates, the primary measurement in supplier scheduling is on-time performance to the delivery date. The number most companies set as a goal is 95 percent or better on-time delivery performance within a specified tolerance. The tolerance will vary by company and industry. A typical tolerance is plus or minus several days. In the case of a daily schedule, a delivery is considered on-time if it arrives on the correct day.

Boeing also measures suppliers on their delivery compared to their need dates. This is different from the measurement above, which is how well the suppliers do compared to their promise dates.

SUPPLIER KANBAN

Kanbans can authorize work from a supplier in the same way they can authorize work within a plant. Beckman Instruments in Palo Alto, California, puts a "faxban" page on its fax machine, and sends the page to its supplier plant in Fullerton. A faxban is a kanban card that is faxed rather than delivered to the supplier (see Chapter 9 for details). As material is used in Fullerton, one of the operators on the kanban line puts a faxban page on the fax machine and authorizes material to be shipped from a steel supplier in Japan. In this way, each of the different levels in the supply chain is notified, and each level is working on the items needed by its customer.

In addition to faxbans, reusable containers are popular as supplier kanbans. An empty container returned to a supplier is an authorization to make more.

When used with a supplier schedule, kanban controls the timing of deliveries, and the supplier schedule provides planning information out into the future. The supplier looks at the supplier schedule to see the overall demand rate, and plans material and capacity to support this rate. The timing of individual quantities to be manufactured, however, is determined by the kanban triggers.

Summary: Supplier Kanban

Where Just-in-Time is being implemented or used, kanbans are an important tool for controlling the delivery of material from suppliers. A kanban can be a faxed page, a reusable container, or a card. Each serves as an authorization for the supplier to deliver material.

Where kanbans are used to trigger the delivery of materials from suppliers, a supplier schedule is also used to give the supplier visibility into the future. The supplier schedule enables suppliers to plan for material and labor, and the kanbans authorize work on specific items.

SUMMARY/CHECKUP

1. Companies today are abandoning the adversarial supplier relationships of the past. Suppliers are part of the team that develops and manufactures the company's products. What are the supplier relationships like in your company?

2. A purchase order is a schedule and a contract rolled into one document. Today, companies are separating these two, with a supplier scheduler managing the schedule and a buyer managing the contract. The supplier scheduler provides a supplier schedule to the suppliers showing the anticipated demands for the future. Does your company separate the contract and the schedule? Do you provide your suppliers with a supplier schedule?

3. In a Just-in-Time environment, a supplier schedule is provided for planning purposes, but the commitment to a supplier is provided by kanbans or faxbans. Do you use kanbans or faxbans with your suppliers?

4. The principle of "silence is approval" applies to suppliers as well as the plant. If the supplier cannot meet the new schedule, then the supplier scheduler needs to know immediately so an alternate solution can be found. Do your suppliers operate under a policy of "silence is approval"?

5. The primary measurement in supplier scheduling is 95 percent or better on-time performance to the order due date within a specified tolerance. The tolerance will vary by company and industry, ranging

from zero to several days. What is the level of supplier on-time performance in your company? What are the tolerances?

The last several chapters have covered the different subjects that constitute an MRP II planning and control system. In the next chapter, we'll look at how you would implement these tools.

SPECIAL ACKNOWLEDGMENT

John Schorr for his work on purchasing and supplier scheduling.

Chapter Eleven

Implementation: The Proven Path

"We didn't stumble too many times in implementation. We followed a good course," says Ed Fitzgerald, General Manager of Valleylab. "One thing that helped us through this whole process was following the proven path. In talking to other companies that are trying to implement MRP II, we learned that they'd get into something and find themselves going completely down the wrong path, then have to redo everything they just did. We didn't find that problem here. Following the proven path, getting the education done, working through the problems, we had very few false starts, if any."

Unfortunately, the approach taken by Ed Fitzgerald at Valleylab is the exception rather than the rule. It appears to be a fundamental characteristic of human nature to read the directions last—and then only if something goes wrong. Do you remember the time you put the swing set together on Christmas Eve? Do you remember getting it halfway assembled only to wonder about those funny little screws, and then realizing you had to disassemble most of what you'd done and start over? It was a long night, wasn't it?

In the world of Christmas presents, such an oversight may only cost you a night's sleep. But in a manufacturing company, leaping into an implementation without "following the directions" first can easily cost you $1 million or more.

Where do companies go wrong? They do what comes naturally, which unfortunately points them in the wrong direction, toward software and systems rather than people, business programs, data accuracy, and accountability. Fortunately, there is a set of directions. It's called the proven path.

WHAT IS THE PROVEN PATH?

The proven path is an approach for implementing MRP II, Just-in-Time, and other people-based technologies. Its 16 steps are based on the accumulated experience of thousands of manufacturing companies over nearly 20 years, so it has been field-tested in the real world.

The earliest version of the proven path dates back to 1975, when it was created by the Oliver Wight organization. This first version was designed solely for MRP II implementations. Today, the proven path has been expanded to provide for the integrated implementation of MRP II, Just-in-Time, total quality, design for competitive advantage, and employee empowerment.

The good news about the proven path is that it's not just theoretical speculation by armchair manufacturing experts. The bad news is that it requires a fair amount of work. But even though implementation of the proven path *is* a lot of work, it's actually less work than doing two implementations: an initial poor job and a "redo." In addition to the cost, you incur immeasurable frustration and demoralization by going a second round.

WHY IS THE PROVEN PATH WORTHWHILE?

It's eye-opening for many companies to calculate the cost of the implementation in terms of a one-month delay—the annual savings minus the annual operating costs divided by 12. In a small organization, the cost of a one-month delay is typically about $300,000. Let's say a company takes an implementation shortcut such as not investing in data accuracy, or makes a poor choice like overstating its master schedule. Or let's say it skips the education phase. Any of these could easily derail the implementation by three or four months, costing the company $900,000 to $1,200,000. So, on a strictly financial basis, the proven path is well worth the effort.

It's also important to factor in expectation levels. Many companies, for example, choose to pursue a Class A implementation (see Chapter 3). If you expect Class A results, then the people in the company have a right to expect a Class A effort. And you won't get Class A results if you don't put effort into data accuracy, sales and operations planning, or any of the other proven path activities.

Success with MRP II correlates with activities and management, not with dollars spent. Figures 11.1 and 11.2 show the results of the Oliver Wight surveys, which were done twice, four years apart. The results were surprisingly consistent, with most answers on the second survey within 2 percent of the corresponding answers on the first, even though the populations were different and four years had elapsed. There were 1,100 and 1,600 companies respectively that responded to the surveys. Of these, approximately half were familiar with the ABCD checklist and ranked themselves on the A–D scale.

The data in Figure 11.1 show that it costs about the same to implement MRP II whether the company achieves Class A results or Class D results. On average, the survey respondents were $65 million manufacturing companies, and most were parts of larger organizations. For larger companies, the cost would be greater; for smaller companies, the cost would be less.

Figure 11.1   Survey Results: Cost/Benefit by Class

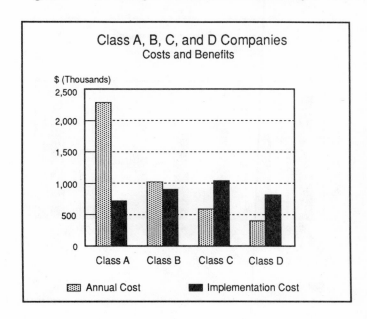

Companies that spend a tremendous amount of money don't necessarily get the best results. Many companies spend a fortune on software and end up operating at a Class D level with very poor payback. On the other hand, companies that spend money on the critical areas, such as education and data accuracy, and work aggressively to identify and solve problems generate significant results. In short, Class A results are dependent on what you do rather than what you spend. Figure 11.2 illustrates this conclusion.

Notice that significantly fewer Class D companies than Class A companies performed the critical implementation activities. While failing to perform a proven path activity does not mean a company cannot achieve Class A levels of performance, each activity that is omitted reduces the chances for success. And why not make it a point to do the activities? It isn't going to cost any more, and if you want Class A levels of results, you'll have to do the work, whether you do it right the first time or have to do it over again. One of the truths in total quality control is that there's never enough time to do it right, but always enough time to do it over again. While this is true in manufacturing

Figure 11.2   Survey Results: Implementation Activities

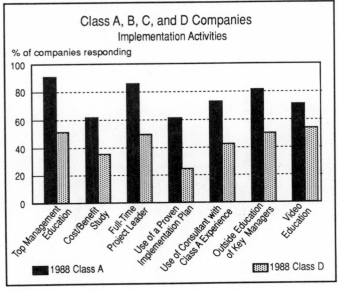

a product, it's also true in implementing MRP II, Just-in-Time, and other technologies.

If a company seeks a Class B implementation, that's all right. The problem comes from companies that say they want Class A results but put forth only a Class D effort. For example, they do a little software training but skip education. They identify problems, but don't solve them. This is a classic mixed message that creates a good deal of chaos and confusion. If a company won't put forth Class A effort, it has no right to ask for Class A results. If an organization is prepared to put out only a Class C effort, then it must expect Class C results. It's much less confusing, and better for everyone, to be honest about the effort and expectations.

Expectations also play a role in determining what resources are available for implementation. There are three controls on an implementation: the work, the resources, and the time. Most companies assume that the work is fixed and that they only have limited resources, therefore time is the variable. This is a common mistake; people don't stay late, come in early, and work on weekends if they don't think the implementation is going to happen in a reasonable time frame. So letting the time stretch out far into the future actually dries up many of the resources needed to do the work.

For most people, two years is a threshold. Beyond two years, people begin believing that "it'll never happen in my lifetime." Something that's going to be implemented in year 3 is too far into the future to be real. And if people are not willing to invest time and energy in the implementation, the work doesn't get done, the time frame for completion slides out further into the future, people lose confidence that the project will ever happen, and a three-year implementation extends to seven or eight years. It's not uncommon to find companies that are in year seven of a two-year implementation.

One approach for dealing with the work-resources-time equation is called *quick-slice*. A quick-slice implementation is different from the more traditional companywide approach because it focuses only on a small segment of the business. Since the work is reduced (only one segment is to be implemented, rather than all), the time can be dramatically shortened. For example, the typical companywide implementation may take a year or so, whereas a slice can typically be completed in about three to five months. Later in this chapter, we'll provide a more detailed explanation of the quick-slice implementation approach.

Finally, the proven path is important because today, in a world of multiple technologies, you may not have the option of implementing one technology at a time—you may have to implement two or more technologies just to remain competitive. If the implementation for a technology takes two years and you have four technologies, you have eight years' worth of implementation activities. Most companies can't wait eight years to get competitive, so an overlap of implementations may be unavoidable. The proven path will allow you to implement multiple technologies as needed.

THE PROVEN PATH IMPLEMENTATION: COMPANYWIDE APPROACH

Figure 11.3 shows a graphic representation of the proven path. The zero, or starting point, is where a formal commitment is made to proceed with the implementation. Notice the number of activities to the left of this commitment. These activities are designed to make sure a company makes an informed decision with a clear understanding of what's involved. Let's look at each element:

1. Audit Assessment #1

This step is a means of assessing where a company is today, in order to establish a starting point. It identifies the greatest opportunities and the most urgent priorities. Often, an audit assessment is done by working with an outside consultant using an assessment tool such as the ABCD checklist.

One reason for hiring an outside consultant is to keep the experience positive. People are generally not motivated to make changes when someone starts criticizing how they currently operate. This puts people in the mode of defending the status quo, and rather than helping them start the change process, it hinders change. But if the checklist is used to develop a consensus about the opportunities that exist if there are changes in the way the business is run, then it becomes a powerful means for mobilizing the organization for change. The results of an audit assessment should be:

- a short-term action plan—what you do next

- identification of opportunities

- a recommendation of an implementation approach (companywide or quick-slice, single or multiple technologies)

Figure 11.3 The Proven Path

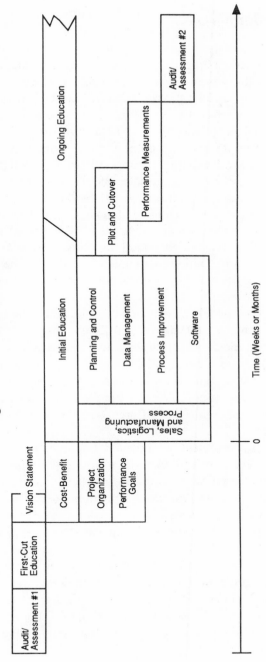

2. First-Cut Education

The goal of the first-cut education phase is to give the key management group an understanding of what is involved in the implementation process. It is fairly typical in many organizations for significant misunderstandings and differing expectations to exist both within the management team and among the employees.

Some people may see MRP II as a computer system—"Put two programmers on it for three months and you're there." Others may see it as a production and inventory control system, in which case why would you need any involvement from sales and finance? Others may see it as a companywide system that integrates all the different groups into a team effort involving all departments with a single set of numbers. And still others may think they're so different that MRP II won't work for them.

Just-in-Time may be perceived as daily deliveries and frequent changeovers, both of which are certain to worry both the manufacturing and purchasing people. Employee empowerment can be misconstrued as democracy.

All but one of these is a misunderstanding. If the management team is composed of people who have these different opinions, then there's little likelihood that members of the team will give a consistent message to the rest of the company. In other words, if the VP of marketing sees MRP II as just a computer system, the VP of finance sees it as an inventory system, and the VP of manufacturing sees it as a companywide system, all will give different signals to the people in their organizations.

When the management team cannot communicate a consistent message, people use a lot of their time to figure out what MRP II is and what their managers want them to do rather than implementing it. In most organizations, a tremendous amount of energy that could be used to do implementation tasks is wasted trying to understand what's expected. Therefore, it's critical for a management group to give consistent messages.

The payoff can be significant. By way of analogy, an Indianapolis 500 race car has more than 700 horsepower. If, however, the driver spins the tires as he accelerates away from a pit stop, the car is riding on a layer of vulcanized rubber and steam, and only about 100 horsepower is applied to the road. Similarly, many companies apply only a small percentage of their available "horsepower" to the implementation tasks, because people lack clear direction or sense a lack of commitment. By eliminating inconsistent messages, a management team can almost double available "horsepower." Best of all, it doesn't cost a cent to communicate a consistent message, nor does it take a tremendous amount of time.

First-cut education is where a management team learns what MRP II, Just-in-Time, and so on, are and how they apply to their company. At the General Dynamics Land Systems Division, manufacturer of the M1A1 tank, the first step in implementing MRP II was to send all top managers to MRP II overview sessions.

It's important for the key management group to reach a consensus about the benefits of the implementation as well as the necessary resources. Most companies do as General Dynamics did and have the top management team (the president, general manager, and the general manager's staff) attend a seminar. They also have the key middle managers who will be involved in the implementation (representatives from manufacturing, production and inventory control, purchasing, engineering or R&D, sales and marketing, and finance) attend a similar, but more detailed, seminar. These people will all play an important role in defining the benefits and understanding their departments' involvement in the activities, consequently each of them needs a working understanding of the technologies being implemented.

Following the seminar, the top management group meets and works to reach a consensus on the benefits to the company and resources that will be required. This consensus helps give a consistent message to the rest of the organization. The top managers can work out differences among themselves, rather than have their people bump into one another in the hall, compare notes, and create confusion.

3. Vision Statement

"If you don't know where you are going, you will never get there. If you know where you are going, you can get there. That's what the visioning process is all about," says George Killianey, a pioneer in this area.

The vision statement is a powerful communications device, one that will make the implementation proceed much more effectively. The vision statement tells your people where you're going—where the company is headed.

According to Killianey, the visioning process is designed for senior executives and is based on the way executives typically think, plan, and problem-solve:

a. The work of most executives deals with issues that are "fuzzy"—not clearly defined, unpredictable, and often conflicting. This is especially true when executives are trying to plan for the long term.

b. Yet most training for executives focuses on how to deal with tangible, concrete issues rather than fuzzy, less tangible issues. Without an established way to deal with these less tangible issues, there is a tendency to avoid addressing them. When this happens, the company becomes a victim of circumstances that it chose not to control.

c. Executives often perceive that they don't have choices. And, without a vision, they're right. The process of developing a vision using techniques designed for this type of activity provides options and establishes a process to ensure that long-term plans are made rather than put on hold.

Jim Sawyer, president of Boeing Canada Technology Ltd., tells of his experience: "During the visioning process, we looked at what we needed to do to survive. In the commercial aircraft industry, it's really a case of survival. We said anything is open for suggestion. We did brainstorming and put 150 ideas up on the board without a challenge. Then we used the visioning tools and techniques to determine what those ideas are worth to the company. We put values on each idea. Through this process, we discovered that it really boiled down to five key issues, or drivers, that we needed to focus on."

The process of developing a vision and mission statement for the company does take some time, but it is well worth the few days' effort when compared to the cost in people's time and energy that results from the lack of such a statement of direction.

4. Cost-Benefit

Many people assume *cost-benefit* means "selling" an implementation— look at the costs, look at the benefit, and if the difference makes sense, do it. And while an attractive cost-benefit is needed to justify an implementation, for most organizations the real motivation for change is a need to change the way the business is run—generally some degree of fear and/or pain. The cost-benefit analysis simply justifies these needed changes financially.

For most companies, the cost-benefit analysis is primarily a resourcing and priority tool. As explained above, the cost justification should be used to calculate the cost of a one-month delay. If this cost of an implementation is about $300,000/month, that implementation will have a higher priority over another activity that costs, say, $50,000 for each month it is delayed. This takes some of the emotion out of the decisions on where to utilize limited resources.

A cost-benefit is also useful if there's an unexpected delay that requires additional funds; you'll know up front whether it's worth the additional resources. If an implementation problem will cost $20,000 to fix, but will delay the implementation two months at a cost of $300,000 per month if it isn't corrected, then the decision is easy.

As you can see, the cost-benefit eliminates a significant amount of emotionalism, and allows you to make rational decisions about intangibles. People still have to use their judgment, but they will be operating from a more solid foundation.

Most implementation cost-benefit analyses are very short—less than 10 pages. They explain the annual benefits—productivity improvement, cost reductions, and the like. They also discuss the implementation costs of computer hardware and software, education, data accuracy, and so forth. Finally, they include the ongoing costs like the costs of cycle counting and software maintenance. Figure 11.4 shows the measurable benefit data for MRP II from the Oliver Wight surveys. Figure 11.5 is an example of a sample MRP II cost-benefit using the benefit data from the Oliver Wight surveys.

A cost-benefit analysis is also used to assign accountability to specific people for specific dollar benefits and costs—for example, someone is accountable for the 10 percent improvement in customer service, and someone else is responsible for the 15 percent improvement in productivity. The same is true for expenses: Someone is responsible for the hardware and software expenses, someone else is responsible for inventory record accuracy expenses, and so on. These budgeted benefits and expenses should appear as objectives against which people are measured during their performance appraisals following implementation.

Figure 11.4   Survey Results: Individual Benefits by Class

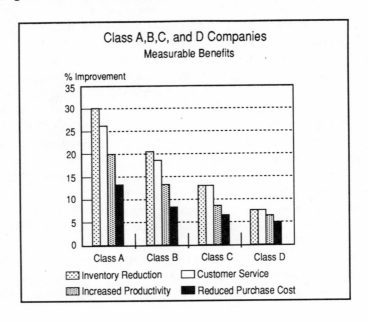

Figure 11.5   Cost-Benefit Analysis

Company Profile

Annual Sales	$ 100M
Cost of Sales	50M
Purchase Cost	25M
Labor Cost	8M
Inventory	15M

Financial Benefits		Costs	
Customer Service	$ 650K	Computer Hardware	$ 400K
Productivity	1,650K	Software	400K
Purchasing	2,500K	Systems Resources	250K
Inventory	900K	Inventory Accuracy	250K
Others	0	Bill of Material Accuracy	150K
		Routing Accuracy	50K
Total Tangible Benefits	5.7M	Education	150K
		Consulting	250K
		Total Costs	$ 1.9M

5. Project Organization

Martin Marietta Astronautics Group in Denver is made up of four companies, plus a central manufacturing operation. Approximately 10,000 people work for the aerospace and defense contractor. After Peter Teets, the president of the astronautics group, issued a mandate that said the group would become Class A, it was up to Mickey Clemons to oversee implementation.

In a nutshell, here's how he approached the project organization:

1. *A steering committee,* made up of Peter Teets and his staff, met once per month (twice per month when the project first started) to assess progress and resolve problems that impeded progress.

2. *A working committee,* or overseeing body, was appointed. This committee, consisting of high-level management representatives from each company, met weekly to work out policy issues, make critical business issue decisions related to the Class A implementation, and track progress.

3. Each company appointed its own *implementation teams* to oversee the projects within the company or business units. The implementations were broken down into logical groupings of business units, manufacturing facilities, and company programs.

While some of the terms are different, the implementation approach used at Martin Marietta Astronautics is typical of most. Figure 11.6 identifies the groups and people generally involved in an implementation.

The *implementation teams* at each Martin Marietta company served the same role as the *project team.* The project team is responsible for the day-to-day management of the implementation. Project team members represent their different functional areas. For example, a project team has representatives (typically the department heads) from engineering, purchasing, sales and marketing, manufacturing, and so on. The members of the project team manage implementation tasks, and may also do work on these tasks. For example, a project team member may have responsibility for working with the group of engineers who

Figure 11.6   Project Organization

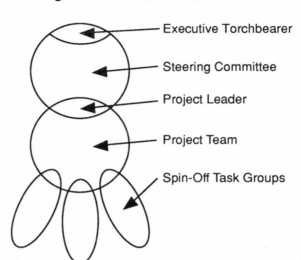

are restructuring the bills of material. In addition, this person may be responsible for actually restructuring the bills of material for a particular product line.

Interestingly, several companies realized in retrospect that they could have trimmed down their project teams. John Mammoser of Schrock Cabinets says, "If I had the whole thing to do over again, I think I'd have fewer people on the project team. I had 14. I think that's too many. I'd reduce it to about 10 at the most." Mike Landrigan at Thunderbird Products echoes this thought: "Our project team was too large. We included too many people in the management meetings themselves. There were just too many individuals. We had 14 on the project team, 11 of whom met day to day. We would have been a lot better off with a group of 6 or 7."

Most companies don't have 14 different departments that all need to be represented on the project team. Consequently, it is realistic to have project teams of the size recommended by Mammoser and Landrigan.

The executive *steering committee* members are concerned less with tactics and more with strategy and resources—they focus on the overall management of the project and make major decisions, such as "Do we have the resources needed to restructure the bills of material?" "Are we going to use modular bills of material?" "Are we going to implement kanban?"

If there's a management problem with the implementation, the project team needs to raise the flag and alert the steering committee. The steering committee in turn needs to make whatever decisions or get whatever resources are needed to correct the situation. For example, the project may be in trouble because the software is untested, creating difficulties. The steering company then needs to ask, "Do we replace or repair the software?" Overall responsibility for the success of the implementation rests with the steering committee.

At Martin Marietta, the *working committee* acted as a corporate coordinator of the various project teams. In a single-company implementation, such a group would not be needed. In an organization in which several implementations are happening simultaneously, however, a number of common issues need to be agreed upon. Policies, methods of measurement, and software issues (where the same software is being used by several locations) are all items on which the different project teams need to reach agreement, and the working committee or corporate project team is the forum for doing so.

The *project team leader* should be a full-time leader, except in a very small company. This is necessary because in most organizations the urgent things get the attention rather than the important things. *Urgent* means it has to be resolved today, or maybe right now. *Important* means it will make a difference in how the company runs five years from now. The difficulty is that what's urgent is not always important, and those things that are important are rarely urgent. When a project leader has day-to-day responsibilities, they need to be taken care of right away, and the next thing you know it's the end of the week and the project management work didn't get done. In company after company, part-time project leaders take considerably longer to implement than full-time project leaders.

In one company, the same person was project leader in two different divisions. At the first division, this leader set a record for the fastest implementation. Several years later, the project leader was transferred to another division and was assigned the role of materials manager and project leader. After three years, this division was still struggling to complete its implementation. At a cost-of-delay expense of several hundred thousand dollars per month, a full-time project leader is one of the best investments a company can make.

The project team leader is also a member of the executive steering committee, and serves as the primary interface between the committee and the project team. The project team leader attends all the steering committee meetings and updates the steering committee on the progress of the implementation tasks.

The *executive torchbearer* represents the top management group, and takes personal responsibility for the success of the implementation. The torchbearer is the person with the "fire in the belly" needed to make the implementation happen. The executive torchbearer puts his or her reputation on the line. In addition, one of the most important roles of the torchbearer is to defend the implementation against diversions. Most companies have more good ideas and more good initiatives than they have the resources to implement. Consequently, someone needs to keep the organization focused on bringing the current implementations through to completion.

The role of the executive torchbearer at Garden America, a manufacturer of turf irrigation systems, has been more difficult than most. The company was sold three times while implementing MRP II/JIT/TQC, making it difficult to deliver a consistent message and remain focused. Even so, both plants achieved Class A levels of performance.

How did Garden America continue its efforts despite all this? "You've got to keep your eye on the ball," says president Rich Gleitsmann. "We maintained our focus through frequent communication—with our employees, suppliers, and customers." When asked about his role as the executive torchbearer, Gleitsmann answered, "The word *champion* is probably overused, but my role is something like that of a champion. As president, I'm the one who keeps saying, 'Yes, I understand that there are day-to-day pressures to get product out, cut costs, improve this and that. But at the same time we're doing all these things, and we are going to stick with the structure that has gotten us this far. That's MRP II, JIT, and TQC. All three of these are tied together in running the overall business.' "

Gleitsmann offers the following advice to presidents of other companies who are implementing MRP II: "Get involved in the detail. Make sure you understand how the various pieces of the business fit together.

Don't allow MRP II to be just a manufacturing program; don't allow it to be just an information systems project. Make it your overall philosophy. And at every opportunity, reinforce the notion that it is the way you're going to run the business."

Spin-off task groups are small groups assigned to do various tasks. These tasks can include revising the process for implementing engineering changes, developing the procedures to attain inventory record accuracy, making sure that the necessary data collection equipment is acquired, and so on.

Spin-off task groups are important for several reasons. First, they are a practical way to get work done in an organization that is already overloaded. The burden of work, rather than falling on a small group like the project team, is spread among a larger group of people. In addition, better decisions are made when the people closest to a situation are part of the problem-solving process.

Finally, spreading the work also spreads the ownership. One of the primary objectives of the implementation is to have people take ownership in the changes and new ways of running the business. When significant numbers of people are included in the implementation process through spin-off task groups, these people have had a say in the changes, and have ownership in the new processes.

There are no firm rules on how much of a person's time should be spent on implementation activities, since the amount will vary from company to company. For example, in a very large organization, the entire project team may be full-time. In a smaller organization, the project team leader may be full-time while the project team members are part-time. Frequently, people on the project team complain that they don't have enough time to do their day-to-day jobs as well as the work they need to do on the implementation. The solution to this problem is not to relieve them of more of their day-to-day work, but rather to have them off-load more of the project work to others in the organization, typically through spin-off task forces.

The spin-off task forces need to be coordinated so that the different groups aren't doing things either in conflict or in duplication of one another, wasting significant time and energy. There are several ways to do this. One is to put the burden of coordination on the spin-off teams. They are responsible for checking with the other teams to make sure their activities are complementary. Another approach is to have one member of the project team on each spin-off task group. This way, the groups are coordinated through the project team.

6. Performance Goals

While the audit assessment #1 (step 1) identifies where you are today and the vision statement describes where you want to go, performance goals represent the *quantitative* measure of what you expect to achieve. It's important to describe these goals quantitatively and in advance, so people know clearly what's expected of them.

Performance goals are stated concretely—for example, "We expect an improvement in customer service from 75 to 95 percent," "We expect a 30 percent reduction in inventory," ". . . an 11 percent reduction in purchased material costs," ". . . a 25 percent improvement in productivity," or ". . . a 10-fold improvement in quality."

If the performance goals are not set properly, then there is the risk of having everyone develop a different set of expectations about what acceptable performance means—"Well, we lowered inventory by 5 percent—that's certainly good, isn't it?" Or, "We increased productivity by 4 percent—that's better than the national average, isn't it?" The best performance goals are "stretch" levels of performance—goals that challenge and motivate people.

Finally, performance goals must be meaningful in terms of the competitive equation. After all, if a company goes to all the trouble and expense of implementing new ways to run the business and sets goals of only 2 or 3 percent improvement, this communicates a low self-assessment of what both the management and the people are capable of doing. A capable and aggressive management team should be able to get substantial improvements on the same order as those reported by Class A companies (see Figure 11.4).

7. Sales, Logistics, and Manufacturing Process

The sales, logistics, and manufacturing process is the next level of detail after the vision statement. These are design decisions about the way you plan to run the business. The result of the sales, logistics, and manufacturing process might be "We're going to implement kanbans instead of shop-floor control," "We're going to have a make-to-order product rather than a make-to-stock product, but we're going to compress the lead time on the make-to-order phase," or "We're going to structure the bills of material in a modular fashion to facilitate easy forecasting and short lead-time deliveries."

Many times these decisions are reached in the early phases of the educational program. The educational program, if done properly, is an exercise in participative management or employee empowerment. The project team and the executive steering committee look at the alternatives, talk about the choices, and weigh the pros and cons.

8. Initial Education

The initial education is designed to educate the mass of people in a company, the people who will make the new ways of doing business work.

Ed Wohlwender, manager of inventory control/central planning at Hillshire Farm & Kahn's, explains that company's education process. "I think early on our senior management realized that because these concepts were new to us, education was going to be significant. Before we even picked software, we went through about two and one half months of meeting twice a week for about two hours using videotapes and written materials to get the concepts out there. If I had to say one thing to anybody getting into this, it's 'Take your best guess at the education you're going to need, and then double it. And there are two types: the conceptual education, and then the specific software training.'

"We dedicated twenty hours of the time of the highest-level managers in this company to get right down into the meat of 'What is MRP II? What's a time fence? Are we make-to-stock or make-to-order? What are some of the organizational impacts?' We went through extensive training on the concepts of MRP II, and I think that's helped me as a project leader. People know what we're talking about, and that knowledge cuts through so much that would otherwise take a great deal of time, and it keeps the commitment alive."

Ed's company is the exception. Most manufacturing companies do as little education as they think they can get away with, and the education they do is usually modeled on basic childhood schooling. In this model, a teacher has the information and communicates it to the students, who soak it all up, then go back and do their work differently. The flow is one way, from teacher to student. And the outcome is predetermined: For example, discussing the Revolutionary War isn't going to change who won, just as discussing algebra isn't going to change the rules of mathematics.

While this model works well for the fourth grade, it's not effective for introducing change in an organization. It generates low levels of enthusiasm and ownership—both of which are necessary before change can actually happen. A better model is a business meeting. In a business meeting, the leader may know more than others in the room, but there's no one with all the answers—the meeting runs on the collective knowledge of the participants. Because this approach recognizes the experience and intelligence of the people in the organization, it builds high levels of ownership and enthusiasm, and it produces better decisions.

General Dynamics Land Systems is a good illustration of this process. The company ran weekly education sessions with key managers, during which video and written materials were used to help people talk about what MRP II would mean to them. The objective was to devise a list of issues everyone wanted to accomplish. Next, the company brought in the key technical people to start the more detailed educational process, which covered the nuts and bolts of MRP II. General Dynamics used its managers to teach what they had learned to the MRP II users in the facility. Again, they relied on video and written materials to assist in focusing their "business meetings" on what needed to be accomplished. The people on the line looked to the project manager for overall direction on MRP II, but it was the line supervisors' responsibility to communicate what they knew to the people on the floor. Ultimately, it was these people who would make everything work, and it was crucial for the managers to teach their own people and to show them that management understood what they were being asked to do. This credibility made the difference between success and failure.

Video and written materials are tremendously effective media for communicating a consistent message to a large number of people, on their time schedule. Even so, they are one-way media—they cannot answer questions.

Therefore, to prepare managers to be effective leaders in their business meetings, the company should sponsor a seminar on the subject, run by a credible instructor with lots of experience. This allows people to ask tough questions and get answers they can use in applying the concepts to their organization. The seminars are intensive, eight hours a day for several days, and they provide a lot of information in a short period of time.

In addition, a number of "subject experts" should be developed within each company. Rather than rely extensively on outsiders, it makes more sense to take people who know your business and people, and educate them. This education would be on subjects such as demand management, master production scheduling, capacity planning, and inventory record accuracy. Not only is this extremely cost-effective, but it builds ownership that leads to success, and creates a valuable resource within your company.

9. Planning and Control

This step in an MRP II or Just-in-Time implementation is the initiation of sales and operations planning. Starting this process early is one of those implementation activities that doesn't have any out-of-pocket cost, but yields enormous financial benefits. If you implement master scheduling, material planning, or kanban, but don't have the top-level plans under control, it's extremely costly. Changes in the top-level plans are magnified many times as they work themselves down to the level of purchased parts and raw materials.

Another way to visualize this is that a "hiccup" at the top translates into an "earthquake" at the bottom. If the number of changes to the top-level plans is too great, the number of changes to the manufacturing and purchasing schedules will be overwhelming—and people won't be able to keep up. And if the initial wave of changes isn't frustrating enough, many of the changes are likely to be reversed a week or two later, compounding the problem. People lose confidence in the information, give up, and the informal system reappears. All this can be avoided if the top-level plans are in order early in the process.

10. Data Management

Years ago, Tom Wallace, in his book *MRP II: Making it Happen* (Oliver Wight Publications), popularized the idea that there are two types of data: forgiving and unforgiving.

Unforgiving Data
Unforgiving data are the type that bite you badly if they're not accurate. These include inventory record accuracy, bills of material, formulas, recipes, and routings.

If the inventory records are incorrect, then the planning will be incorrect. If you think you have 100 on hand and you only have 50, then all the rescheduling action messages will be incorrect, the planned orders will be incorrect, and so on. If the planned orders are incorrect, then the lower-level requirements will likewise be incorrect. So, one "strategically placed" inventory error could create hundreds of items with incorrect planning data.

Bill of material, formula, and recipe data are also extremely unforgiving. If the bill of material calls for a particular IC chip, but what's really used is a different IC chip, you can be certain of four things: (1) you'll have IC chips that you don't need, (2) you'll be short on those chips that you do need, (3) you'll find out about the shortage at the last minute, and (4) you won't be able to make the product. When these things happen, you can be sure of one other thing: As you miss your dates, the informal system will rear its head again.

Routings pose similar problems. If the routings are incorrect, the operation sequences are incorrect, the work centers are incorrect, or the time standards are off significantly, the validity of shop-floor control and capacity requirements planning will be seriously affected. Shop-floor control might recommend moving work to one work center when it really should go to another. Capacity planning might indicate an overload or underload where none exists. When these things happen, people lose confidence in the system, and the informal system becomes the order of the day.

The minimum data accuracy levels for Class A operation are: inventory records—95 percent; bills of material, formulas, or recipes—98 percent; and routings—95 percent.

Note that the 95 percent inventory record accuracy is not calculated in net dollars (the way accounting measures a physical inventory).

Using the net dollars method, an error of plus 50 square yards of neoprene sheet and an error of minus 50 square feet on a different type of neoprene sheet result in a very small error, or no error, in terms of dollars. While such an error has little impact on the company's financial books, it can have a significant impact on the ability to make and ship product.

The target of 95 percent inventory record accuracy used for planning and scheduling means that 95 percent of the individual items are within the counting tolerance for that item. If 100 items were cycle counted, and 10 were found to have differences between the on-hand balance and the actual count that were greater than the counting tolerance, the resulting accuracy would be 90 percent. The tolerance is generally based on how the items are counted: 2 percent or so for weight-counted items, zero percent for larger items. In no cases should the tolerance exceed 5 percent. A 95 percent accuracy measured this way is better than 99 percent accuracy in terms of net dollars, and more accurate than a physical inventory.

A bill of material, formula, or recipe accuracy of 98 percent means that 98 percent of the single-level bills show all the correct components or raw materials, in the correct quantities. If three single-level bills, formulas, or recipes are tested and one shows an incorrect raw material, the second has an incorrect quantity, and the third is correct, the resulting accuracy is 33 percent. Again, 98 percent accuracy measured this way is far higher than the accuracy many companies are used to maintaining.

A 95 percent routing accuracy means that 95 percent of the routings show the correct operations sequence, at the correct work centers, and with a reasonable time standard. If four routings are examined, and one has an operation out of sequence, another has an incorrect work center number, a third has a time standard that is significantly in error, and the fourth was correct, the resulting accuracy is 25 percent.

As you might expect, a great deal of energy is required to achieve these levels; in fact, in many implementations, data accuracy is one of the most time- and energy-intensive efforts. But it has to be done for MRP II or Just-in-Time to work properly. In addition, it is part of a total quality initiative. *Quality* refers not only to the product, but also to the information used to manufacture the product. In addition, the total quality problem-solving approach is used to achieve these levels of accuracy.

You may wonder, "Do we have the ability to achieve such high levels of accuracy?" The answer is Yes, you do have the ability. There is a tested and proven process for achieving inventory record accuracy; bill of material, formula, or recipe accuracy; and routing accuracy. It's done every day, by companies populated by normal people.

That process includes the following steps:

1. Educate.

2. Assign responsibility.

3. Provide the tools.

4. Achieve audit accuracy.

5. Correct the causes of errors.

Let's look at how this basic process would be applied:

In all three cases (inventory records; bills of material, formulas, or recipes; and routings), the first step is to *educate* people so they understand why it's important to have accurate information and how other companies have been successful in achieving the established goals.

Again, in all three instances, *responsibility* needs to be assigned to an individual or a group for the accuracy of the records. In the case of inventory record accuracy, it is typically assigned to the people in the stockroom, raw material warehouse, finished goods warehouse, and distribution centers. In the case of bills of material, formulas, or recipes, it might be assigned to the product development or engineering group. For routings, it might be assigned to the process or manufacturing engineering people.

Providing the tools for inventory record accuracy requires a simple and easy-to-use transaction recording system and, depending on the manufacturing environment, it may include limited access so that only authorized people can make inventory transactions. For bills of material, formulas, recipes, and routings, the tools are simple systems to maintain this information quickly and easily.

The methods for *achieving audit accuracy* vary, depending on what's being audited. For inventory records, the most common method is cycle counting, in which a sample of items is counted on a periodic basis and compared to the on-hand balance. Over some period of time, all the items in inventory are counted in this manner.

There are several different methods for auditing the accuracy of bills of material, formulas, or recipes: the unplanned issues/receipts method, the audit method, and the product teardown method. For an assembled product, the unplanned issues/receipts method works well. Material is issued to manufacturing based on the bill of material. Any additional items that are needed, or any items that are left over after manufacturing the product, trigger a review of the bill. In the audit method, people from the plant and/or office who are knowledgeable about the products take the bills of material, formulas, or recipes and review them for accuracy. Product teardown is rarely used because it requires disassembling a product to see what items were used to manufacture it.

In the case of routings, an audit in the plant works well. The manufacturing people, or auditors who circulate throughout the plant, note any situations in which the routing shows an operation, sequence, work center, or time standard that is different from what is actually used to manufacture the product. These trigger a review of the routing.

The most important reason for these audits is to *correct the causes of errors.* The approach used to provide high-quality (accurate) information is the same one used to provide high-quality products. Information is a product provided to the internal customers (sales people; manufacturing, planning, and scheduling people; and so on), just as the products a company manufactures are provided to their external customers. The total quality approach is to find the root cause of a problem and fix it so it can never happen again.

Likewise, the primary purpose of the audits is to find the causes of the inaccurate data and fix them so they cannot happen again. In the same way that you cannot inspect quality into a product, you cannot audit accuracy into the information. It is not possible to cycle-count your way to 95 percent inventory record accuracy, or audit bills of material, formulas, or recipes to achieve 98 percent accuracy. The root causes of the errors must be uncovered and corrected.

People do not have to be able to leap tall buildings in a single bound to achieve these levels of data accuracy, but they must possess a tenacious determination to find the causes and fix them.

Forgiving Data
With forgiving data, reasonable accuracy is acceptable—and generally fairly easy to achieve. The forgiving data are the order quantities, lead

times, and safety stock levels. There are a number of "right" numbers for each of these. If the order quantity is 500, is 600 incorrect? No, 500 may be better than 600, but neither is wrong. In other words, you won't risk destroying the formal system if the accuracy of forgiving data isn't perfect. This brings up the next point—with this type of data, the objective is to change them.

Take order quantity. In the spirit of JIT, you start with a number and progressively reduce it. The same holds true for lead times and safety stock. In all of these cases, the emphasis isn't on getting the right number, but on making the numbers smaller. The effort required to get reasonable lead times and order quantities isn't enormous, but continuous effort will provide steady dividends well beyond the implementation.

11. Process Improvement

As mentioned in Chapter 1, we live in a world of multiple technologies, and competitive pressures are such that most companies cannot restrict themselves to implementing only one technology. In such a multiple technology implementation, several different initiatives may be implemented under this heading. These could include: Just-in-Time, employee empowerment, total quality control, and design for competitive advantage.

The Just-in-Time pilot implementation at Tellabs is an excellent example. Tellabs chose an area that was small enough to ensure success but large enough to command attention and serve as a learning model. For the pilot project Tellabs chose its digital loop product line, which accounted for 10 percent of its total production output.

The first order of business was to assemble the pilot team. Tellabs initiated the pilot program on the third shift, which meant team meetings were held at 6:00 A.M. Few people were willing to sign on in the beginning. "They had to be pretty committed people to show up at 6:00 A.M.," recalls Grace Pastiak, who was in charge of the Just-in-Time pilot program. They were.

Four months of training, preparation, and strategy sessions were necessary before the pilot could begin. A pilot "cell" was put together, and two days after the Just-in-Time pilot began production, throughput time was reduced by one third. What had taken 20 days to produce in batch mode took 6½ days to build using Just-in-Time. After the second week, once-reluctant participants were filing into Pastiak's office asking if they were going to be part of the next Just-in-Time pilot project. Pastiak laughs. "They were afraid to be on the first pilot," she says. "Now they were afraid not to be picked for the next one. Just-in-Time really did affect the culture."

That is not all it affected. "We did more the first month we were on Just-in-Time—with fewer people—than we had ever done on *any* line in the past," said Ed McDivitt, Tellabs's vice-president of operations. Other key measures that support McDivitt's claim: Work-in-process (WIP) inventory went from 4,500 circuit boards to 900, an 80 percent reduction; lot sizes shrank from batches of 100 down to 40, a 60–70 percent drop; engineering design revision time, the time it took to make changes on the boards in WIP, was decreased from 200 hours to 20 hours, a 90 percent time savings; throughput time went from 20 days to 2 days, a 90 percent drop.

Business results and enthusiasm like these are a strong incentive for companies to implement several technologies as part of a proven path implementation. As Oliver Wight used to say, "Nothing sells like success," and the pilot approach generates success. Even in situations in which companies feel constrained by resources, a small pilot in one of these process improvement areas can be a boost. In most cases, the benefit of success is significant, and the resource constraints can be managed because in most cases the resources are different from those needed for other implementation tasks.

In other cases, the implementation proceeds more smoothly and quickly through the use of other technologies. At Hillshire Farm & Kahn's, management was able to evaluate the effect of employee empowerment on its quick-slice implementation in two locations. "We've implemented team training at one of our locations, and that has proved significant in the progress that location has made on the quick-slice implementation," says Ed Wohlwender. "The word gets down lower in the organization more quickly at that location. The comment that the manufacturing superintendents made was 'We went through team training and it was great, but now we're actually able to apply the things we learned in team training to this project.' They're able to use those team building skills in this slice implementation."

Stan Grubbs of Boeing Defense & Space reinforces this idea: "I think we've learned that preparing people for change and working with them a little bit before throwing them into it can have a lot of benefit. We realized that after we got into the implementation. If I had to give some advice, I'd definitely recommend that managers spend some time with successful organizations and make sure they're ready to change. It's time well spent. It will definitely remove many of the conflicts, and cut time off the overall project."

Process improvements do not conflict with one another, nor do they conflict with a planning and control system like MRP II, so it's no surprise that many companies choose to implement a number of these initiatives at the same time.

12. Software

While software is essential for MRP II, the best software package is no guarantee of Class A performance. As stressed above, what correlates with Class A performance is good management. To make an analogy with golf, it's not the cost of the set of clubs, but how you hit the ball.

Today, there is good, tested MRP II software for most of the computers being used. Some software is even available for personal computers. Over the years, a number of companies have attempted to write their own MRP II software. While there are one or two successes, the overwhelming majority of these experiences have been mistakes. The typical MRP II software package represents an investment of more than 100 man-years of systems and programming work. Even if a company were to put 5 or 10 people on the project, the most that can be used efficiently, they will need to work beyond the time frame for implementation.

The best analogy for MRP II software is that of the catapult on an aircraft carrier. The catapult takes the airplane from 0 to 170 miles per hour in a little over three seconds. But after that, the airplane's own engines have to do the work. Similarly, a software package gets a company from 0 to 100 man-years of systems effort in a few months, but then it's the company's responsibility to adapt the package to its specific needs and maintain the software. Every company does have individual needs, but these typically require only minor changes. The way a picking list is printed, or the addition of a back-scheduling calculation in capacity planning and shop-floor control, would be a good example of these kinds of needs. Companies do not change the basic material or capacity planning logic unless there is a flaw in their software.

13. Pilot and Cutover

There are three ways to begin using a new system (like MRP II) or a new approach to running the business (like Just-in-Time). Let's use MRP II as an example, although the same explanation works for other technologies as well:

1. *Parallel approach.* This is great if you're replacing a system that already works. Take payroll—you can simultaneously run the old and new payroll systems and compare the checks as they come out of both systems. If the checks match over a period of time, you can safely disconnect the old system and run the new one. The problem is that most companies are implementing an MRP II system for the first time, not replacing one piece of software with another, so they don't have a system that gives them accurate information. Consequently, if the new system agrees with whatever they were using before, they're in real trouble. So the parallel approach is not workable. The only exception is where an existing piece of MRP II software is working and this software is being replaced by another MRP II software package.

2. *"Cold turkey."* This is appealing to many people, but it's not recommended. Cold turkey means you throw the switch on Friday and you're on the new system on Monday—all items, all products, everything at once. Some people argue that this approach forces everyone to sink or swim on Monday. But in fact, it might sink the entire operation. As Oliver Wight CEO Walt Goddard puts it, "The drowning man doesn't die from lack of motivation—he's overwhelmed." If your data aren't as accurate as they should be, if your people aren't as well trained as they need to be, then you run the risk of major chaos, reduced shipments, and financial pain. A few companies have survived a cold-turkey cutover, but most suffer major damage. Not surprisingly, those that have survived a cold-turkey cutover swear they'd never do it again.

3. *Pilot approach.* This is the recommended implementation approach. The pilot is a cold turkey approach, but it is applied to only a limited

number of items—you "flip the switch" on a small enough piece of the business that the risk is low if things go wrong. No one will be overwhelmed. You can fix whatever problems appear, and continue. After about a month of pilot, most of the problems will have been identified. Once they are fixed, it's time to take another product or group of products and begin running the new system on these items. Fix the problems that emerge, settle in, and continue until all products have been included. Clearly, this is the least risky and most orderly approach, the one most likely to lead to a successful implementation, and the one pursued by nearly all companies these days.

14. Performance Measurements

How do you know that the pilot is working? How do you know whether to continue with it or fix it? Some of these questions can be answered subjectively: Do people believe the schedules? Are you getting good information? In a Just-in-Time implementation, is kanban controlling the flow of material? Yet there are other questions that can be answered only by establishing performance measurements. Most of the performance measurements relate to goals established during step 6. Now you're actually measuring yourself against those goals.

Some of the measurements or goals that you set for yourself won't be apparent in the pilot program—it's unlikely that overall customer service will improve significantly with just a pilot program. So you might start tracking customer service on specific product lines. Some companies compare items that are on the pilot with items that are not. The same holds with productivity, although that's more difficult to measure on a product-by-product basis.

At this point, the key is to start measuring against the goals. People often don't realize that the planning and scheduling system just clears the water, making previously hidden problems visible. The problems don't go away, but at least people can see what has to be done.

"It really took people a while to realize there was no magic in the solution," recalls Boeing's Stan Grubbs. "It was really an issue of focus, of continuing to work issues and resolve them. I think some people thought we'd give them new computing tools and they'd magically start to attain schedules.

"One thing that was a real shot in the arm for our shop-floor control efforts was getting all the cost centers to focus on their particular measures and post them in their areas," Grubbs explains. "And we made sure all the people in the cost centers understood what was expected, what we were trying to achieve, and why it was important. Initially, we were working with the management people. But when we got the people in the cost centers focusing, we received almost a step function of improvement."

As the people at Boeing demonstrated, the way to improve performance measurements is to solve problems—the speed at which measurements improve is the speed at which the problems are solved. As mentioned before, companies that do well with their MRP II implementation know not only how to identify the problems, but also how to take corrective action.

15. Audit Assessment #2

"Where are we?" "Did we achieve the goals we set for ourselves in the beginning?" "What's next?" "What other things should we be working on?"

Audit assessment #1 (step 1) identified the opportunities for improvement, triggering a series of implementation activities. If those activities worked well, then the operation of the business has improved significantly. Audit assessment #2 might reveal that while you've done certain things well—like data accuracy—you are not managing MRP II well. Perhaps the S&OP process is not being managed well, or the master production schedule is overstated. Those kinds of deficiencies will become apparent through audit assessment #2. You can then focus on those areas and pour your energy into fixing them.

It also may be the case that you've done all of the steps quite well—not 100 percent, but approaching Class A levels—and now you need to consider implementing other technologies that were not included in the previous implementation effort. The world doesn't stand still—what was competitive two years ago may not be so today. Audit assessment #2 can point you in the right direction.

Audit assessment #2 therefore becomes audit assessment #1 for the next pass through the proven path. The proven path should be seen not as a project, but as a continual structured process for improvement. Companies string together successive passes through the proven path—end to end—forming an uninterrupted chain of operational improvement.

16. Ongoing Education

Most people assume that once the initial education is complete and the company is operating in a new and different way, there's no point to further education. The assumption is that if people are using the system every day, their proficiency will grow. Yes, people do maintain a degree of proficiency through their daily use of the system. But there are a number of important reasons for continuing education.

First, new people are constantly entering the organization—if they don't get the opportunity for education early on, some damage can result. For example, in one organization a new VP of manufacturing was hired from the outside. He was not experienced with formal systems, and he said things like "We never had accurate inventory records in the other companies where I've worked" and "We have to put more on the master schedule so we can be sure we won't miss the shipping plan. I like to put 15 million in the schedule in order to get 10 million out." When a person like this assumes a position of authority, he or she can lose the respect and confidence of people both above and below. Worse, experience shows that it's a long road back once that kind of first impression has been made.

In addition, businesses change—especially these days. The decisions you made two years ago on how to apply the tools of MRP II to your business might—and typically would—be made differently today. Therefore, each company should regularly reexamine the way it's currently running its business, asking the question "How would we use these tools to most effectively run the business today?"

Finally, there's the proficiency issue. While people are proficient at their piece of the business, they tend to lose the global perspective that enables them to work effectively with other groups as a team; in other words, they get tunnel vision. Ongoing education can force everyone to take a step back from his or her little corner of their business and review the big picture.

THE PROVEN PATH IMPLEMENTATION: QUICK-SLICE APPROACH

Instead of a companywide implementation, a company may choose to implement a new technology on only a "slice" or small part of the business. Quick-slice can be used for MRP II and Just-in-Time implementations, as well as with other technologies. The quick-slice approach is not to be confused with the pilot approach. With the pilot approach, tasks are done companywide before the pilot is initiated.

For example, in a companywide MRP II implementation, data accuracy is brought up to the required levels for all items, education is done for all people, performance goals are set for the entire business, and so on, before the pilot is begun. In a slice implementation, the proven path activities are completed only for the slice and for the people involved in the slice. In an MRP II quick-slice implementation, data accuracy is brought to the required levels only for the items in the slice, education is done only for the team working on the slice, the cost-benefit is done only for the slice, and so on.

With the slice approach, the work to be done is dramatically reduced, and given the same resources, a slice can be accomplished in much less time than a companywide implementation.

Consider the case of KMS Fusion, Advanced Products, which manufactures rugged microcomputers primarily for NASA and the military. The company was only three years old and experiencing rapid growth, with sales expected to double in the following year, when its executive committee became convinced that MRP II would help improve the company's performance. There was only one drawback: Full implementation would take at least one year, and that was too long. Shipping orders on schedule had become more difficult, which was problematic since the division had always considered its guaranteed 60-day lead time a competitive advantage.

"In the beginning, we were relatively successful at shipping product within 60 days. But as sales continued to grow, we were rapidly losing control of our ability to manage the manufacturing cycle and know when shipments were actually going to be made," Fred Augspurger, director of materials, explains.

The symptoms were evident: Inventories "blossomed," and shortage and hot lists grew longer each month.

"We had few planning tools, and we were about to lose one important advantage—the ability to maintain a 60-day lead time," says Augspurger.

When the executive committee members learned about the quick-slice approach, with its 100-day implementation, they realized that they had what they needed.

Implementation of quick-slice posed two primary challenges at KMS Fusion: (1) using the new practices of MRP II in one area of the business while the current practices and systems were used in the other areas, and (2) the commitment required by the team members to successfully implement quick-slice in a "compressed" time frame.

KMS Fusion faced the challenge of maintaining customer service while implementing a new process for managing the business—at the same time that the number of orders nearly doubled compared to the previous year.

The nature of quick-slice—it focuses on a narrow target within the operation—makes implementation easier. It is less complex for 10 to 12 people to concentrate on implementing MRP II in one segment of the business than for more than 200 people to implement the MRP II process throughout the company. You don't have to carry the rest of the organization along with you to get MRP II going.

Quick-slice also serves as a proving ground for MRP II. It becomes a success story that helps gain acceptance for the future implementation throughout the rest of the company.

The division is seeing inventory reductions and productivity increases in the business segment in which quick-slice was implemented, according to Augspurger. In addition, Advanced Products has maintained its customer service levels—even though the business has grown dramatically.

"If we hadn't implemented quick-slice, we would still be trying to recover our ability to ship orders within 60 days," Augspurger states.

Experiences like those of KMS Fusion show that companies can accomplish quick-slice implementations in a three-to-five-month time frame. As a result, they can show results quickly. The difference between a quick-slice approach and a pilot approach is that in the former the process of gaining data accuracy and educating workers is repeated when the company moves to the next slice. In a pilot implementation, the next group of products can be brought onto the system more quickly because the data are already at the required levels of accuracy and the people have already been educated. In terms of total time, however, it may be possible to do several slices in the time that would be required for a companywide implementation, so the overall implementation time is about the same.

Another reason for choosing quick-slice is to sell the system to reluctant top managers. If the middle managers are convinced a technology will work in their company, but top managers aren't sold, a quick-slice approach is an excellent way to prove that the technology can really work. The investment is relatively small, and the time frame is short.

Most Just-in-Time implementations are quick-slice. A section of the company is selected for a "breakthrough pilot" and the focus is on getting this area up and running. Similarly, many employee empowerment programs are implemented using a quick-slice approach. A department or other group is selected, and the education and empowerment work is done with this group to create initial successes, rather than companywide.

RESOURCE CONFLICTS

One of the biggest problems with implementation is that the technologies discussed in this book need to be implemented as quickly as possible for companies to become more competitive.

"Everybody feels overloaded," says John Mammoser of Schrock Cabinets' simultaneous multiple technology implementation. "A big increase in production has thrown a wrench into this whole thing. We've had an increase in sales and we're really busy, on top of all this project stuff. So that's made it doubly tough on everybody. However, the people in the plant and the people on the manufacturing side have seen the benefits, and I don't hear much complaining from them.

"A lot of times I just felt I was groping in the dark, and I wondered how in the world I was ever going to get all these things going and keep everything going at once. I just told myself, 'You can't get involved with all the details.' If I have something to say about JIT, I usually go to the JIT leader and talk to him. I'm not out talking to these teams on a regular basis, pushing them or asking them what they're doing.

"Our general manager is very much in favor of change, and he's the driving force. If it hadn't been for him, it would have never gotten off the ground. Our torchbearer has provided a lot of support too. He's not a flamboyant or a 'rah-rah' sort of guy, but he's always supported it in his own way, and he expects everybody to follow along. A core of people on the project team, about six or eight, are very much in favor of change. We're going to do anything to see this thing through. We have a rather young work force, a lot of people for whom this has been their only job, and it's the only way they really know. With some of these people we have run into some resistance to change, but I think we're overcoming it because people have seen the good things that are happening, especially in the JIT area. They're starting to come around."

The experience at Schrock illustrates an obvious concern for resources and leadership. Like most companies, Schrock has found that while the resource demands are enormous, there are some mitigating factors. One of the basic principles of implementation is ownership. A guaranteed route to frustration and failure is to have someone go into a dark room, redesign someone's job, and present it to that person as carved in granite and closed to change. Spreading the load to as many people in the organization as possible serves two purposes, both essential for success: First, the resource demands that fall on any one person are reduced; second, because many different people are actively involved in the work and the decision making, ownership of the changes is much higher than would be the case otherwise.

Yet the amount of time and money required to implement many technologies simultaneously may be prohibitive. So every company has to make some decisions about what it can realistically do. This becomes a matter of determining priorities and timing.

The best approach is to create a realistic plan from the outset. But not every company is able to do that. It can be difficult to accurately assess the size of some tasks, and what appear to be "stretch" goals may prove to be unattainable. Therefore, it makes sense to have a process for continuing to verify the validity of the implementation plans. Start by taking all the technologies to be implemented and develop a detailed implementation plan for each—a list of all the different tasks that have to be accomplished, who will be accountable, and when each task should be done. (*The Proven Path,* published by Oliver Wight Publications, includes detailed implementation plans for a number of technologies.) Then honestly evaluate the plan. Sort the plans by person responsible and date, and ask the question "Can the people responsible for these tasks really do them, plus complete their regular jobs, so that product still makes it out the door on time?" If so, start to work the plan. If not, something has to be cut from the plan.

Many times a company says, "We can do that," when it really cannot. Most people, especially top managers, are driven to put more into a plan than is realistic. If people are consistently missing the due dates for tasks, it will be necessary to go back and find out why. If people are just overwhelmed by the amount of work they have to do, it will be necessary to back off and take something out of the plan.

Consequently, one of the major issues in implementation is evaluating how much you can realistically do. It's better to say you're going to do less and make it happen than to make big promises and not deliver. If the task is manageable and people achieve success, everyone is motivated to take on additional challenges. If people can never be winners, they'll be unmotivated and the entire organization will achieve less. An excellent test of the maturity of a management team is its ability to set realistic goals and objectives for people. A company may need everything yesterday, but if it can't be done, the management team needs to step up to its responsibilities and produce realistic plans.

SUMMARY/CHECKUP

1. There is a proven path, a tested way to implement new technologies like MRP II, Just-in-Time, Total Quality Management, and employee empowerment. If your company is implementing new technologies, is it following the tested and proven approach?

2. The three controls on implementation are the work, the resources, and the time. Time should not be allowed to be the variable, as it can dry up the resourcing. Instead, resources should be managed, or an approach like quick-slice should be utilized. In your company, is time the variable?

3. Consistent messages from the top of the organization can roughly double the available "horsepower" applied to an implementation. In your company, how consistent are the messages from the top?

4. The cost of delay value is a resourcing and priority-setting tool. Does a cost of delay value exist in your company?

5. Most companies do an inadequate job of educating their people for change. As Ed Wohlwender said, "If I had to say one thing to anybody getting into this, it's 'Take your best guess at the education you're going to need, and then double it.'" How well is your company handling the need to educate your people for change?

6. Data accuracy is a major stumbling block for many companies. Inventory records need to be 95 percent accurate; bills of material, formulas, or recipes, 98 percent; and routings, 95 percent. How accurate are these data in your company?

7. Most companies today are doing multiple technology implementations. Because of competition, organizations cannot afford to wait and implement new technologies sequentially. Does your implementation include multiple technologies?

8. The pilot approach is the recommended method for implementation. Does your implementation plan call for a pilot?

9. Quick-slice is an implementation approach that allows results in three to five months. Has quick-slice been evaluated as a possible element in your implementation?

10. There is a tendency to include more in an implementation than is realistic. Are your company's implementation plans realistic? Are they being achieved? Do they need to be changed?

At this point we've seen how a comprehensive planning and scheduling system would be implemented. We've looked at what such a system is and how it works. And we've identified the links between the planning and scheduling system and the other people-based technologies that all companies need to consider. It should be obvious that we're no longer living in the manufacturing world of the past. Things have changed, significantly, and they will not go back to the way we all remember them. This leads us to the subject of the epilogue, adapting to the new world of manufacturing.

SPECIAL ACKNOWLEDGMENTS

Tom Wallace for his pioneering work and dedication to the field of MRP II implementation.

Epilogue

The Road Less Traveled

The rate of change in manufacturing management knowledge is so great that most organizations have enough work to occupy them for the next several years. During this time, the world will not be standing still. The progress that brought us to this point will continue and will likely accelerate.

On the plus side, life has never been better for people in manufacturing. Given the basic planning and control tools that they've needed for years, people can now do an excellent job in areas in which excellence was simply not achievable before. The participative aspects of technologies such as Just-in-Time, employee empowerment, total quality, and design for competitive advantage leave people feeling excited and satisfied.

If there is a downside, however, it's the clash of two cultures, typified by the two differing sets of beliefs about manufacturing described in the first chapter:

- "Changing the way we manage is the most significant action we can take to improve the bottom line."

- "Changing the way we manage isn't the way it's 'done,' and everybody knows that. Let's get back to fundamentals—faster feeds and speeds, attacking labor costs, automation, things like that. . . ."

Fear and pain motivate a company to change. But what about an individual? Are those people who don't easily conceptualize new processes to be relegated to the bottom of the manufacturing totem pole?

257

No, they cannot be. They're too valuable to lose.

Companies are beginning to understand that one of the significant competitive constraints in the future may be the process by which an organization internalizes change—makes itself different without tearing itself apart. And as new ideas continue to pour into the competitive body of knowledge, it will be the implementation of change by individuals that forms the bottleneck.

Companies will continue to address the clash of the old and new cultures by bringing people to a common base of understanding. The old model is gone, and things have changed. Most successful companies put this fact on the table and discuss it. That's why the proven path implementation includes so much emphasis on people, education, goal setting, and spreading ownership throughout the organization. In nearly every case, even the most entrenched skeptics become converts as they get into detailed discussions of how things will be done differently. At some point, "the light goes on" for people and they see things differently.

CREATING THE FUTURE

If the effort to resolve the clash of the old and new cultures by replacing one model with another seems like a lot of work, it is. But it's worth every bit of energy. People in manufacturing have long demonstrated that they are not afraid of work. What they do dislike, though, is a situation in which they expend a great deal of energy and don't receive the expected rewards. Fortunately, the satisfactions that come from changing the organization are substantial. They include a sense of accomplishment, producing something of worth and value, greater job security, having ideas accepted and implemented, and the recognition of competitive superiority compared to other organizations.

The decision to make this kind of change is your own. The *need* to change, however, is controlled externally. Sooner or later the competitive equation will force change within your organization.

Ideally, companies will see these changes coming before they become painful, and will act in advance of the threat. While this does happen, as mentioned earlier, most companies wait for the pain before making changes. Largely, that's because these changes require shifting the model or paradigm so that people understand that the manner in which a manufacturing company is managed can be a powerful competitive weapon.

If you choose to wait until the pain and fear are present, you're living dangerously. Not every organization will be a survivor, because some of its key managers simply will not be able to make the transition from the old culture to the new one. Remember that the corporate battlefield is strewn with the bodies of companies that *used* to be number one.

All companies, and all those who are in management positions in these organizations, need to take an honest and unbiased view of where they are competitively. The questions to ask are "How do we compare with top-notch organizations?" "How biased are we against change and against accepting new management technologies?" "What do we have the resources to accomplish?" and "What happens if we don't change?"

If you do choose to change, you're taking the path that too few companies follow. In that case, the tools you've read about in this book will help you achieve your goals. They'll help you to identify opportunities and make significant improvements in cost, quality, and delivery. In short, they'll enable you to take the high road to running your business.

Index

Scheduling (*continued*)
  and formal vs. informal systems, 22, 23, 27
  and honesty, 32
  and the single-set-of-numbers approach, 31, 33
  and the universal manufacturing equation, 39. *See also* Master production scheduling; Supplier scheduling
Schrock Cabinets, 12, 14, 15, 230, 251
Sealed Power, 97, 159, 188
Shop, James Correll, 202
"Silence is approval" principle, 139, 143, 150, 210, 214
Single-set-of-numbers approach, 31, 33
Soccio, Tom, 74
Software. *See* Computer(s)
Spin-off task groups, 233–34
Steelcase, 29, 116
Steering committees, 229, 230–31, 232
Stevens, Al, 122
Subcontractors, 30
  and capacity planning, 161, 172, 173–74
  and informal systems, 38
  and sales and operations planning, 60
Supplier(s)
  and capacity planning, 171
  communication of material plans to, 44
  and firm planning orders, 142
  and the human body analogy, 15–16
  integration of, 15–17
  and interplant demands, 91
  and master production scheduling, 109, 110
  and material requirements planning, 100–101, 129–32, 135, 138–40, 142, 143, 145, 147–48, 150
  and padding lead times, 148
  and safety stock, 148
  and the "silence is approval" principle, 139, 143, 150, 210, 214. *See also* Supplier scheduling

Supplier scheduling, 203–15
  and committed and material zones, 206–8, 210
  and formal systems, 42
  individuals involved with, responsibilities of, 209
  and JIT, 208, 213–14
  and kanbans, 208, 213–14
  and master production scheduling, 111, 116, 122
  and material requirements planning, 127–28
  and performance measures, 211–13, 214–15
  and the planning zone, 208, 210
  and providing scheduling information to suppliers, 204–5
  and sales and operations planning, 55
  and the supplier scheduler, definition of, 138–39. *See also* Suppliers

T

Taxation, 51
Teamwork, 14, 17, 230–34
  and the ability to come to consensus, 68
  and communication, 6
  and customer service, 56
  and formal systems, 40
  and implementation, 224–25, 230–34, 243–44, 248, 253
  and JIT, 12
  and R&D plans, 67
  and sales and operations planning, 68
  and supplier scheduling, 204, 214
Teets, Peter, 229
Tektronics, 179
Tellabs, 119, 242–43
Tennant, 116, 151, 152
Thanksgiving, 39
Thomas, Mary, 23
Thunderbird Products, 51–53, 60, 71–72, 230